Cognitive Assessment
A Multidisciplinary
Perspective

PERSPECTIVES ON INDIVIDUAL DIFFERENCES

CECIL R. REYNOLDS, *Texas A&M University, College Station*
ROBERT T. BROWN, *University of North Carolina, Wilmington*

A Continuation Order Plan is available for this series. A continuation order will bring delivery of each new volume immediately upon publication. Volumes are billed only upon actual shipment. For further information please contact the publisher.

Cognitive Assessment
A Multidisciplinary Perspective

Edited by

Cecil R. Reynolds

Texas A&M University
College Station, Texas

PLENUM PRESS • NEW YORK AND LONDON

Library of Congress Cataloging-in-Publication Data

Cognitive assessment : a multidisciplinary perspective / edited by
  Cecil R. Reynolds.
      .p.   cm. -- (Perspectives on individual differences)
    Papers presented at a conference, held Oct. 1991, at Texas A&M
  University.
    Includes bibliographical references and index.
    ISBN 0-306-44434-8
  . 1. Cognition--Testing--Congresses.   2. Psychometrics--Congresses.
  3. Neuropsychological tests--Congresses.   4. Individual differences-
  -Congresses.   I. Reynolds, Cecil R., 1952-   . II. Series.
  BF311.C55117   1993
  153.9'3--dc20   93-34142
                                                               CIP

ISBN 0-306-44434-8

© 1994 Plenum Press, New York
A Division of Plenum Publishing Corporation
233 Spring Street, New York, N.Y. 10013

Printed in the United States of America

Contributors

Patricia A. Alexander, Department of Educational Psychology, Texas A&M University, Harrington Tower, College Station, Texas 77843-4225

Peter M. Bentler, Department of Psychology, University of California, Los Angeles, California 90024-1563

Erin D. Bigler, Department of Psychology, Brigham Young University, Provo, Utah 84602

Robert L. Brennan, Research Division, American College Testing, Iowa City, Iowa 52243

D. S. Calkins, Krug Life Sciences, Houston, Texas 77058

J. F. DeFrance, University of Texas Medical School at Houston, Houston, Texas 77025; HCA Gulf Pines Hospital, Houston, Texas 77090

J. Degioanni, National Aeronautics and Space Administration, Houston, Texas 77058

Susan Embretson, Department of Psychology, University of Kansas, Lawrence, Kansas 66045

S. Estes, HCA Gulf Pines Hospital, Houston, Texas 77090

Robert C. Graf, Motor Behavior Laboratory, Pennsylvania State University, Pennsylvania 16802

C. Hymel, Graduate School of Biomedical Sciences, University of Texas at Houston, Houston, Texas 77025

R. Hymel, HCA Gulf Pines Hospital, Houston, Texas 77090

Jonna M. Kulikowich, Department of Educational Psychology, University of Connecticut, Storrs, Connecticut 06269

Stanley A. Mulaik, School of Psychology, Georgia Institute of Technology, Atlanta, Georgia 30332

J. N. Rutledge, Austin Radiological Associates, Austin, Texas 78756

Robert Schultz, Child Study Center, Yale University, New Haven, Connecticut 06520

F. C. Schweitzer, HCA Gulf Pines Hospital, Houston, Texas 77090

Charles H. Shea, Human Performance Laboratories, Texas A&M University, College Station, Texas 77843-4243

John B. Shea, College of Human Sciences, Florida State University, Tallahassee, Florida 32306-2033

Lee Willerman, Department of Psychology, University of Texas, Austin, Texas 78712

Victor L. Willson, Department of Educational Psychology, Texas A&M University, Harrington Tower, College Station, Texas 77843-4225

David L. Wright, Human Performance Laboratories, Texas A&M University, College Station, Texas 77843-4243

Preface

This volume is an outgrowth of an invitational conference held in October 1991 on the main campus of Texas A&M University and sponsored by a grant from the Dean's Office of the College of Education. The expressed purpose of the conference was to allow researchers from too often disparate areas of research related to individual differences to come together and discuss their approaches to the topic, share ideas, and critique their differing paradigms to shorten the time it takes for researchers in parallel disciplines to discover advances that may aid their own work.

We sought to bring together world-class psychometricians and statisticians, cognitive scientists, and neuroscientists focused on the common theme of individual differences. Each reviewed advances in his or her own work that has clear implications for enhancing our understanding of individual differences — from defining and partitioning variance components to modeling individual differences to structural and functional cortical variations that produce individual differences.

The Chair of the Department of Educational Psychology at Texas A&M University, Bruce Thompson, took a lead role along with Victor L. Willson in organizing and conceptualizing the conference. The support of the Dean of the College of Education, Jane A. Stallings, was central to its success. Rebecca Kocurek of the Department of Educational Psychology assisted the editor as well in tracking the progress of the volume and its contributors as the work was under way. Appreciation is also due Eliot Werner, Plenum's Executive Editor, for his continued faith and interest in our work.

CECIL R. REYNOLDS

Contents

CHAPTER ONE

Neuroimaging and Neuropsychological Assessment

ERIN D. BIGLER

Within the first 30 years of this century, patients with various forms of brain damage began to be evaluated with test instruments designed to assess "mental abilities" (Anastasi, 1988). In 1935 Ward Halstead began his systematic research in brain–behavior relationships which, in turn, led one of his students, Ralph Reitan, to initiate his clinical research and standardization of tests designed specifically to evaluate brain function through behavior (Reitan & Wolfson, 1985). During this period, the typical methodology in defining "brain damaged" or "organic" groups under investigation was to take cases with objective physical exam criteria (e.g., paralysis on one side of the body following a stroke or head injury, specific type of EEG abnormality, etc.) or patients who had been operated on neurosurgically wherein the brain could be directly inspected (see review by Bigler, Yeo, & Turkheimer, 1989). The obvious limitations of such methodologies lie with their inability to specifically quantify exact areas/regions of structural brain damage. What this fostered early in this century and through the decades up until the 1970s was a unitary concept of "brain damage" or "organicity" (see Bigler & Erfurth, 1983). During this era this conceptualization of "brain injury" resulted in a clear lack of precision in defining independent variables (IV) for the study of brain–behavior relationships in humans. This restriction in what could be defined as an IV in the classification of brain injury was due to the lack of

ERIN D. BIGLER • Department of Psychology, Brigham Young University, Provo, Utah 84602.

Cognitive Assessment: A Multidisciplinary Perspective, edited by Cecil R. Reynolds. Plenum Press, New York, 1994.

any standardized in vivo method to quantify structural brain damage. For example, in 1964 Reitan stated:

> Even though a surgeon's instruments may impose themselves upon the situation in one way or another, the underlying condition of pathology is inevitably difficult to describe in complete or fully accurate terms. Consequently, many unknowns are undoubtedly present to influence the variance of psychological measurements even in the best-designed investigations. (pp. 295–296)

During this period it is likely that the most precise IV measures of actual structural damage to the brain came from extirpation studies, exemplified by Milner's work (1964, 1991). With this methodology, actual cerebral tissue was removed in the treatment of an invasive neurological disorder (typically a brain tumor) and from surgical notes, as well as detailed examination of the removed tissue, regions of structural damage were outlined and quantified. This procedure has significant limitations, however, and is quite unsatisfactory for a number of reasons, most important of which is the inability to quantify the amount of surrounding tissue damage left in the brain (Bigler, 1991). Thus, even the best of methods during this era fell short of the most rigorously defined IV's for brain–behavior research.

Coinciding with the early development of mental abilities testing (from around 1900 to 1930) was the development of various X-ray procedures, including pneumoencephalography (Oldendorf, 1980). Unfortunately, none of these procedures, including the radioisotope brain scan, provided a direct image of the brain (see review by Bigler et al., 1989). Thus, the technology of that era provided no means of direct analysis of brain structure. The state of neuroimaging changed dramatically in the 1970s, however, with Hounsfield's Nobel prize winning work on the physics of computerized tomography (CT) (Oldendorf, 1980). By 1974 the first clinical use of CT scanning was underway and by the mid-1970s CT scanning had met universal acceptance as *the* brain imaging technique. CT scan analysis could now be utilized as a method to quantify underlying structural abnormalities that related to postmortem findings (see Figure 1). In the 1980s a new method of image analysis became available—magnetic resonance (MR) imaging (Pykett, Newhouse, Buonanno, Brady, Goldman, Kistler, and Prohost, 1982), which utilized the universal magnetic fields of any given tissue. MR analysis of brain tissue yields an exquisite image that permits detailed visualization of gross brain anatomy and pathology (see Figure 2). In comparison to CT scanning, MR scanning results have led to further refinement and resolution in identifying brain structure and pathology.

Thus, beginning as early as the mid-1970s and certainly by the mid-1980s, clinical neuroscience had reached a level where greater preci-

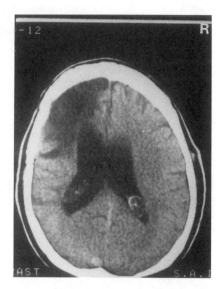

FIGURE 1. (left) Ventral view of whole brain at postmortem depicting pronounced cavitation in the inferior left frontal region and wasting of the left lateral and anterior aspect of the temporal lobe. This damage was the result of a high-velocity impact closed head injury. (right) Horizontal CT scan depicting frontal cavitation and how it is imaged with CT. In this image, the dark areas reflect less dense, nonviable tissue analogous to what is observed in the postmortem specimen.

sion could be used in defining central nervous system (CNS) IV's by utilizing anatomic information from the CT or MR scan. Unfortunately, for the most part this did not happen. Most neuropsychological research during this era utilized CT and/or MR in its most simplistic form—clinical interpretation rather than any type of quantitative image analysis. This point will be demonstrated below by analyzing the frequency of CT and/or MR identified IV's in neuropsychology research.

THE LACK OF USE OF NEUROIMAGING DATA AS IV'S IN NEUROPSYCHOLOGICAL RESEARCH

Figures 3, 4, and 5 depict the use of neuroimaging data as IV's in neuropsychological research in several journals that are prominent in the field. For a more detailed analysis, *Neuropsychologia* (Figure 3) and *Brain* (Figure 4) were selected because both of these journals were publishing in the field during the era of CT and MR development and on

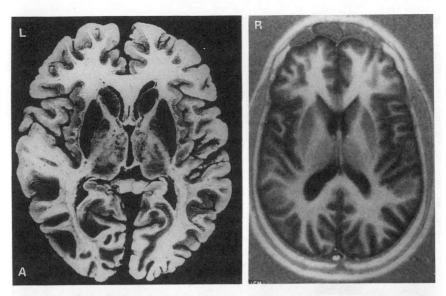

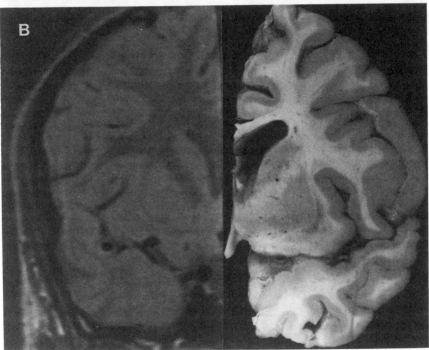

FIGURE 2. (A) Postmortem stained horizontal section (left) compared to MR imaging (right). (B) Postmortem nonstained coronal section compared to MR. (C) Posterior dorsal view of a severely damaged (closed head injury) postmortem brain with a large right hemisphere subdural hematoma which has been reflected back and is resting on top of the left hemisphere. Note the generalized compression of most of the lateral surface of the right hemisphere. (D) Horizontal MR depicting (in white) a massive subdural hematoma as a consequence of severe closed head injury. Notice the structural detail that can be achieved by MR techniques. Compare to Figure 1.

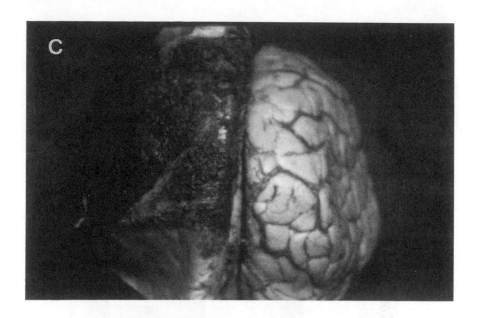

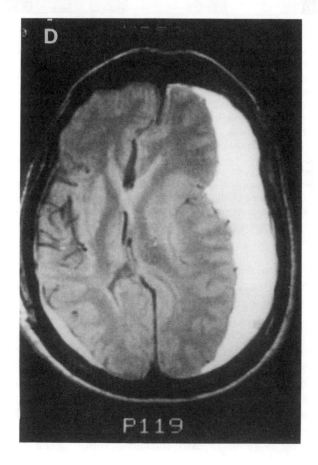

P119

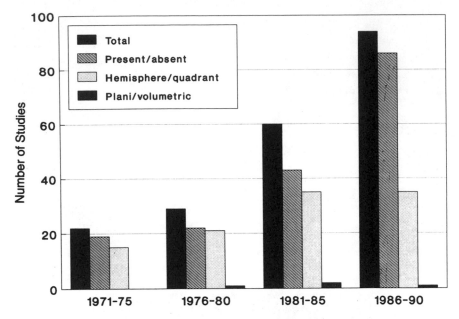

FIGURE 3. Comparison of various methods of measurement in neuropsychological research from 1971 to 1990 wherein some form of neuroimaging data were used in the journal *Neuropsychologia* to define "brain damage." Black bars represent the total number of studies wherein some form of neuroimaging was employed including pneumoencephalography, technetium brain scan, CT, MR, single photon emission computed tomography (SPECT), and position emission tomography (PET). The reason that the total always exceeds any of the subcategories is that several studies reported only that some form of imaging had been done but did not utilize imaging data in any other fashion. The present/absent classification refers to a simple dichotomy as to whether the scan was "normal" or "abnormal." Hemisphere/quadrant classification signifies that an abnormality was present and whether the pathology was in the left or right hemisphere and/or anterior verses posterior. The plani/volumetric distinction is based on whether a linear or area/volume quantification was made. Note the marked lack of use of any quantitative method of analysis. These same classifications are used for Figures 4 and 5.

through the period when these methodologies gained universal acceptance in neurodiagnostic assessment. Figure 5 depicts several other journals that published significant neuropsychological research but were either not in existence in the early 1970s (*Journal of Clinical and Experimental Neuropsychology*) or were not publishing significant numbers of neuropsychological studies during that period (*Journal of Clinical Psychology*). There is only one conclusion to be made from this analysis of published research, namely, that the majority of neuropsychological studies have simply ignored quantitative neuroimaging data as IV's. This is a remarkable circumstance given the exquisite detail that can be derived from current generation CT and MR scanners.

Neuropsychology has been all too satisfied during the last 20 years to

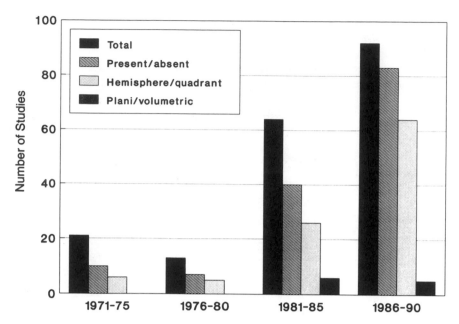

FIGURE 4. Comparison of various methods of measurement in neuropsychological research from 1971 to 1990 wherein some form of neuroimaging data were used in the journal *Brain* to define "brain damage." See Figure 3 for discussion of figure captions. Note the marked lack of use of any quantitative method of analysis.

continue to study groups of "brain damaged" subjects by classifying them into "right" or "left" hemisphere damaged groups or by some clinical diagnosis. For example, in traumatic brain injury (TBI) research the standard of the past has been to study groups of patients that had TBI so identified by a history (i.e., hospital emergency room report) of some traumatic accident wherein the patient either experienced a loss or alteration in consciousness or had some outward, observable, physical evidence for brain injury (e.g., hemiplegia, aphasia, skull fracture, etc.). Traumatic brain injury may produce a widespread pathologic effect, however, that may have little relationship to physical findings or alteration in level of consciousness. These points will be discussed below.

THE "BRAIN DAMAGED" MODEL IN NEUROPSYCHOLOGY AS REPRESENTED BY NEUROIMAGING IN TBI

Figure 6 depicts postmortem sagittal sections of the brain of a head injury victim who sustained a severe TBI. These sections capture the typical pathological changes that may occur in TBI which are represented by ventricular expansion (which signifies loss of white matter due to

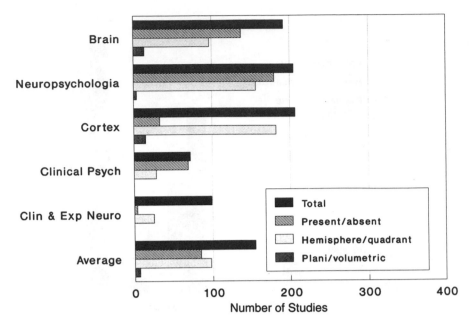

FIGURE 5. Comparison of various methods of measurement utilizing neuroimaging methods in neuropsychological research across five journals that have produced significant numbers of neuropsychological publications. *Brain* is from 1971 to 1990; *Neuropsychologia* is from 1971 to 1990 (see Figure 1), *Cortex* is from 1971 to 1990; *Journal of Clinical Psychology* (*J. Clin. Psychol.*) is from 1975 to 1990; *J. Clin. & Experiment. Neuropsychol.*) is from 1979 (its inaugural year of publication) to 1990. See Figure 3 legend for discussion of figure captions. Note across all journals the marked lack of any quantitative method of analysis.

diffuse axonal injury; see Bigler, 1990) and cerebral contusions (bruising of the brain). The relevance of these types of injuries to behavioral function may be best demonstrated by an individual case, which will be presented next.

Figures 7, 8, and 9 and Table 1 present the neuroimaging and neuropsychological data on a young adult male who when 20 years of age and a college junior sustained a severe traumatic brain (closed head) injury. For comparison purposes some estimate of premorbid ability level is necessary and at the time of injury this patient had an overall college grade point average of 3.57 and had a college admittance SAT score of 1140. Accordingly, such tests would suggest premorbid ability level to be considerably above average, with premorbid intellectual level to be conservatively estimated >110. With uniform ventricular expansion secondary to the trauma-induced degenerative effects, there is typically a significant loss of measured intellectual function that is correspondingly uniform (Cullum & Bigler, 1986). In this patient's case his postinjury (18 months) intellectual scores indicated a three standard deviation drop

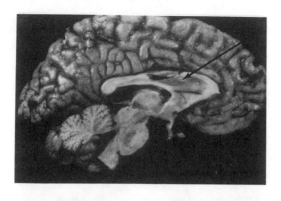

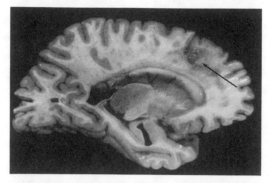

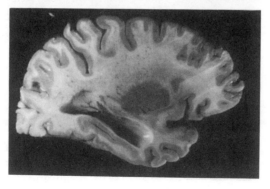

FIGURE 6. Postmortem sagittal views from a patient who sustained a severe traumatic brain injury. (top) Midsagittal depicting thinning of the body of the corpus callosum (arrow). Since the corpus callosum is comprised of a large bundle of white matter (myelinated fiber tracts) that course back and forth between the hemispheres, it is particularly vulnerable to brain injury because of rotational and shearing effects (Yeo & Bigler, 1991). (middle) Deep white–gray matter interface contusion (arrow) along with ventricular dilation. (bottom) Temporal horn dilation of the lateral ventricular systems indicating substantial tissue loss in the temporal lobe region (see Bigler, 1990).

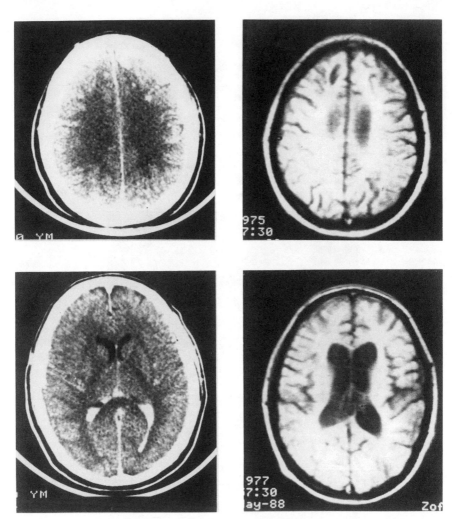

FIGURE 7. Horizontal CT (left) and MR (right) scans in a TBI patient whose neuropsychological data is presented in Table 1. The CT scans on the left were obtained on admission to the hospital approximately 2 hours postinjury. The CT scans depict blood in the ventricle, and multiple, small punctate hemorrhages (indicated by small, focal hyperintense white areas) spread throughout the brain, particularly in the frontal regions. The MR scans on the right were taken approximately one year postinjury and are at approximately the same level as the CT scans obtained on the day of injury. Note the marked dilation of the ventricles. This signifies considerable brain tissue loss and because the expansion is rather uniform, this would indicate generalized tissue loss. The scan in the top right also depicts the presence of focal white matter wasting due to the deep white hemorrhagic contusions as depicted in the CT scan analysis on the day of injury. (The images are reversed in terms of radiologic left and right. The CT scans are oriented with the patient's left on the reader's left.)

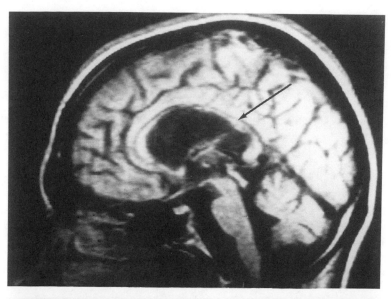

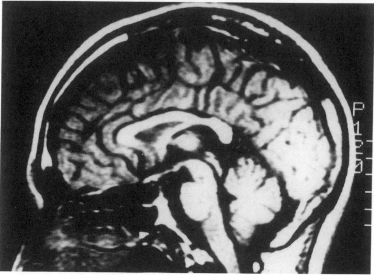

FIGURE 8. (top) MR Sagittal view of the TBI patient presented in Figure 7. (bottom) Age-matched non-brain-injured control. Note (arrow) the marked atrophy of the brain of the corpus callosum. Such lesions typically disconnect the two cerebral hemispheres, resulting in impaired cerebral integration. As depicted in Figure 9 the patient has a severe left-hand spelling apraxia and dysgraphia. The sagittal view (top) also depicts a withered fornix, which is likely the basis, in part, of the pronounced short-term memory deficits in this patient.

WRAT-R Spelling List
Level 2

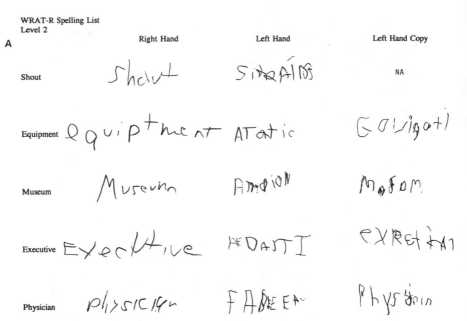

FIGURE 9. (A) Left-hand spelling apraxia and dysgraphia in a TBI patient with specific damage to the corpus callosum (see Figure 8). The words are from the Wide Range Achievement Test—Revised (Jastak & Wilkinson, 1984). Although the patient makes a mistake in spelling "equipment," his handwriting is legible (although below what would be expected of a college student) and the remainder of the words are correctly spelled (the live above "o" in "shout" was the patient's attempt to close the open "o" and likewise the straight line following the letter c in spelling the word *executive* was the patient's attempt to equal the length on both sides of the letter "u"). In stark contrast is the patient's complete inability to write/spell with the left hand when the words are given by dictation (middle column). The patient's left-hand spelling apraxia and dysgraphia is not quite as severe with visual copy of the word (right column), but remains very prominent. The neuropsychological deficits reflect generalized cognitive impairment. (B) Right-hand constructional dyspraxia is greater than left in the same patient. For visual-spatial and perceptual-motor functioning the corpus callosum disconnection creates the opposite effect from spelling. In this situation the right hand is more impaired than the left.

from premorbid estimates (see Table 1). A number of studies are currently in progress wherein the dynamic relationship between brain volume loss and neuropsychological function is being examined (Bigler, Snyder & Abildskov, 1992) and these studies suggest some linear relationship between brain volume loss and intellectual/cognitive impairment.

Memory impairment is commonplace in TBI (Bigler, 1990). The basis for memory deficits in TBI is usually related to direct injury to temporal-limbic areas that subserve memory or to white matter pathways that transfer memory information. Often the structural basis to the memory

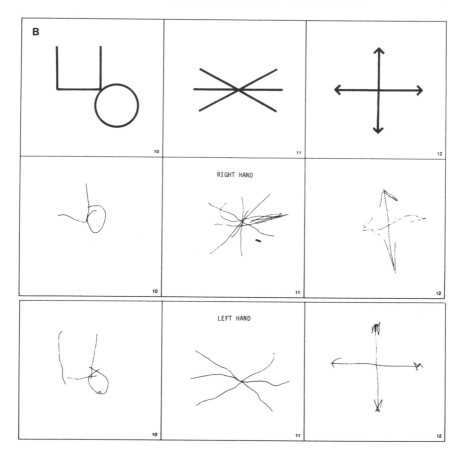

FIGURE 9 (*Continued*)

impairment can be identified by detailed inspection of the MRI. For example, Figure 8 depicts a sagittal view of this patient in comparison to an age-matched noninjured control. It is apparent that there is marked thinning of the fornix, the major pathway from the hippocampus to other cerebral structures in the transfer of memory information.

The damaged fornix eliminates the projection of information from the hippocampus to other cortical areas, hence a profound short-term memory impairment. Additionally, this sagittal view (see Figure 8) demonstrates marked thinning of the corpus callosum, particularly through the body. This level of injury disrupts the transfer of information from one hemisphere to the other which impairs cerebral integration. Such a degenerative effect often produces a deficit on any task that requires integration of information. Accordingly, this patient demonstrated a pronounced left-hand spelling apraxia as depicted in Figure 9. Figure 9

TABLE 1. Neuropsychological Test Results

Age: 21   Sex: Male   Education: 15   Dominance: Right hand and foot, mixed ocular

Intellectual
  WAIS-R   Full Scale IQ Score = 76

  Verbal IQ Score = 90   Performance IQ Score = 63
    Information   9   Picture completion   5
    Digit span   8   Picture arrangement   4
    Vocabulary   11   Block design   5
    Arithmetic   6   Object assembly   3
    Comprehension 6   Digital symbol   NA
    Similarities   10

Memory
  WMS   Delayed   RAVL   Rey-Osterrieth
    Memory quotient   70   Recall   Trial   CFD
    Information   5   I 4   Copy
    Orientation   2   II 5   4
    Mental control   3   III 4   Recall
    Logical memory   3   0   IV 4   0
    Digits   10(5,5)   V 4
    Visual memory   3   3   Delayed recall 0
    Associate learning 8.5   3(4,1)   Recognition recall 3

Achievement	Standard Score	Percentile	Grade Equivalent
Reading	107	68	>12
Spelling	103	58	>12
Arithmetic	54	0.2	3E

Motor	Strength of Grip (kg)	Finger Oscillation (10 sec average)
Right	14.7	37.3
Left	29.6	40.4

Sensory-Perceptual Exam
  Intact Simple touch bilaterally. Bilateral tactile hand extinction to DSS hand-face stimulation. Intact auditory perception with no extinction. Left visual field extinction to DSS. Bilateral finger dysgnosia, dysgraphesthesia and dystereognosis.

Other
  Raven's CPM   25/36   time: 10'45"   TM: A = 101 sec, B = 125 sec

---

demonstrates that the left hand was not affected in terms of copying simple geometric form but cannot write or spell to verbal command.

As this case presents, a detailed analysis of neuroimaging findings makes the neuropsychological explanation for the deficit more powerful. There are numerous factors that need to be taken into consideration, however, when using TBI neuroimaging data as IV's. These factors will be discussed below. Many of the points made with TBI can also be generalized to other neurologic disorders such as cerebral vascular accidents, brain tumors, and brain infections.

UTILIZING NEUROIMAGING DATA AS INDEPENDENT VARIABLES

As alluded to previously in this discussion, in TBI the point of impact may or may not have specific bearing on the residual pathology (see review by Bigler, 1990). This is due to the tremendous pressure of forces exerted throughout the cranium during the initial milliseconds postinjury, along with the shearing and torsion effects exerted throughout the brain. Once these initial effects have occurred, then the secondary effects begin to accumulate in the form of hemorrhages, tissue swelling and secondary ischemic changes, both focally as well as generally. If a hemorrhage is large or focal edema is present, then it also may produce a significant shift in brain structures which in turn may produce tissue compression as a result of displacement.

The result of these neuropathological effects on IV selection when using neuroimaging data is that the researcher has to be very careful, because each variable tends to be interrelated. Accordingly, in TBI research if one were to select patients with left and right hematomas thinking that this would be some index of greater hemispheric injury, one would have drawn a very incorrect conclusion. This point is well demonstrated in Figure 10.

The issue of the degree of pathologic change is also problematic. Figures 11, 12, and 13 depict a case of significant TBI wherein the patient had received an MR scan 3 months prior to injury. In this case, having the preinjury scan permits a direct quantification of change in cerebral size and structure. Unfortunately, it is extremely rare to have such preinjury imaging data and so one has to rely on estimates of preinjury values. One technique used to obtain an estimate of preinjury values is to study the CT scan taken immediately upon admittance to the hospital. It is routine in every trauma center to obtain an admission CT scan, and often the initial CT scan is taken early enough so that the full effects of cerebral edema have not been manifested. In these cases it is best to use just the ventricular system. This is depicted in Figures 14 and 15 by utilizing three-dimensional image analysis (Bigler et al., 1992). The three-dimensional image also assists in improved volumetric quantification of damage as well as the simultaneous viewing of all areas damaged. This is depicted in Figure 16.

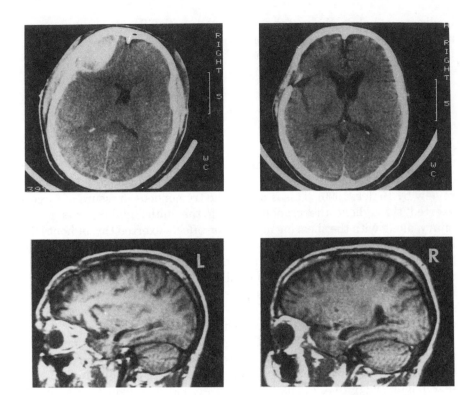

FIGURE 10. (top left) CT scans on hospital admission in a 39-year-old college educated male who sustained severe traumatic brain injury in a motor vehicle accident. The scans depict the presence of a massive hematoma with marked brain displacement and midline shift. (top right) CT scan at same level as day of injury scan at 3 months postsurgery demonstrating significant ventricular dilation and frontotemporal lobe atrophy. (bottom) Left and right MRI sagittal views through the temporal horn depicting bilateral anterior temporal lobe encephalomalacia, temporal horn dilation, and scattered cerebral atrophy. Note that even though the hematoma was on the left that the greater degree of tissue loss/ventricular dilation is in the right temporal lobe region. When tested 9 months post-trauma he had a prominent left hemiplegia and hemisensory deficit with global cognitive impairment (VIQ=89, PIQ=62, FSIQ=76, WMS MQ=64). When retested 6 months later verbal intellectual functions had improved somewhat (VIQ=101) but performance (PIQ=64) and memory (WMS MQ=64) functions remained unchanged. Even though this patient has lateralized left-body side sensory and motor deficits along with greater impairment in spatial perceptual functioning than verbal, it would be inappropriate to characterize this as a true "right hemisphere" syndrome because the damage is diffuse and generalized. Accordingly, it would be inappropriate to place this patient in a "right hemisphere" group because of his left hemiplegia or in a "left hemisphere" group because he had a left-side hematoma (adapted from Bigler, 1991).

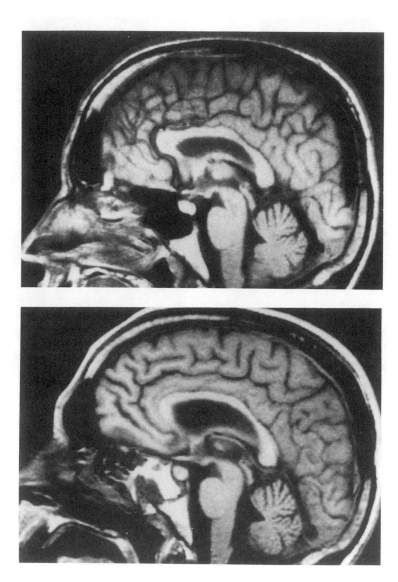

FIGURE 11. Posttraumatic degenerative changes identified in sagittal MR scanning one month postinjury (bottom) in comparison to normal preinjury MR findings (top). Note the atrophy of the corpus callosum and corresponding enlargement of the ventricular system. Compare and contrast the bottom MR scans with Figure 6. Coronal and horizontal views of the same patient are depicted in Figures 12 and 13.

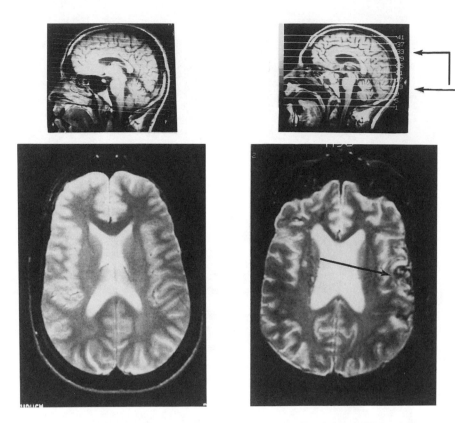

FIGURE 12. Posttraumatic degenerative changes identified in coronal MR scanning one month postinjury (bottom) in comparison to normal preinjury MR findings (top). Note the distinct enlargement of the ventricular system and the greater prominence of some sulcal regions in the bottom scan. This is an indication of generalized atrophy.

THE INTEGRATION OF NEUROIMAGING DATA WITH NEUROPSYCHOLOGICAL TEST FINDINGS: IMPORTANCE FUNCTION ANALYSIS

The problem of quantifying underlying pathological changes in brain structure with neuropsychological performance is a complex one. The issue is more than just volume or site of the lesion. This is well demonstrated by the results of one of our previous studies (see Turkheimer, Yeo, & Bigler, 1990). In this study, we analyzed CT data in 52 patients with singularly focal, lateralized lesions in either the left or right hemisphere. Figures 18 and 19 depict the relationship between left- and right-hand tactile processing errors, a presumably very lateralized function of the contralateral hemisphere (Bigler, 1988) and volume of the lateralized

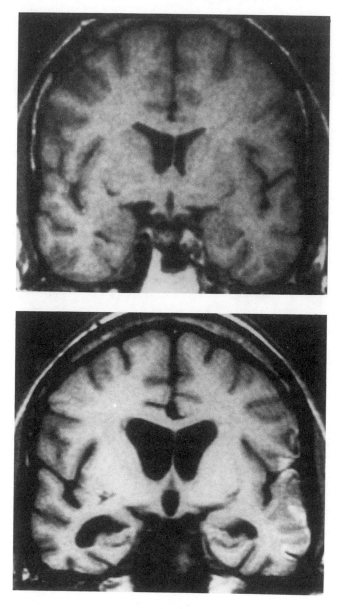

FIGURE 13. Posttraumatic degenerative changes identified in horizontal MR scanning one month postinjury (bottom) in comparison to normal preinjury MR findings (top). The sagittal views above indicate level where horizontal sections were taken. Note the generalized enlargement of the ventricular system postinjury which represents a generalized tissue loss throughout the brain and signifies generalized cerebral atrophy. There is also necrotic tissue on the brain surface that signifies residual damage as a consequence of cortical contusions.

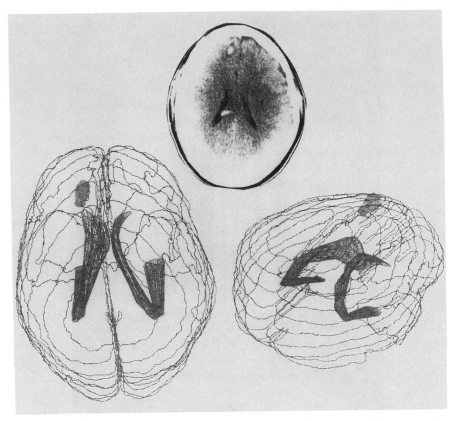

FIGURE 14. (top) CT scan images depicting acute injury effects from a CHI wherein the ventricles are used to establish an estimate of preinjury volume and morphological integrity for critical brain structures. (bottom) MR scans at identical levels as the CT images above 18 months postinjury depicting ventricular enlargement, representative of degenerative changes throughout the brain. Based on volumetric measures taken from the day of injury scan, the degree of change postinjury can be readily demonstrated in two- (bottom MR scan) or three-dimensions (see Figure 15).

lesion. As can be seen by these scatter plots, the linear relationship is minimal. This should come as no surprise. Accordingly, what this suggests is that when considering the relationship between a given brain lesion and its effects on neuropsychological performance, at a minimum one needs to consider location, laterality, and size of the lesion. None of these potential IV's should be examined in isolation or an incomplete picture of lesion effects will be obtained.

In an attempt to develop such an analysis Turkheimer (1989) developed a method capitalizing on the mathematics of "Importance Functions" in examining the interaction of brain lesion and neuropsychological

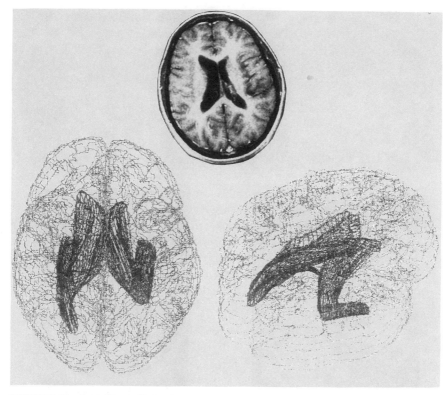

FIGURE 15. (top) Three-dimensional (3-D) representation based on CT image analysis from the CT obtained on the day of injury. The hemorrhagic lesion observed in Figure 14 (top) is depicted in the left frontal region. This 3-D image is based on a wire-frame outline of the outer surface of the brain and ventricles (shaded area). (top) Horizontal plane 3-D image. (top) Eight posterior oblique 3-D image. (bottom) Postinjury degenerative effects characterized by enlarged ventricular system. The bottom left and right views are in the identical plane as the similar views presented on top.

outcome. The application of such importance functions have been examined in several studies (see Turkheimer, Yeo, Jones, & Bigler, 1990; Yeo, Turkheimer & Bigler, 1990) and will be presented below. The discussion and illustrations that follow are taken from Yeo et al. (1990).

QUANTITATIVE REGIONAL ANALYSIS OF BRAIN FUNCTION

We recently described quantitative procedures for inferring localization of function based on systematic covariation of behavioral deficits and lesion locus, as determined by structural neuroimaging (Turkheimer, 1989; Turkheimer et al., 1990). A major difference between our approach

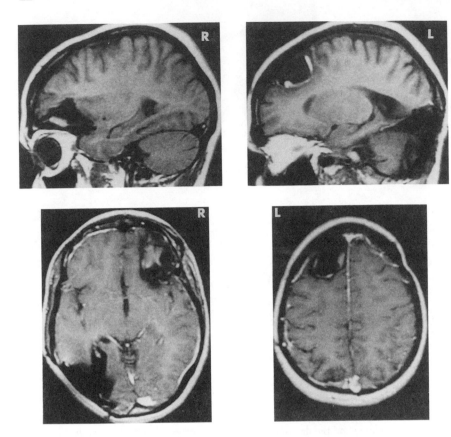

FIGURE 16. MR findings in TBI depicting residual effects of bilateral frontal contusions and a coup (left posterin) and contre-coup (right inferior frontal) injury in two dimensions.

and others (see Gur, Trivedi, Saykin, & Gur) is that we determine brain–behavior relationships empirically. Quantitative analysis of localization of function involves three sets of operations: procedures for quantification of structural neuroimaging data, statistical procedures for determining structure–function relationships, and graphical procedures for presentation of such relationships.

In our method, CT or MR images are obtained for a sample of focal lesion patients who have been administered several neuropsychological tests. The scans are either placed on a lightbox or the image is digitized using a "Frame Grabber" routine (see Bigler, 1992; Bigler, Kurth, Blatter, & Abildskov, 1993; Bigler, Snyder, & Abildskov, 1992). The outer perimeter of the brain is traced, as are the outlines of ventricles, cisterns, and the lesion (see Figure 20). Previous research has shown this to be a highly reliable procedure (Yeo, Turkheimer, & Bigler, 1983). Scan slices are then coded according to prominent landmarks. The greatest length

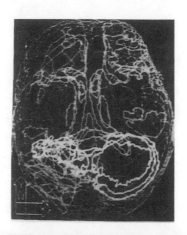

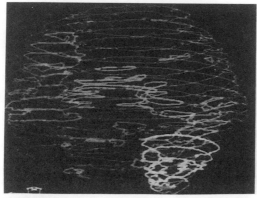

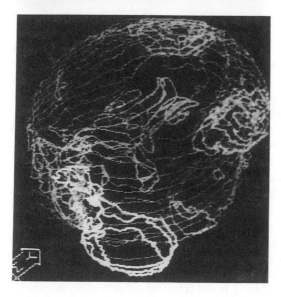

FIGURE 17. 3-D image analysis of MR results in the patient depicted in Figure 16. (top) Horizontal view. (middle) Left lateral view. (bottom) Left posterior oblique.

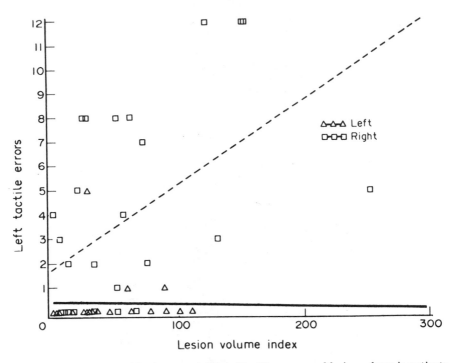

FIGURE 18. Relationships between left-hand tactile errors and lesion volume in patients with left and right hemisphere lesions. (From Turkheimer et al., 1990)

and width of each slice is measured in centimeters. The greatest left and right extensions of the lesion from the interhemispheric fissure are measured, with leftward distance measured by negative numbers. These horizontal measures are divided by the greatest width of the slice, resulting in standardized left and right lesion extension values. Similarly, we measure the distance from the greatest anterior and posterior extensions of the lesion to the midpoint of the hemispheric tissue on that slice, and we divide each value by the total length of the brain on that slice. These procedures thus estimate the extent of the lesion as a rectangle, with sides parallel to the x and y axes, as shown in Figure 21.

These measures of lesion characteristics and neuropsychological function are fit to a mathematical model describing the relationship between lesions and their neuropsychological consequences (Turkheimer et al., 1990). The model postulates an unknown importance function, invariant across subjects, that describes the relative importance of each location in the brain to a particular measure of neuropsychological function. The importance function is analogous to the expert judgments in the Gur et al. method, but it is determined empirically.

The importance function for each measure is estimated in terms of a

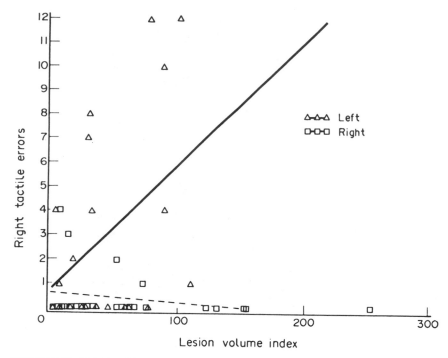

FIGURE 19. Relationships between left-hand tactile errors and lesion volume in patients with left and right hemisphere lesions. (From Turkheimer et al., 1990)

postulated empirical relationship between lesion characteristics and test scores. According to the model, the score on a given test for a given subject is given by

$$P_{nk} = \int L_n I_k(x,y) + M_k \tag{1}$$

where P_{nk} is the score of subject n on measure k, L_n is that subject's lesion, $I_k(x, y)$ is the importance function for measure k, and M_k is a regression intercept for each test. In discrete terms, this is equivalent to saying that the expected test score is equal to the sum of the importance values at all lesioned locations.

In a study of localization of function, one is given a set of measurements describing the size and location of each subject's lesion and a set of test scores for each subject; the aim is to find an importance function for each measure that fits the model. Elsewhere (Turkheimer et al., 1990), we have shown how least-squares polynomial regression can be employed to obtain importance functions based on this model. In this article, we apply a somewhat simpler version of the model to the problem posed by Gur et al., that is, predicting lesion locus from neuropsychological test

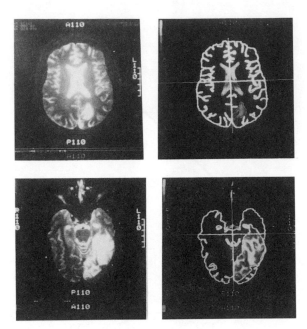

FIGURE 20. Trace technique for representing lesion characteristics in preparation for quantification in an x-y coordinate system. These images are from a CHI patient with subsequent cerebral infunction. The MR scans on the left are approximately one week postinjury. The scans on the right depict the computerized tracing of the cortical surface, ventricles, and lesion.

scores once importance functions have been estimated from previous research.

ESTIMATION OF IMPORTANCE FUNCTIONS

We have used our model to estimate importance functions drawn from portions of the Halstead-Reitan Neuropsychological Battery. The data were collected from 53 patients with focal cerebral lesions (for additional descriptive data see Turkheimer, Yeo, & Bigler, 1990; Yeo, 1989; Yeo, Turkheimer, & Bigler, 1983). Equation 1 was fit to a polynomial of the form

$$I(x,y) = b_1x^3 + b_2y^3 + b_3x^2 + b_4y^2 + b_5x + b_6y + b_7xy + b_8 \tag{2}$$

where $I(x, y)$ is the importance function and $b_1 - b_8$ are parameters to be estimated.

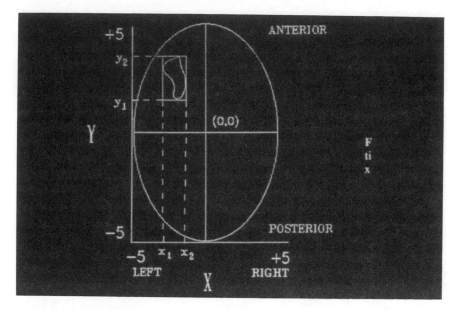

FIGURE 21. Estimation of lesion location as a rectangle extending from x_1 to x_2 and y_1 to y_2 (From Yeo et al., 1990)

Estimated importance functions for left- and right-hand tactile errors from the Reitan-Klove Sensory Perceptual Examination, Reitan-Indiana Aphasia Screening errors and right visual field errors (Reitan & Wolfson, 1985) are depicted in Figures 22 to 24. They are represented as a contour map on a single horizontal brain slice, with anterior regions at the top and posterior regions on the bottom. High-importance values indicate that a lesion at a particular location will produce relatively greater deficits. One contour band has been included for each 5% of variance accounted for by lesion location. Table 2 provides data on the proportion of variance accounted for by lesion volume and location for the entire sample. The R^2 values for such a small sample involve substantial capitalization on chance, so they should be evaluated relative to one another, rather than to a null hypothesis of no relationship.

PREDICTION OF LESION LOCUS

Once importance functions (I_k) have been estimated for a set of k measures, expected test scores can be computed for a given subject by integrating the importance function for each measure over the extent of the subject's lesion. The relations among lesion size and shape and the

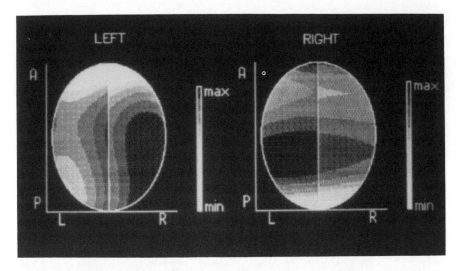

FIGURE 22. Importance functions for tactile errors for left and right hand. (Adapted from Yeo et al., 1990)

resulting neuropsychological test profile are extremely complex. Two lesions with the same center may produce very different expected test profiles if they extend in different directions.

We describe an approach using the simplification employed by Gur et al., in that lesions are considered as single points rather than regions.

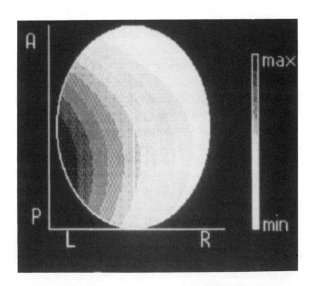

FIGURE 23. Importance functions for errors on the Reitan-Indiana Aphasia Screening Test (Reitan & Wolfson, 1985). (Adapted from Yeo et al., 1990)

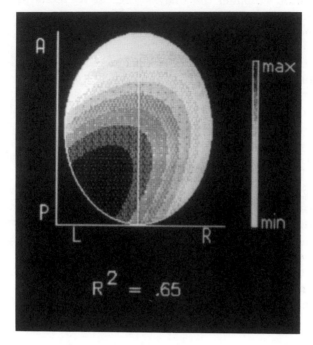

FIGURE 24. Importance functions for right visual field errors on sensory-perceptual examination.

TABLE 2. Correlations between Neuropsychological
Measures and Lesion Volume for Left and Right
Hemisphere Lesion Subjects

Test	Left Side Measures		Right Side Measures	
	Hemisphere of Lesion			
	Left	Right	Left	Right
	r	r	r	r
Finger tapping	0.05	0.25	0.23	0.01
Strength of grip	0.03	0.13	0.04	−0.13
Tactile errors	0.03	0.49	0.42	−0.22
Auditory errors	−0.01	0.13	0.15	−0.14
Visual errors	0.16	0.09	0.37	−0.27
Finger-tip writing	0.21	0.42	0.14	0.33
Finger recognition	0.28	0.12	0.32	−0.14
Aphasia verbal			0.42	0.02

This assumption simplifies the analysis because it eliminates the need to consider points contiguous to the center of a lesion, which will in general not be expected to produce precisely the same deficits as those resulting from the center point, because the importance function is not uniform across the brain. According to the model, a lesion to a single point will produce small deficits on each test, equal to the value of each importance function at that point. Ignoring nonuniformity in the importance function, larger lesions centered on the point will produce an additional unit deficit on each test for each additional volume of lesioned tissue. Under this simplification, therefore, the location of the lesion determines the pattern of deficit, and the size of the lesion determines the magnitude of deficit averaged across tests.

The algorithm Gur et al. employ is a method of assessing the degree of correspondence between a neuropsychological profile and that predicted by an importance function. The weighted mean of the test scores is an imperfect measure of correspondence, as demonstrated above. A simple alternative is to calculate at each point the correlation across tests between the actual and predicted scores.

In terms of equation 1, a lesion to a single point (x, y) will produce a deficit equal to the value of the importance function for each test evaluated at the point,

$$P_{nk} = I_k(x,y) + M_k \tag{3}$$

Ignoring local differences in importance, the expected deficit resulting from a larger lesion with volume v will be given by

$$P_{nk} = V[I_k)x,y) + M_k \tag{4}$$

From this we can see that the difference between a subject's observed score and the intercept M_k from the importance function is a linear function of the expected deficit produced by a lesion to any single point (x,y). We can therefore assess the fit between a set of observed test scores and those expected on the basis of lesions to a given point (x,y) in terms of the linear correlation between them.

We have applied this analysis to the test scores of a patient who was not included in the sample from which the importance functions were estimated. His CT scan is shown in Figure 25A, revealing a low-density area in the temporal-parietal-occipital region and a separate lesion in the frontal periventricular white matter. These lesions were apparently simultaneously caused by a shower of emboli of cardiac origin. Figure 25B shows the predicted lesion locus with its center point indicated by the

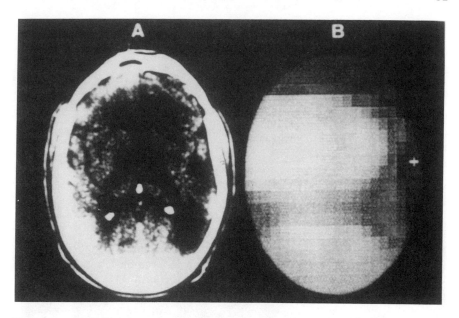

FIGURE 25. (A) CT scan of patient with left hemisphere lesions (left is on the reader's right). (B) Predicted lesion loci for the same patient based on importance function data from patients with focal left and right lesions.

white cross; darker regions have a greater probability of being damaged, based on this importance function methodology.

PROBLEMATIC ISSUES

As with any new technology, there will be limitations. It should not be assumed that the elegance and fine detail of MR imaging tells us all that need be known about brain damage. It needs to be clearly specified that MR and CT quantification techniques only specify certain anatomic boundaries and may tell little about physiological integrity of the brain. For example, Figure 26 depicts the comparison between CT, MR, single photon emission computed tomography (SPECT), and positron emission tomography (PET) in a patient who suffered a stroke (cerebral infarction) in the region of the posterior middle cerebral artery (from Pawlik & Heiss, 1989). As is readily evident, MR provides more precise definition in the regions of damage than CT, but neither captures the extent of metabolic aberration produced by the stroke. Thus, the physiological changes produced by a focal lesion may produce deficits in diverse ways that may not necessarily be predicted by the locus of the lesion.

Another factor that will remain problematic, is the issue of brain

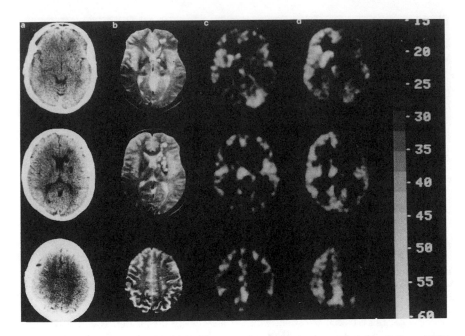

FIGURE 26. Characteristic CT (a), T$_2$-weighted MR (b), cerebral blood-flow (CBF) (Ml/100 g per min) (c) and cerebral metabolic rate (CMR) for glucose (remol/100 g per min) PET images (d) of a right-handed patient with aphasia consequent to recurrent ischemic attacks in deep left arterial border zone. Note that despite the lesions being relatively focal and small on CT and MR imaging, the changes in metabolic functioning extend beyond the regions of specific anatomic damage.

development and compensatory changes with early brain injury or mal-development (see Bigler, Lowe, & Yeo, 1989). Thus, in some (or possibly most) individuals with early onset brain abnormalities their course of brain–behavior development will be different from those not so affected. It also may be that there are subtle morphological differences associated with early environmental effects, disease/disorder effects, and/or other developmental variables that may affect brain development and organization in unique ways. Accordingly, this will require a large data base of normative studies across infancy, childhood, and adolescent years. Very recent breakthroughs in MR technology will soon permit much faster image acquisition times, thereby permitting the development of large data bases for various clinical populations (Stehling, Turner, & Mansfield, 1991). Thus, we can expect in the future a large data base system of morphological variables and their statistical relationship to outcome. These advances also hold considerable promise for functional neuroimaging using MR techniques (Belliveau, Kennedy, McKinstry, Buchbinder, Weisskoff, Cohen, Vevea, Brady, and Rosen, 1991).

CONCLUSIONS

Neuropsychology can no longer ignore neuroimaging data or utilize it in a simplistic fashion. The interface of in vivo neuroimaging with neuropsychological data results in a more powerful outcome than either technique separately. Even though we are in the infancy of both of these fields, it is anticipated that this line of quantitative assessment of brain structure and physiology with behavioral outcome will constitute the future of assessment in neuropsychology.

REFERENCES

Anastasi, A. (1988). *Psychological testing* (6th ed.). New York: Macmillan.

Andrews, M. P., & Milner, B. (1991). The frontal cortex and memory for temporal order. *Neuropsychologia, 29*, 849–859.

Belliveau, J. W., Kennedy, D. N., McKinstry, R. C., Buchbinder, B. R., Weisskoff, R. M., Cohen, M. S., Vevea, J. M., Brady, T. J., & Rosen, B. R. (1991). Functional mapping of the human visual cortex by magnetic resonance imaging. *Science, 254*, 716–719.

Bigler, E. D. (1988). *Diagnostic Clinical Neuropsychology*, Revised Edition. Austin, Texas: University of Texas Press.

Bigler, E. D. (1991). Neuropsychological assessment, neuroimaging and clinical neuropsychology: A synthesis. *Archives of Clinical Neuropsychology, 6*, 113–132.

Bigler, E. D. (1990). Neuropathology of traumatic brain injury. In E. D. Bigler (Ed.), *Traumatic brain injury: Mechanisms of damage, assessment, intervention, and outcome.* Austin, TX: PRO-ED.

Bigler, E. D. (1992). Three-dimensional image analysis of trauma-induced degenerative changes: An aid to neuropsychological assessment. *Archives of Clinical Neuropsychology, 7*, 449–456.

Bigler, E. D., & Erfurth, J. W. (1981). The inappropriate continued singular use of the Bender Visual Motor Gestalt test. *Professional Psychology, 12*, 562–569.

Bigler, E. D., Kurth, S., Blattor, D., & Abildskov, T. (1993). Day-of-injury CT as an index to pre-injury brain morphology: degree of port-injury degenerative changes identified by CT and MR neuroimaging. *Brain Injury*, 125–134.

Bigler, E. D., Snyder, J. L., & Abildskov, T. J. (1992). PC-based 3-dimensional neuroimaging of MRI in cerebral trauma: An aid to neuropsychological assessment. *Journal of Clinical and Experimental Neuropsychology, 14*, 78.

Bigler, E. D., Yeo, R. A., & Turkheimer, E. (1989). *Neuropsychological function and brain imaging.* New York: Plenum Press.

Cullum, C. M., & Bigler, E. D. (1986). Ventricle size, cortical atrophy and the relationship with neuropsychological status in closed head injury: A quantitative analysis. *Journal of Clinical and Experimental Neuropsychology, 8*, 437–452.

Gur, R. C., Trivedi, S. S., Saykin, A. J., & Gur, R. E. (1988). Behavioral imaging: A procedure for the analysis and display of neuropsychological test scores: I. Construction of the algorithm and initial clinical evaluation. *Neuropsychiatry, Neuropsychology & Behavioral Neurology, 1*, 53–60.

Halstead, W. C. (1947). *Brain and intelligence: A quantitative study of the frontal lobes.* Chicago: University of Chicago Press.

Jastak, S., & Wilkinson, G. S. (1984). *Wide range achievement test-revised.* Wilmington, Delaware: Jastak Associates.

Milner, B. (1964). Some effects of frontal lobectomy in man. In J. Warren and K. Ackert (Eds.), *The frontal granular cortex and behavior.* New York: McGraw-Hill, 313–334.

Milner, B., Corsi, P., & Leonard, G. (1991). Frontal-lobe contribution to recency judgments. *Neuropsychologia, 29,* 601–618.

Oldendorf, W. H. (1980). *The quest for an image of brain.* New York: Raven Press.

Pawlik, G., & Heiss, W. D. (1989). Positron emission tomography and neuropsychological function. In E. D. Bigler, R. A. Yeo, & E. Turkheimer (Eds.), *Neuropsychological function and brain imaging* (pp. 65–138). New York: Plenum Press.

Pykett, I. L., Newhouse, J. G., Buonanno, F. S., Brady, T. T., Goldman, M. R., Kistler, J. P., & Prohost, G. M. (1982). Principles of nuclear magnetic resonance imaging. *Radiology, 143,* 157–168.

Reitan, R. M., & Wolfson, D. (1985). *The Halstead-Reitan neuropsychological test battery.* Tucson, AZ: Neuropsychology Press.

Stehling, M. K., Turner, R., & Mansfield, P. (1991). Echo-Planar imaging: Magnetic resonance imaging in a fraction of a second. *Science, 254,* 43–50.

Turkheimer, E. (1989). Techniques of quantitative measurement of morphological structures of the central nervous system. In E. D. Bigler, R. A. Yeo, & E. Turkheimer (Eds.), *Neuropsychological function and brain imaging* (pp. 47–64). New York: Plenum Press.

Turkheimer, E., Yeo, R. A., & Bigler, E. D. (1990). Basic relations among lesion location, lesion volume and neuropsychological performance. *Neuropsychologia, 28,* 1011–1019.

Turkheimer, E., Yeo, R. A., Jones, C. L., & Bigler, E. D. (1990). Quantitative assessment of covariation between neuropsychological function and location of naturally occurring lesions in humans. *Journal of Clinical and Experimental Neuropsychology, 12,* 549–565.

Yeo, R. A., & Bigler, E. D. (1991). Callosal morphology in closed head injury patients. *Journal of Clinical and Experimental Neuropsychology, 13,* 63.

Yeo, R. A., Turkheimer, E., & Bigler, E. D. (1990). Neuropsychological methods of localizing brain dysfunctions: Clinical versus empirical approaches. *Neuropsychiatry, Neuropsychology and Behavioral Neurology, 3,* 290–303.

Yeo, R. A., Turkheimer, E., & Bigler, E. D. (1983). Computer analysis of lesion volume: Reliability, utility and neuropsychological applications. *Clinical Neuropsychology, 5,* 45.

CHAPTER TWO

Brain Structure and Cognitive Function

LEE WILLERMAN, ROBERT SCHULTZ, J. N. RUTLEDGE, AND ERIN D. BIGLER

Only the most hidebound or ideologically driven can still maintain that genetic variation has a negligible impact on general mental ability (e.g., Bouchard, Lykken, McGue, Segal, & Tellegen, 1990; Plomin, DeFries, & McClearn, 1990). Nevertheless, the specific mechanisms by which genes shape and are manifested in brain structure and function have remained elusive. Impediments to progress have included the absence of good animal models and the multifactorial nature of intelligence. Multifactorial inheritance implies multiple genetic and environmental influences so that no single gene, whether regulatory or structural, can dominate IQ variance in the normal range. Identifying individual genes with only modest effects on intellectual function is daunting, but as new techniques from molecular biology become applicable to human intellectual variation (McClearn, Plomin, Gora-Maslak, & Crabbe, 1991), rapid progress can be expected. Until now, most human behavior geneticists necessarily have

Acknowledgment. We thank J. C. Loehlin for comments on an earlier version of this paper.

LEE WILLERMAN • Department of Psychology, University of Texas at Austin, Austin, Texas 78712. ROBERT SCHULTZ • Child Study Center, Yale University, New Haven, Connecticut 06520. J. N. RUTLEDGE • Austin Radiological Association, Austin, Texas 78756. ERIN D. BIGLER • Department of Psychology, Brigham Young University, Provo, Utah 84602.

Cognitive Assessment: A Multidisciplinary Perspective, edited by Cecil R. Reynolds. Plenum Press, New York, 1994.

relied on low-tech methods like twin and adoption designs for untangling genetic and environmental influences on intelligence. However, even these low-tech procedures have provided a remarkably convergent body of findings over the years.

Behavior genetic studies have helped clarify the extent to which the social and biological environment contribute to intellectual variation. Surprisingly, certain classes of social variation, often used to explain intellectual differences, have far less impact than theorized. For example, genetically unrelated adolescents and adults reared together from infancy resemble each other not one whit for IQ, although they resemble each other when younger (see Loehlin, Horn, & Willerman, 1989). Several of these studies have also included genetically related siblings, revealing that they correlate more highly with each other than do the adoptively related pairs. Studies of intelligence comparing younger and older twins also have shown declining effects of shared family environment with age (Chipuer, Rovine, & Plomin, 1990). Given the nigh unshakable faith among many professional and laypersons in the decisiveness of family environment for shaping intelligence, the absence of noticeable familial environmental effects persisting through adolescence is surely one of the most counterintuitive discoveries in psychology. The pertinent social or biological environmental factors that do affect general ability are unshared among family members. These unique influences may include prenatal and postnatal disease, diet, toxins, and trauma, as well as caretaking practices, birth order, age, and gender, or other systematic differences in experiences of children growing up together.

What might be responsible for the *decline* in shared environmental effects with age? A prominent hypothesis is that as children begin to differentially extend their social networks outside the family, qualities of the home environment decreasingly contribute to intellectual development. This hypothesis has not yet been rigorously tested, but would require that such elements as differences in friends, schools, reading habits, and TV preferences, have demonstrable *causal* effects on differences in intelligence within a family. An alternative hypothesis is that some early environmental events may not have noticeable effects on intellectual functioning until adolescence, perhaps precipitated by declines in dendritic density and cerebral oxygen consumption normally occurring during that period (Fineberg, 1987).

Although the identification of specific genes affecting general ability is in the future, current neuroimaging methods can reveal structural and functional characteristics of the brain that covary with intelligence. We now review recent evidence for relations between structural brain features as assessed by magnetic resonance imaging (MRI) and cognitive function in healthy subjects.

THE HUMAN BRAIN

Relative to body size, the human brain is the largest among the species (Jerison, 1973), with extensive cortical folding resulting in greater cortical surface area and a very high fraction of white matter interconnecting information-processing modules (Hofman, 1989). These modules are columnar units of roughly 80–120 neurons depth (columnar width is more ambiguous, Swindale, 1990) descending nearly perpendicularly from the cortical surface to the underlying cortical white matter. This pattern, however, is only truly applicable to the crowns of gyri; along sulcal banks and fundi, orientations of the cortical columns may extend more obliquely from the surface (Welker, 1990). Nevertheless, the columns form a mosaic of functional information processing units, most operating independently with fairly narrow duties, which are then integrated into larger systems via intermodular connections (Gazzaniga, 1989). Individual cortical columns arise from undifferentiated proliferative units that are fully in place by day 40 of embryogenesis, each unit then giving rise to a cortical column of neurons through successive mitotic divisions that stop about halfway through gestation (Rakic, 1988).

Differences in cortical surface area across species depend on the number of proliferative units. Rakic (1988) estimates that humans have 150 to 200 million such units, about 10 times more than the macaque. Since the number of proliferative units appears fixed by human embryo day 40, it suggests that events occurring very early in pregnancy (often before conception is even known) may be predictive of eventual differences in brain size and perhaps intelligence.

Across related species, regional brain size seems to obey the principle of "proper mass"—species specializing in one function more than another (e.g., vision more than audition) have relatively more brain tissue subserving the more dominant function (Jerison, 1973, 1988). This principle is also evident in maps of sensory and motor homunculi where cortical area is proportional to the resolution or precision needed for controlling the corresponding body part (Geschwind, 1979; Welker, 1990). If the principle of proper mass were substantiated for human cognition in the normal range, it would enable strong predictions about brain structure-function relations; for example, more regional brain mass lending to better information processing power. That the proper mass principle also applies to patterns of intellectual function and to special talents, seems a plausible hypothesis. Magnetic resonance imaging studies of those with learning disabilities have shown smaller size of specific brain regions to be a marker for some of these conditions (e.g., Jernigan, Hesselink, Sowell, & Tallal, 1991), but whether symmetry prevails such that a relatively larger regional size predicts special abilities remains to be demonstrated.

BRAIN SIZE AND INTELLIGENCE

Investigations of brain size and intelligence historically were prompted by the intuition that larger size meant more information processing power, analogous to larger muscles implying more strength. Unfortunately, the subtext of many early studies was to justify the social superiority or inferiority of one or another racial, ethnic, or national group (Gould, 1981). Many of these studies were compromised by inadequate appreciation of the complexities of measuring brain size and the absence of standardized measures of intelligence. Postmortem brain weight was itself problematic because of artifacts introduced by brain fixation methods, varying intervals between death and fixation (Coleman & Flood, 1987), lack of control for causes of death (Tobias, 1970), or decreases in brain size with age (Dekaban & Sadowsky, 1978; Ho, Roessman, Straumfjord, & Monroe, 1980). Correlating intelligence with brain size in youthful samples at the height of their intellectual powers or using intracranial volume (which presumably does not decrease with age) might have avoided some of these difficulties, but such studies were not done.

Intelligence most often has been related to extracranial measurements, from which intracranial volume was estimated (e.g., the panracial equation of Lee & Pearson, 1901). Extracranial size is not ideal because of a typical 7 mm range of adult skull thickness (Rogers, 1984) and because of variation in head shape (Beals, Smith, & Dodd, 1984). The latter researches estimate that 13% of the variation in intracranial volume arises from globularity differences in the brain case. With equal perimeters, the more spherical the head or less thick the skull, the greater the intracranial volume. Van Valen (1974) estimated the true correlation of brain size with intelligence to be about $r = .30$. This result was derived from a path analysis of correlations of extracranial with intracranial size, and extracranial size with objective or teacher-rated ability. Many more correlations between external head size and intelligence have since been collected (see Jensen & Sinha, 1993; Rushton, 1990; Lynn, 1990). The results have been remarkably consistent; all correlations have been small and positive, though not all studies partialed out body size to ensure specificity of brain size per se as responsible for the correlations.

It has been thought important to control for body size because of allometric considerations; namely, that larger brain size would in part reflect more brain mass required to control somatic and visceral functions in larger bodies (Jerison, 1973). Different growth curves for brain and body make questionable the precise applicability of adult body size as a control. MRI brain volumes in healthy children (ages 8–10 years) and adults (ages 25–39) show modest and nonsignificant differences between these years (Jernigan & Tallal, 1990), which concurs with findings from postmortem brains (Ho et al., 1980), yet body weight doubles, height increases 20 to 30%, and skull thickness increases about 15%, with a further increase in extracranial size because of added scalp adiposity (Tanner, 1990). Perhaps body size during the preteen years might serve as a better control than adult body size, but even this is uncertain because the brain reaches 60% of its total mass by the end of the first postnatal year (Konner, 1991), when infant body size is much less than half of what it will be in adulthood (Tanner, 1990). If brain size does not increase much during adolescence, partialing out adult body size seems poorly justified and after the fact. While some control may be better than none, adult size seems dubious as the ultimately proper "statistical knife" for carving out that fraction of the brain involved in noncognitive activity. Evidence indicates that the cross-sectional area of motor neuron cell bodies correlates with adult height, but that the sizes of hippocampal neurons do not (Ho, Gwozdz, Hause, & Antuono, 1992). Thus, body size is likely to be associated with brain size in only certain regions, and future work will require finer differentiation of brain anatomy to obtain the proper correction for body size on a region by region basis.

Since noninvasive neuroimaging technology now makes possible in vivo brain size estimates, it seems quite unnecessary to worry further about the limitations of extracranial measures. Magnetic resonance imaging may be the neuroimaging method of choice because it can simultaneously provide data on potentially important physical characteristics other than overall brain size (e.g., regional surface area, white and gray matter proportions, and degree of myelination). Numerous image processing software packages are commercially available which enable segmentation (separation) of tissue into theoretically important regions so that a range of hypotheses about structure–function relations can be tested without simultaneously destroying the raw material. New advances now permit imaging of relatively small structures like the hippocampus, amygdala, and thalamus, all of which have figured in theories of cognitive or language function, but had been directly observable only after disease or death. As these smaller structures and their interrelations become foci of MRI research, the biological substrates of intellectual variation should become somewhat better defined (e.g., Squire & Zola-Morgan, 1991). Before providing selected results from an MRI study of brain structure and intelligence, we briefly review MRI methodology.

MAGNETIC RESONANCE IMAGING

Conventional magnetic resonance images are digitized representations of hydrogen density of water and the interaction of hydrogen protons with other tissue molecules. Hydrogen protons are diamagnetic and therefore can be systematically manipulated to glean their spatial location for purposes of image generation. The MRI signal generated from brain tissue is relatively strong because gray and white matter have a high density of hydrogen protons as a consequence of their high water content, 82 and 72%, respectively (Suzuki, 1972).

Production of an MR image requires both a strong static external magnetic field and a disruptive radiofrequency (RF) pulse. The static magnetic field causes a small majority of the hydrogen protons to align in one direction along an axis, conventionally called the longitudinal axis. The strength of the magnetic field in our research was 1.5 Tesla, or about 30,000 times the earth's magnetic field. The aligned hydrogen protons precess approximately 64 million times per second (64 MHz) with this field strength, just below FM radio frequencies. A brief (3.2 msec) 64 MHz pulse orthogonal to the longitudinal axis tips the aligned protons away from the main field (by 90°) into the transverse plane. Rotation of the protons within the transverse plane induces voltages in surrounding receiver coils at 64 MHz, and it is these voltages that are used to reconstruct the origins of the signal to produce an image.

The "behavior" of tissue water is indexed by two relaxation times—T1 and T2. T1 is defined as the time required for protons to realign with the main field after the 90° tipping pulse. Immediately after the 90° pulse, protons continue to precess about the longitudinal axis, but they are now in the transverse plane. Local tissue biochemistry, however, causes the protons to dephase or lose synchronized precession with one another, thus reducing signal strength and pixel brightness. T2 is defined as the time it takes the precessing protons to dephase.

Images are formed from a matrix of picture elements or pixels. Pixel brightness, other things being equal, is a function of T1, T2, and tissue water content (proton density). Magnetic resonance imaging acquisition procedures which emphasize proton density will create images where gray matter is brighter than white matter, because gray matter has relatively more protons per unit volume capable of emitting a signal (i.e., cell bodies contain more water). T1 and T2 also contribute to gray–white matter contrast. With our image acquisition procedures, contrast was mainly a function of differential gray–white water content and differential T2; T1 contributions to the signals were minimal. As will be described later, image contrast and white matter T2 are predictive of differences in intelligence.

Contrast enables definition of boundaries between tissue types and simultaneously implies something about the microstructural environment in which the protons reside. Contrast is virtually absent in newborns (Holland, Haas, Norman, Brant-Zawadzki, & Newton, 1986), but evolves during the first two years, during which time the cholesterol concentration, a marker of myelination (Koenig, 1991), more than doubles (Dobbing

& Sands, 1973). Thus, the decline in T2 values between birth and toddler-hood reflects the dramatic increase in myelination.

Hydrogen proton T1 and T2 are a function of interactions with macromolecules such as lipids and proteins which comprise neuron membranes. Water in tissue exists in one of two states—free or bound to membranes. Although an oversimplification, the more water bound to membrane surfaces, the shorter the T1 and T2 relaxation times, and the less intense the signal emitted (Cameron, Ord, & Fullerton, 1984). Two ways in which greater gray–white matter contrast can be achieved are by increasing the fraction of bound water within white matter, and/or decreasing the percentage of bound water in gray matter. Increasing the number of surfaces or increasing the number of myelin wrappings about axons, should shorten white matter T2 relaxation time, and net any changes in gray matter, accentuate gray–white matter contrast.

Figure 1 shows horizontal brain "slices" from two female college students who differ greatly in WAIS-R IQ. These images illustrate two pertinent aspects of the brain to be discussed. The brains differ in size and contrast (and also in shape). Notice that contrast between white and gray matter in the brain on the left is lower than in the brain on the right. This is because the white matter is darker in the subject on the right. To quantify image contrast, ventricular cerebrospinal fluid (CSF) first had to be deleted with a cursor tracing. A computer program then segmented the brain image into white and gray matter before calculating the average intensities of white and gray matter pixels, their difference in average

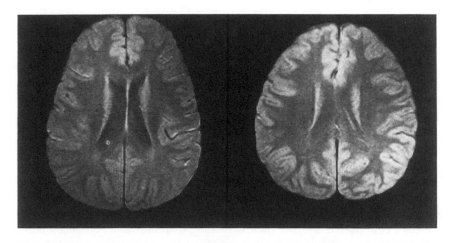

FIGURE 1. Gray and white matter image contrast at the midventricle level in two women (frontal lobes at the top). The brain from an average IQ subject (left) has low contrast between gray and white matter while the brain from a high IQ subject (right) shows high gray–white contrast. The light symmetrical crescent shapes on both sides of the inter-hemispheric fissure represent cerebral spinal fluid in ventricles.

pixel intensity being the definition of contrast. Greater image contrast has been found to be associated with higher intelligence (Schulz, Willerman, Rutledge, & Bigler, 1989; Raz, Millman, & Sarpel, 1990; Schultz, 1991), the evidence for which will be reviewed below.

METHODS

Magnetic resonance imaging was obtained on 40 right-handed college students satisfying a requirement in their introductory psychology course. Equally divided by sex and IQ category, potentially eligible students were first screened for high ($\geq$ 1350) or more modest SAT total scores ($\leq$ 940) so as to increase the yield of subjects who would differ substantially in mean IQ when tested individually. To be eligible for an MRI, students had to obtain prorated WAIS-R Full Scale IQs of either $\geq$ 130 or $\leq$ 103. The prorated IQ was based on four subtests, Vocabulary, Similarities, Picture Completion, and Block Design. This four-subtest aggregate correlated $r = .93$ with FSIQ in the Wechsler standardization sample (Sattler, 1988). Subjects also had to have negative neuropathology histories and be free of metallic implants.

Imaging was performed at a nearby MRI facility, where handedness and family background questionnaires were completed, and height and weight were recorded from a balance scale. Horizontal images were acquired using a multispin echo pulse sequence, where TR = 2000 msec and TE = 30 (proton density) and 80 msec (T2-weighted). There were 18 images of each type. Each image or "slice" was 5 mm thick, separated by gaps of 2.5 mm. The pixel matrix was 256 $\times$ 256, with an 8-bit gray scale. The MRI tapes were read into a VAX/780 computer in the Advanced Graphics Laboratory at the University of Texas, where all analyses were done blindly with respect to sex and IQ.

BRAIN SIZE

Most of the skull, meninges, surface vasculature, and CSF at the brain's perimeter have intensity values that can be easily distinguished from gray and white matter; they are eliminated by thresholding gray scale intensity and converting all such pixels to zero. Often a small amount of nonbrain tissue remains at the perimeter and is deleted manually with a cursor tracing. The brain is then enclosed using the cursor and the number of pixels with values greater than zero within and across slices is counted by the computer to obtain slice or brain size. Interrater reliability for slice area and overall brain size was $r = .99$.

CONTRAST

An edge detection program segmented white from gray matter on three of the slices using the average pixel intensity difference between the two types of tissue. These slices were at the level of the lateral ventricles or higher and were selected after having revealed substantial size differences as a function of intelligence level (Willerman, Schultz, Rutledge, & Bigler, 1991). The program exploits pixel intensity differences at the white–gray border by applying a Laplacian of Gaussian segmentation strategy (Marr & Hildreth, 1980) to the proton-density weighted images (i.e., TE = 30 msec). Typically, the program makes 5 to 15 "errors" per slice, which are corrected manually with a cursor.

Separating ventricular CSF and subcortical gray (e.g., caudate) from the surrounding white matter was necessary for two of the three slices. This was done manually with the cursor. Both gray–white segmentation and removal of nontarget tissue were done very reliably (test–retest reliability $r = .99$).

RESULTS

PRIMARY DATA

Descriptive data on the sample are provided in Table 1. Parental education was high for these subjects, from which we infer that histories of gross nutritional or social deprivation were unlikely. After controlling for sex, body weight and height were negligibly correlated with brain size, $rs = .10$ and $.09$, respectively. Nevertheless, body size was partialled out because brain size adjusted for body size is believed to more closely approximate, even within a species, the proportion of brain tissue devoted to cognitive processing.

TABLE 1. Means (SDs) for Major Variables

	Average IQ		High IQ	
	Men ($n = 10$)	Women ($n = 10$)	Men ($n = 10$)	Women ($n = 10$)
Midparent Education (Years)	15.8 (2.0)	16.2 (1.9)	17.4 (1.8)	16.5 (1.7)
Prorated full scale IQ	91.5 (8.8)	89.5 (7.7)	138.5 (3.7)	134.3 (3.1)
Verbal IQ	92.5 (8.2)	89.8 (10.7)	138.0 (13.1)	129.1 (4.4)
Performance IQ	91.1 (12.1)	91.1 (11.2)	132.1 (9.6)	129.8 (7.7)
VIQ-PIQ	1.4 (12.8)	−1.3 (16.7)	5.9 (20.1)	−0.7 (10.8)

BRAIN SIZE

Sex and high versus average IQ classification were significant predictors of adjusted brain size. The high IQ group had a larger adjusted brain size (r_{pb} = 40,p < .05), as did the men (r_{pb} = .35, p < .05), with no significant interaction. The correlation of adjusted brain size with FSIQ was r = .51, p < .01), higher than expected because of the selection of extreme groups. Using a correction for range restriction (Guilford & Fruchter, 1973) predicted an adjusted brain size × FSIQ correlation of r = .35 in a sample more representative of the IQ distribution in the general population. A stepwise regression in which the dichotomous IQ classification (high versus average IQ group) was entered first and the FSIQ scores themselves entered second, revealed an additional significant effect for the residualized FSIQ scores (r = .41, p < .05), suggesting generalizability to a more continuous IQ distribution.

Figure 2 gives the corresponding scattergrams for Verbal and Performance IQ. Adjusted brain size × IQ correlations with VIQ (r = .47) and PIQ (r = .54) were significant. The PIQ correlation with brain size was somewhat higher than the corresponding correlation with VIQ, despite an r = .78 between VIQ and PIQ. Whether the correlation difference between PIQ and VIQ actually reflects more brain size influence on fluid than crystallized abilities is a question that immediately comes to mind, but would require a diverse battery of fluid and crystallized ability tests to answer properly.

Not all levels of the brain contributed equally to the adjusted brain size × IQ correlation. Those horizontal brain levels nearest to the lateral ventricles show greater brain size differences as a function of IQ than levels above or below (see Figure 3). This result is hardly surprising because language and association circuits (e.g., angular gyrus, arcuate fasciculus) that figure prominently in distinguishing humans from other primates are included in these levels (Deacon, 1988), and presumably ought to capture intelligence-related structural brain differences within humans as well.

Recent MRI research has now confirmed the relations just reported in an older and more variable sample (Mean age = 38 years, SD = 16) (Andreasen, Flaum, Swayze, O'Leary, Alliger, Cohen, Ehrhardt, & Yuh, 1993). They obtained IQ × intracranial volume correlations for men and women of r = .40 (n = 37) and r = .44 (n = 30), respectively, after adjusting for height. Correlations of total brain size with IQ were not given, but volumes as the left and right cerebrums, hippocampi, and temporal lobes correlated with IQ, as did the volume of the cerebellum. Another analysis used volumes of gray and white matter in the total sample to predict IQ; gray matter volume × IQ was significant (r = .35), but not white matter volume × IQ (r = .12). The gray and white matter

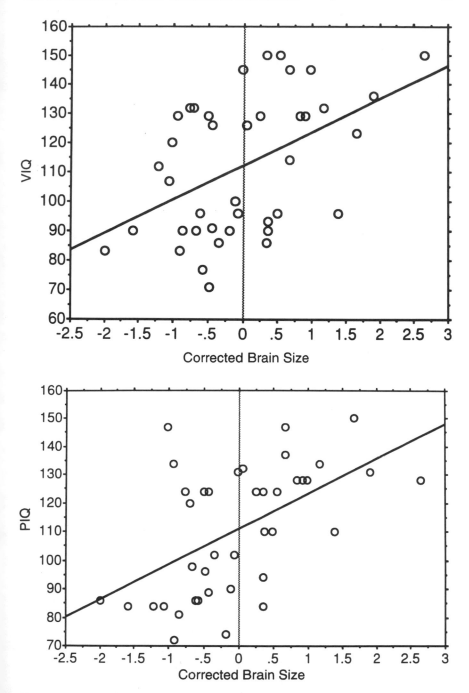

FIGURE 2. Scattergrams for corrected brain size with Verbal IQ and Performance IQ. The horizontal axis is in standard score units ($M = 0 \pm SD = 1$).

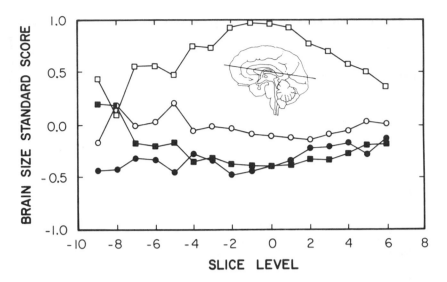

FIGURE 3. Brain area in standard scores ($M = 0 \pm SD = 1$) by high versus average IQ group and sex, adjusted for height and weight. Squares refer to men and circles to women; empty symbols refer to high IQ and filled symbols to average IQ groups. Slice 0 is at the midventricle level as shown in the insert. Brain sizes above or below graphed levels are not shown because all subjects could not be represented. (From Willerman et al., 1991).

correlations are slightly lower than would have been obtained had age and sex been partialled out in addition to stature (Jensen & Sinha, 1993).

CONTRAST

Figure 4 presents scattergrams of gray–white matter contrast with Verbal and Performance IQ our subjects (Schultz et al., 1989; Schultz, 1991). Contrast × IQ *rs* were higher for PIQ ($r = .62$) than for VIQ ($r = .45$), a pattern that was also characteristic of the brain size correlations. The contrast × FSIQ correlation was $r = .54$ ($p < .01$). Stepwise regression revealed that both brain size and image contrast made statistically significant contributions to predicting FSIQ, VIQ, and PIQ.

Schultz (1991) found that the contrast–IQ relation was due primarily to shorter white matter T2 times being associated with higher IQ. Since shorter T2 times can result from an increased number of membrane surfaces to which water binds (Cameron et al., 1984), Schultz hypothesized that shorter T2 times in high IQ subjects implied either a greater number of myelinated fibers and/or more wrappings of myelin around each axon. We should add, however, that variation in the biochemistry of myelin might also account for the findings. Myelin normally contains "sinks" to bind hydrogen protons; subtle differences in its structure conceivably might affect the extent to which free hydrogen protons become bound to its surfaces (Koenig, 1991).

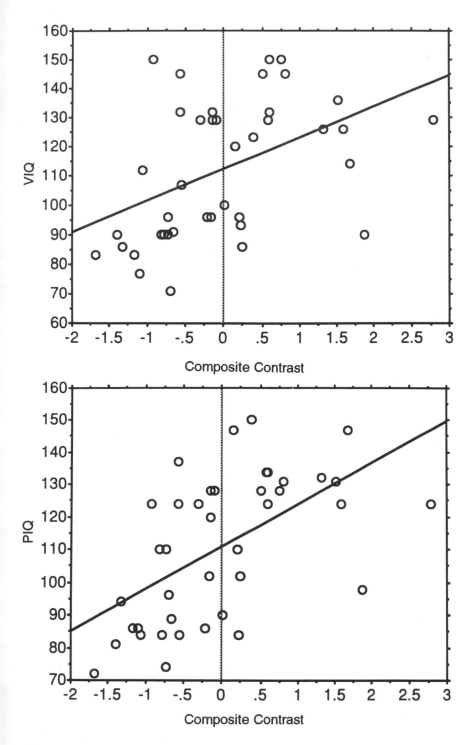

FIGURE 4. Gray minus white matter image contrast ($M = 0 \pm SD = 1$) with Verbal and Performance IQ.

Although applicability of findings from pathological or experimentally induced demyelination studies is uncertain here, myelin loss reduces nerve conduction velocity, lengthens refractory periods, temporally disperses impulses, and increases transmission failures (Konner, 1991). Evoked brain potential studies of normals have inferred greater fidelity of neural transmission to be associated with higher intelligence (Barrett & Eysenck, 1992; Stough, Nettlebeck, & Cooper, 1990), so that a specific connection between myelin quantity or quality and intelligence or speed of information processing seems a reasonable working hypothesis.

With a sample of 26 ostensibly healthy adults ranging in age from 18 to 78, Raz, Millman, & Sarpel (1990) measured gray–white contrast based on T1 relaxation time. Contrast declined with age and increased with intelligence. Both Raz et al. and Schultz (1991) have specifically implicated white matter properties as significant in healthy populations. Parallel declines in fluid ability and contrast with age make it tempting to explore the connection between these two findings, as perhaps both are related to axonal–myelin integrity.

Since speed of mental processing figures prominently in many theories of intelligence and myelin enhances nerve conduction velocity (NCV), age-related declines in mental speed (Salthouse, 1991) also could reflect compromised myelin integrity. That myelin-related variation could influence intelligence in a younger sample seems plausible because NCV and general ability are correlated in college students (Reed & Jensen, 1992). Brain NCV as estimated from latency between retinal stimulation and the first (~70 msec) and second (~100 msec) evoked potential peaks in primary visual cortex is correlated with Raven Advanced Progressive Matrices scores $r = .27$ and .37 (after corrections for anterior–posterior head length, unreliability, and range restriction). Since myelinated fibers are largely responsible for the fastest transmission times along this nerve tract, myelin quality or quantity is implicated.

Vernon and Mori (1992) have recently reported two studies with ns of 85 and 88 showing significant correlations between IQ and NCV in the median nerve of the arm in college students. Several NCVs were obtained for wrist to finger, wrist to elbow, and wrist to axilla. The correlations of IQ with wrist to finger NCV were consistently higher, rs ranging from .38 to .48, than the other NCVs, rs ranging from .15 to .30. The hypothesis that shared qualities of myelin in the peripheral and central nervous system (e.g., the thickness of the myelin or the spacing of the nodes of Ranvier) are responsible for the correlations with intelligence is seductive, but myelin in the peripheral (PNS) and central nervous system (CNS) have different embryonic origins (Schwann cell myelin in the PNS arises from the neural crest while oligodendrocytes for CNS myelin arise from the neural tube). The NCV × IQ correlations tended to be higher for efferents (wrist to finger) than afferents is perhaps significant because efferents originate in the CNS, whereas afferents arise from ganglia adjacent to the spinal cord, from which they simultaneously grow toward the peripheral target structure and toward the brain. At this stage it is too early to know whether axonal or myelin qualities are responsible for the correlations with intelligence. Moreover, two studies of similar design, but with negative results, already exist (Barrett, Daum, & Eysenck, 1990; Reed & Jensen, 1991). The Barrett et al. study probably did not provide sufficiently intense stimulation to ensure that all fibers in the median nerve were firing and will not be considered further. The large Reed and Jensen study, however, is more comparable to the Vernon and Mori research. They correlated wrist to elbow afferent NCV with intelligence in two groups of college students. The statistically negligible correlations of NCV with IQ ranged from $r = -.09$ to .04. Methodological differences might account for the discrepant results, but if the Vernon and Mori results prove replicable, it could lead to novel ideas about biological substrates for general intelligence.

SEX DIFFERENCES

A major interpretive complication of the brain size–intelligence relation is that women tend to have smaller brains than men even after adjusting for body size (Ankney, 1992; Gur, Mozeley, Resnick, Gottlieb, Kohn, Zimmerman, Herman, Atlas, Grossman, Berretta, Erwin, & Gur, 1991; Peters, 1991; Willerman et al., 1991), yet women do not have lower general intelligence. Wechsler's tests and the Stanford-Binet were designed with an eye to minimizing sex differences so that strong conclusions about an absence of cognitive sex differences based on these tests cannot be made. The Raven Progressive Matrices, however, which is a good measure of general mental ability, also shows no sex difference, though sex was ignored in its standardization (Raven & Court, 1989).

What are the possible explanations for the fact that women and men do not differ in general intelligence? Sex differences in brain organization may permit females to accomplish similar adaptive goals via somewhat different strategies or neural substrates (Willerman, Schultz, Rutledge, & Bigler, 1992). Also, Haug (1987) has found that women's brains have greater cortical neuron-packing density, so that their cortical neuron numbers may in fact be equal to those of men. He suggests that larger brain size in men is due to greater dendritic proliferation and/or thicker axons. Ankney (1992) has hypothesized that the difference in brain size is the result of the sexual selection which provided pressures for better three-dimensional visualization in males. This hypothesis is interesting because disproportionately large hippocampi characterize males of species who range widely in their foraging or sexual activities (Sherry, Jacobs, & Gaulin, 1992). Rich connections between the hippocampus and the parietal cortex, a lobe figuring importantly in human three-dimensional visualization, suggests that a larger male brain may arise from these specific adaptations.

Is there evidence for sex differences in brain organization? Focal left hemisphere (LH) damage is less likely to result in aphasia or apraxia in women, except for damage in a region of the frontal lobe, where it is more likely to produce symptoms in women (Kimura, 1987). Moreover, electrical stimulation of LH cortex in patients about to undergo surgical resection for epilepsy is relatively less likely to interfere with language production in females than in males. (Ojemann, Ojemann, Lettich, & Berger, 1989). Finally, female patients with LH lesions seem to show impairments in both verbal and nonverbal intellectual functions, whereas men with LH damage show reductions only in verbal abilities (see Inglis & Lawson, 1982; Turkheimer & Farace, 1992). The trend is for LH lesions in women to produce relatively smaller within-subject differences between VIQ and PIQ.

Since these studies all were of brain injured patients, we wanted to learn whether greater LH involvement in nonverbal functions was observable in healthy college women. Four horizontal MR slices surrounding the middle of the lateral venticles were divided into left and right hemispheres as defined by a line drawn through the interhemispheric fissure (Willerman, et al., 1992). The slices were selected because they showed the largest size differences as a function of high versus average IQ classification (see Figure 3). One high IQ woman was excluded from further analysis because the size difference between her two hemispheres was twice as large as the next largest difference. As asymmetry index was created by subtracting left hemisphere size from right hemisphere size (LH−RH) and dividing by average hemisphere size (LH+RH)/2. A positive asymmetry index indicates a relatively larger LH than RH, while a negative value indicates a relatively larger RH. Prorated Verbal minus Performance (V−PIQ) was the major dependent variable.

An analysis of variance in which sex and asymmetry (LH > RH; LH < RH) were the independent variables and V−PIQ was the dependent variable, revealed a significant sex difference in slope direction. This interaction ($p < .001$), illustrated in Figure 5, shows that for men a LH > RH was associated with VIQ > PIQ, while a LH < RH pattern was associated with a VIQ < PIQ. The asymmetry index correlated with the V−PIQ discrepancy, $r = .44$ ($p < .06$) in the men. In women, the asymmetry index correlation was opposite in direction, $r = -.55$ ($p < .05$). Women with a LH > RH tended to have relatively higher PIQs than VIQs, while those with LH < RH showed the opposite pattern.

A parallel analysis was run on the Vocabulary minus Block Design scale scores alone, with similar results. The asymmetry index in men was correlated with Vocabulary − Block Design scale scores, $r = .62$ ($p < .05$), while in women, the corresponding $r = -.41$ ($p < .09$) was opposite in direction. The interaction with sex was again significant ($p < .01$),

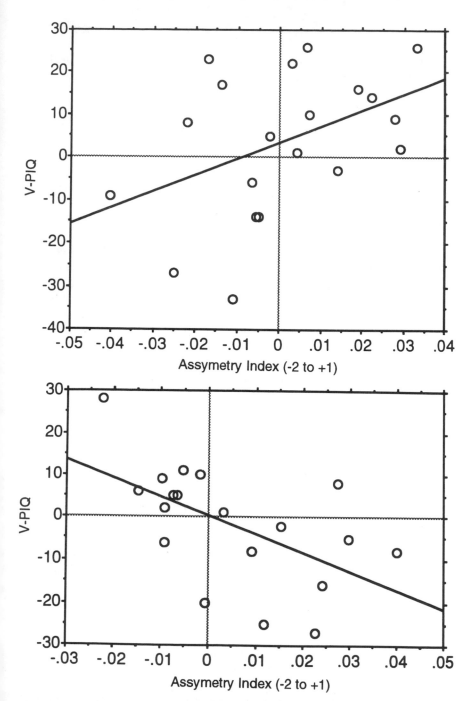

FIGURE 5. Scatterplots of VIQ minus PIQ with hemisphere asymmetry by sex (Males in upper panel, females in lower panel). The Asymmetry Index in LH−RH/(LH+RH)/2. A positive asymmetry index indicates a relatively larger LH than RH. A negative asymmetry index indicates a relatively larger RH than LH (From Willerman, Schultz, Rutledge, & Bigler, 1992).

indicating that the relative size of the LH or RH had different effects on the pattern of within-subject verbal and nonverbal function in each sex. We conclude that sex differences in brain organization affecting cognitive function do exist.

NATURE OF g

Since Spearman (1904) first documented positive correlations among diverse mental tests, the underlying nature of general mental ability or g has been the subject of considerable factor analytic research and theory (Carroll, 1989). One unresolved issue is whether g is unitary or characterized by multiple processes. Kranzler and Jensen (1991) noted that even if entities A, B, C, etc. independently contributed to g, conventional mental tests have included all the entities in unknown proportions, producing the positive correlations among mental tests. Without independent data on the nature of A, B, and C, progress is hardly possible, though it now seems clearer that multiple factors contribute to g. Using stepwise regression, Kranzler and Jensen (1991a,b) found that g was predicted by four factors derived from a battery of elementary cognitive tasks (ECTs). If g were a unitary process, only a single predictor would have emerged because this procedure partials out the influence of predictors entered earlier. Similar results have been recently obtained by Vernon and Weese (1993).

Our MRI findings also suggest multiple factors underlying g. One component is brain size, which presumably indexes greater resolving power or redundancy of information processing mechanisms (Glassman, 1987). The second component is myelination as indexed by white matter T2 relaxation time, which probably has consequences for neural conduction velocity and/or signal reliability.

It would be interesting to correlate mental tasks having a wide range of g loadings with each of these two biological variables. To the extent that mental tests correlated differentially with them, it would provide clues to processes underlying performances on those tests. Extending this analysis to other brain features such as the size of specific structures or cortical surface areas could enrich the picture even further.

REFERENCES

Andreasen, N. C., Flaum, M., Swayze, V., O'Leary, D. S., Alliger, R., Cohen, G., Ehrhardt, J., & Yuh, W. T. C. (1993). Intelligence and brain structure in normal individuals. *American Journal of Psychiatry, 150*, 130–134.

Ankney, C. D. (1992). Sex differences in relative brain size: The mismeasure of women, too? *Intelligence, 16*, 329–336.

Barrett, P. T., & Eysenck, H. J. (1992). Brain evoked potentials and intelligence: The Hendrickson paradigm. *Intelligence, 16,* 361–381.

Beals, K. L., Smith, C. L., & Dodd, S. M. (1984). Brain size, cranial morphology, climate, and time machines. *Current Anthropology, 25,* 301–330.

Bouchard, T. J. Jr., Lykken, D. T., McGue, M., Segal, H. L., & Tellegen, A. (1990). Sources of human psychological differences: The Minnesota study of twins reared apart. *Science, 250,* 223–228.

Cameron, I. L., Ord, V. A., & Fullerton, G. D. (1984). Characterization of proton NMR relaxation times in normal and pathological tissues by correlation with other tissue parameters. *Magnetic Resonance Imaging, 2,* 97–106.

Chipuer, H. M., Rovine, M. J., & Plomin, R. (1990). LISREL modeling: Genetic and environmental influences on IQ revisited. *Intelligence, 14,* 11–29.

Coleman, P. D., & Flood, D. G. (1987). Neuron numbers and dendritic extent in normal aging and Alzheimer's disease. *Neurobiology of Aging, 8,* 521–545.

Deacon, T. W. (1988). Human brain evolution. II: Embryology and brain allometry. In H. J. Jerison & I. Jerison (Eds.), *Intelligence and evolutionary biology* (pp. 363–381). New York: Springer-Verlag.

Dekaban, A. S., & Sadowsky, D. (1978). Changes in brain weights during the span of human life. *Annals of Neurology, 4,* 345–356.

Dobbing, J., & Sands, J. (1973). Quantitative growth and development of human brain. *Archives of Diseases in Childhood, 48,* 757–767.

Fineberg, I. (1987). Adolescence and mental illness. *Science, 236,* 507.

Gazzaniga, M. S. (1989). Organization of the human brain. *Science, 245,* 947–952.

Geschwind, N. (1979). Specializations of the human brain. *Scientific American, 241,* 180–199.

Glassman, R. B. (1987). An hypothesis about redundancy and reliability in the brains of higher species: Analogies with genes, internal organs, and engineering systems. *Neuroscience and Biobehavioral Reviews, 11,* 275–285.

Gould, S. J. (1981). *The mismeasure of man.* New York: Norton.

Guilford, J. P., & Fruchter, B. (1973). *Fundamental statistics in psychology and education.* New York: McGraw-Hill.

Gur, R. C., Mozley, P. D., Resnick, S. M., Gottlieb, G. L., Kohn, M., Zimmerman, R., Herman, G., Atlas, S., Grossman, R., Berretta, D., Erwin, R., & Gur, R. E. (1991). Gender differences in age effect on brain atrophy measured by magnetic resonance imaging. *Proceedings National Academy of Sciences, USA, 88,* 2845–2849.

Haug, H. (1987). Brain sizes, surfaces, and neuronal sizes of the cortex cerebri: A stereological investigation of man and his variability and a comparison with some species of mammals (primates, whales, marsupials, insectivores, and one elephant). *American Journal of Anatomy, 180,* 126–142.

Ho, K., Roessman, U., Straumfjord, J. V., & Monroe, G. (1980). Analysis of brain weight. II. *Archives of Pathology and Laboratory Medicine, 104,* 640–645.

Ho, K., Gwozdz, J. T., Hause, L. L., & Antuono, P. G. (1992). Correlation of neuronal cell body size in motor cortex and hippocampus with body height, body weight, and axonal length. *International Journal of Neuroscience, 65,* 147–153.

Hofman, M. A. (1989). On the evolution and geometry of the brain in mammals. *Progress in Neurobiology, 32,* 137–158.

Holland, B. A., Haas, D. K., Norman, D., Brant-Zawadzki, M., & Newton, T. H. (1986). MRI of normal brain maturation. *American Journal of Neuroradiology, 7,* 201–208.

Inglis, J., & Lawson, J. S. (1982). A meta-analysis of sex differences in the effects of unilateral brain damage on intelligence test results. *Canadian Journal of Psychology, 36,* 670–683.

Jensen, A. R., & Sinha, S. N. (1993). Physical correlates of human intelligence. In P. A.

Vernon (Ed.), *Biological approaches to the study of human intelligence*. Norwood, NJ: Ablex.

Jerison, H. J. (1973). *Evolution of the brain and intelligence*. New York: Academic Press.

Jerison, H. J. (1988). The evolutionary biology of intelligence: Afterthoughts. In H. J. Jerison & I. Jerison (Eds.), *Intelligence and evolutionary biology* (pp. 447–466). New York: Springer-Verlag.

Jernigan, T. L., Hesselink, J. R., Sowell, E., & Tallal, P. A. (1991). Cerebral structure on magnetic resonance imagining in language- and learning impaired children. *Archives of Neurology, 48*, 539–545.

Jernigan, T. L., & Tallal, P. A. (1990). Late childhood changes in brain morphology observable with MRI. *Developmental Medicine and Child Neurology, 32*, 379–385.

Kimura, D. (1987). Are men's and women's brains really different? *Canadian Psychology, 28*, 133–147.

Koenig, S. H. (1991). Cholesterol of myelin is the determinant of gray–white contrast in MRI of brain. *Magnetic Resonance in Medicine, 20*, 285–291.

Konner, M. (1991). Universals of behavioral development in relation to brain myelination. In K. R. Gibson & A. C. Petersen (Eds.), *Brain maturation and cognitive development* (pp. 181–223). New York: Aldine de Gruyter.

Kranzler, J. H., & Jensen, A. R. (1991). Unitary g: Unquestioned postulate or empirical fact? *Intelligence, 15*, 437–448.

Lee, A., & Pearson, K. (1901). Data for the problem of evolution in man. VI. A first study of the correlation of the human skull. *Transactions of the Royal Society of London, 196A*, 225–264.

Loehlin, J. C., Horn, J. M., & Willerman, L. (1989). Modeling IQ change: Evidence from the Texas Adoption Project. *Child Development, 60*, 993–1004.

Lynn, R. (1990). New evidence on brain size and intelligence: A comment on Rushton and Cain and Vanderwolf. *Personality & Individual Differences, 11*, 795–797.

Marr, D., & Hildreth, E. (1980). Theory of edge detection. *Proceedings Royal Society of London, 207*, 187–217.

McClearn, G. E., Plomin, R., Gora-Maslak, G., & Crabbe, J. C. (1991). The gene chase in behavioral science. *Psychological Science, 2*, 222–229.

Peters, M. (1991). Sex differences in human brain size and the general meaning of differences in brain size. *Canadian Journal of Psychology, 45*, 507–522.

Plomin, R., DeFries, J. C., & McClearn, G. E. (1990). *Behavioral genetics: A primer* (2nd ed). New York: W. H. Freeman.

Rakic, P. (1988). Specification of cerebral cortical areas. *Science, 241*, 170–176.

Raven, J., & Court, J. H. (1989). *Manual for Raven's Progressive Matrices and vocabulary scales: Research Supplement No. 4*. London: H. K. Lewis.

Raz, N., Millman, D., & Sarpel, G. (1990). Cerebral correlates of cognitive aging: Gray–white matter differentiation in the medial temporal lobes, and fluid versus crystallized abilities. *Psychobiology, 18*, 475–481.

Reed, T. E., & Jensen, A. R. (1991). Arm nerve conduction velocity (NCV), brain NCV, reaction time, and intelligence. *Intelligence, 15*, 33–47.

Reed, T. E., & Jensen, A. R. (1992). Conduction velocity in a brain nerve pathway of normal adults correlates with intelligence level. *Intelligence, 16*, 259–272.

Rogers, S. L. (1984). *The human skull*. Springfield, IL: Thomas.

Rushton, J. P. (1990). Race, brain size and intelligence: A rejoinder to Cain and Vanderwolf. *Personality & Individual Differences, 11*, 785–794.

Salthouse, T. A. (1991). Mediation of adult age differences in cognition by reductions in working memory and speed of processing. *Psychological Science, 2*, 179–183.

Sattler, J. M. (1988). *Assessment of children*. San Diego, CA: Jerome M. Sattler.

Schultz, R. T. (1991). *The relationship between intelligence and gray–white matter image contrast: A MRI study of healthy college students.* Unpublished Doctoral Dissertation, University of Texas at Austin.

Schultz, R., Willerman, L., Rutledge, J. N., & Bigler, E. (1989). MRI contrast and intelligence. *Archives of Clinical Neuropsychology, 5,* 212 (Abstract).

Sherry, D. F., Jacobs, L. F., & Gaulin, S. J. C. (1992). Spatial memory and adaptive specialization of the hippocampus. *Trends in Neuroscience, 15,* 298–303.

Spearman, C. (1904). "General intelligence", objectively determined and measured. *American Journal of Psychology, 15,* 201–293.

Squire, L. R., & Zola-Morgan, S. (1991). The medial temporal lobe memory system. *Science, 253,* 1380–1386.

Stough, C. K. K., Nettlebeck, T., & Cooper, C. J. (1990). Evoked brain potentials, string length and intelligence. *Personality and Individual Differences, 11,* 401–406.

Suzuki, K. (1972). *Chemistry and metabolism of brain lipids.* In R. W. Albers, G. J. Katzman, & B. W. Agranoff (Eds). *Basic neurochemistry* (pp. 207–225). Boston: Little, Brown.

Swindale, N. V. (1990). Is the cortex modular? *Trends in Neurosciences, 12,* 487–492.

Tanner, J. M. (1990). *Fetus into man.* Cambridge, MA: Harvard University Press.

Tobias, P. V. (1970). Brain size, grey matter, and race—fact or fiction? *American Journal of Physical Anthropology, 32,* 3–26.

Turkheimer, E., & Farace, E. (1992). A reanalysis of gender differences in IQ scores following unilateral brain lesions. *Psychological Assessment, 4,* 498–501.

Vernon, P. A., & Mori, M. (1992). Intelligence, reaction times, and peripheral nerve conduction velocity. *Intelligence, 16,* 273–288.

Vernon, P. A., & Weese, S. E. (1993). Predicting intelligence with multiple speed of information-processing tests. *Personality and Individual Differences, 14,* 413–419.

Welker, W. (1990). Why does cerebral cortex fissure and fold? In E. G. Jones & A. Peters (Eds.), *Cerebral cortex (Vol. 8B) Comparative structure and evolution of cerebral cortex, Part II* (pp. 3–136). New York: Plenum Press.

Willerman, L., Schultz, R., Rutledge, A. N., & Bigler, E. D. (1991). *In vivo* brain size and intelligence. *Intelligence, 15,* 223–228.

Willerman, L., Schultz, R., Rutledge, A. N., & Bigler, E. D. (1992). Hemisphere size asymmetry predicts relative verbal and nonverbal intelligence differently in the sexes: An MRI study of structure-function relations. *Intelligence, 16,* 315–328.

CHAPTER THREE

Assessment of Cognitive Function: Exploration of Memory Processing to Topographical Mapping Techniques

J. F. DeFrance, C. Hymel, J. Degioanni, D. S. Calkin, S. Estes, F. C. Schweitzer, and R. Hymel

> Lull'd in the countless chambers of the brain,
> Our thoughts are link'd by many a hidden chain;
> Awake but one, and lo, what myriads rise!
> Each stamps its image as the other flies.
>
> Alexander Pope

Human memory function has been the subject of intensive study. Nevertheless, little is known as to how the brain integrates its operations during the learning process so that an individual memory can "stamp its image" during recollection or recall. Electrophysiological approaches hold

J. F. DeFrance • University of Texas Medical School, Houston, Texas 77025; HCA Gulf Pines Hospital, Houston, Texas 77090. C. Hymel • Graduate School of Biomedical Sciences, University of Texas at Houston, Houston, Texas 77025. J. Degioanni • National Aeronautics and Space Administration, Johnson Space Center, Houston, Texas 77058. D. S. Calkin • Krug Life Sciences, Houston, Texas 77058. S. Estes, F. C. Schweitzer, and R. Hymel • HCA Gulf Pines Hospital, Houston, Texas 77090.

Cognitive Assessment: A Multidisciplinary Perspective, edited by Cecil R. Reynolds. Plenum Press, New York, 1994.

great promise in helping to unlock some of the mysteries of memory processing. While behavioral, lesion (e.g., clinical case studies), and laboratory studies such as magnetic resonance imaging (MRI), computerized tomography (CT), and positron emission tomography (PET) can be very helpful, only physiological studies can directly measure changes in brain activity in real time, that is associated with the various operational stages of mnemonic function. The focus here was on what we think to be one of the more interesting aspects of human memory—the "proactive interference" effect.

Proactive interference (PI) involves a deterioration in apparent memory function due to an interaction with previously learned material (Underwood, 1957; Wickens, 1970, 1973). Because the PI effect has been easily demonstrated in normals (e.g., Wickens, Born, & Allen, 1963)—and especially so in various clinical populations (Cremak & Butters, 1972; Stuss, Kaplan, Benson, Weir, Chiulli, & Srarzin, 1982)—it has been of considerable interest to psychologists and other cognitive neuroscientists. It is not unreasonable to speculate that the ability to process information effectively in the face of interfering material is a sign of a healthy nervous system. The deterioration in a person's ability to cope with interference accompanies various pathological conditions, ranging from frontal lobe trauma (Stuss et al., 1982), certain dementias (Beatty & Butters, 1986; Wilson, Como, Garron, Klawans, Barr, & Klawan, 1987), to serious alcohol abuse (Cremak & Butters, 1972; Cremak, Butters, & Moreines, 1974).

Since Underwood (1957) demonstrated the importance of PI in the forgetting of material from long-term memory, there has been little debate as to the existence of the effect. It is not yet firmly established whether or not the impairment is due to an encoding or retrieval difficulty, although the bulk of the research has emphasized the importance of the encoding side of memory processing. Wickens (1973) has argued that PI resulted from the very nature of encoding functions, based upon the fact that elements which are homogeneous with respect to a specific psychological class, are not only encoded as a unique item, but also as a member of that psychological class. Hence, we presume that the elements or members of the same class have less to distinguish them for the retrieval process. Supporting the role of failure of encoding have been a number of clinical studies. For instance, Cremak & Butters (1972) studied patients with Korsakoff's syndrome and concluded that for these patients, their encoding was not precise enough to allow categorical retrieval. Putting a slight turn on the encoding hypothesis, Thomson & Tulving (1970) believed that the critical point was not that the retrieval cue be presented at input, but that the recalled items were encoded in a fashion appropriate to the retrieval cue.

In a slightly different slant to that of Wickens (1970), a study by Gardiner, Craik, & Birstwistle (1972) questioned the encoding characteristics role in PI by investigating the role of retrieval cues in the buildup and release from PI. They found evidence that a retrieval cue will be effective in improving recall provided that the material is specifically encoded with respect to that cue at the time of its storage. Thinking along these lines tends to blur the absolute distinction between encoding and retrieval stages of memory processing.

Recording electrical brain activity through the human scalp, which is synchronized with a stimulus while an individual is engaged in active processing, produces a family of identifiable and highly reliable components which make up the cognitive event-related potential (ERP). Generally speaking, components of interest occur up to 700 msec after the onset of the stimulus and includes a sensory evoked response and a collection of higher order processing components. These various processing components reflect the various stages involved in the information processing (Donchin, Ritter, & McCallum, 1978; Halgren & Smith, 1987; Hillyard, 1985), but not the content per se. Smith and Halgren (1986a,b) have studied a negative–positive (N4 and LPC) complex which followed the elementary sensory component and appeared to correlate with higher order cognitive processing. The negative component was referred to as an associative negativity. This late positive component has been termed the "late positive component" (Hillyard & Kutas, 1983; Picton & Stuss, 1980). The LPC is equivalent to the P3 or P300 (Sutton, Braren, Zubin, & John, 1965) and is most prominent in those performance paradigms where a decision is to be made (Halgren, Squires, Wilson, Rohrbaugh, Babb, & Crandall, 1980; Hillyard, 1985; Hillyard, Hink, Schwent, & Picton, 1973).

Smith and Halgren (1986) have found that the N4 component declines as material becomes familiar, whereas the P3 (i.e., LPC) becomes larger. It was suggested that the LPC reflect a sort of "perceptual closure." Of prime importance, both components of the ERPs appear very much dependent upon temporal lobe function. Smith and Halgren (1986) found that with left temporal lesions, there is a preserved N4 component but that there was no regulation of the N4 between familiar and unfamiliar words. This had led to the notion that the N4 reflects "context retrieval" which is important in the recall process (Halgren & Smith, 1987; Jacoby, 1983). In any event, it is reasonable to conclude at this time that the N4 component reflects a modulatory operation of the temporal lobe. Furthermore, it has been shown that for such paradigms the N4 is closely related to semantic processing generated by the semantic context (Hillyard & Kutas, 1983; Polich, 1985). For instance, the N4 develops in the presence of semantic change, not differences in the physical attributes such as differing typeface (Kutas & Hillyard, 1984). Thus, semantic processing capable of activating associative processing may evoke the N4 component. This study explored the electrophysiological correlates of the verbal "proactive interference" effect, especially in regard to the N4 and LPC components—in part to illustrate how a coupled behavioral and electrophysiological approach can be exploited.

METHOD

SUBJECTS

This report is based upon data from 45, right-handed, nonreferred male and female volunteer subjects. They were recruited from a local medical school and were free of any known psychological, neurological, or psychiatric conditions. The ages ranged from 21 to 34.

BEHAVIORAL PROBE

The behavioral probe was organized into separate "acquisition" and "retrieval" sections, each with its own set of evoked potentials. Words for the acquisition phase were taken from the following semantic categories: four-footed animals, sports, weather phenomena, natural earth formations, birds, and parts of buildings, according to Battig and Montague's (1969) category norms. The word groups were organized in terms of three trials over six blocks. Each trial consisted of 10 acquisition and recall words. Three trials formed a block, where the items were all taken from the same semantic category. Word frequency and syllables were equated within a block.

In the retrieval phase, words were presented one at a time on the screen and the subject was asked to press the right mouse button if the word was in the list just presented, or the left button if it was not. In each recall list, 50% of the items were from the immediately preceding list. The number of correct responses as well as the reaction times were recorded.

There was also a preliminary phase where scrambled letters were presented and the subjects were instructed to merely sit and watch the screen. The ERPs from this section were used to compare with those where active memory processing was demanded.

RECORDING SCHEME

The EEG was recorded from 28 active recording sites referenced to linked earlobes (A1-A2). The montage is based on the international 10-20 system (Jasper, 1958), with additional electrodes placed in the frontotemporal (FTC1, FTC2), centroparietal (CP1, CP2), temporoparietal (TCP1, TCP2), and occipital (PO1, PO2) regions. Low-noise tin electrodes were used in all cases and the impedance kept at less than 5 KOhm. Additional electrodes were used to monitor extraocular artifacts. Vertical eye movements and blinks were recorded via electrodes placed immediately above and below the orbit of the left eye. Horizontal eye movements were monitored with an additional pair of electrodes located at the external canthi. The EEG and EOG was amplified with a 32-channel NeuroScience Brain Imager (0.1–40 Hz, 6 dB/octave lowpass, 36 dB/octave highpass). The raw EEG was sampled in 800 msec periods by 16-bit analogue-to-digital converters (TECMAR Labmaster DMA) under control of the SCAN EP/EEG acquisition and analysis system (NeuroScan, Inc.). Topographic maps were constructed by weighting interpolated map voltage values by the inverse of the linear distance of the four nearest electrode sites (Buchsbaum, Rigal, Coppola, Cappelletti, King, & Johnson, 1982).

The analytic approach described herein has important advantages over earlier mapping approaches in its ability accurately to identify and remove eye movement and blink artifacts (Corby & Kopell, 1972; Semlitsch, Anderer, Schuster, & Presslich, 1986; Verleger, Gasser, & Mocks, 1982). These represent a serious source of artifact in topographic maps, especially for detection of frontal and temporal lobe function. These artifacts generally diminish both the sensitivity and accuracy of topographic mapping. Electrooculargram (EOG) artifacts originate from a steady-state dipole between the retina and the cornea. Blinks and/or eye movements affect this dipole by creating large potential fields that sweep across the scalp thereby distorting the EEG. The influence of these artifacts is greatest in the anterior leads (i.e., those closest to the eye muscles). Vertical EOG (VEOG) artifacts are characterized by a wave that is maximal over FP1 and FP2 and diminishes over posterior electrode sites. Horizontal EOG (HEOG) artifacts are characterized by a wave that is maximal over the F7 and F8 electrodes and diminishes over posterior electrodes. They are further characterized by an inversion in polarity at left/right electrode sites. EOG contamination of the ERP data was corrected by using a regression-based weighting coefficient unique to each subject.

For the topographical mapping of the ERPs, waveform averages were constructed from an 800 msec epoch of EEG recorded with the presentation of each word item. Sampling began 100 msec prior to the stimulus presentation to establish a prestimulus baseline. The single-sweep data was baseline corrected by subtracting the mean of the prestimulus period.

In the acquisition phase, the subjects were instructed to simply watch—try to "remember" the words. The retrieval phase involved recognition memory, where the subject was forced to make a yes or no decision with respect to the items presented. The recall lists were made up of five target items and five distractors items, or foils. The subject's performance was evaluated across the three trials, which were made up of the six collapsed blocks. Each trial consisted of 120 items, formed from six blocks and again, there were six acquisition and six recall sections per trial.

The emphasis of evoked potential studies was on the P200, N4, and the Late Positive Component (LPC). There were three parameters examined, each of which may have varied according to the efficiency of an individual's memory processing. These parameters were: (1) latency, (2) amplitude, and (3) spatial distribution of the components of the ERPs.

Data Analysis

The data analyses proceeded stepwise. First, the topographical maps were evaluated for sites of likely significance, then critical electrode sites were selected for additional study. For the formal statistical analyses, the latency and amplitude data were collected repetitively on subjects which resulted in a factorial arrangement with experimental conditions (acquisition and retrieval), trial (trial and trial 3), electrode site (Fz, Cz, Pz, T5, and T6), and ERP component (P200, N4, and LPC; or N150 and LPC for T5 and T6) as factors. These latency and amplitude data were analyzed separately with a completely within subject four-way analysis of variance (ANOVA) using SuperANOVA (Abacus Concepts), considering each of the above factors to be a fixed independent variable and obtaining a multivariate solution. Twelve specific hypotheses that are germane to this article, which involve possible differences in particular cell means, were tested using estimates of error variance obtained in the ANOVAs. The hypotheses were: (1) Are the means for trial 1 and 3 latency and amplitude different for site Pz and components N4 and LPC during acquisition and retrieval? (2) Are the means for trial 1 and 3 latency and amplitude different for sites for T5 and T6? Null hypotheses were rejected if adjusted probabilities were the greater of the values from the Huynh and Feldt or the Greenhouse and Geisser corrections.

RESULTS

As the EEG data were accumulated for the construction of the ERPs, so were performance data. A summary of that data is presented in Figure 1, in terms of percentage correct for the retrieval trials. Suffice it to say, the profile of the recall pattern evinced a robust proactive interference effect. On trial 1, for instance, the subjects scored at an average correct rate of 91.1%. On the second and third trials, with the buildup of the proactive interference effect, their collective performance fell to 77.5 and 75.15%, respectively. This is a typical pattern, consistent with those of other PI studies (e.g., Craik & Birstwistle, 1971), where the greatest decrement in performance generally occurs in the second trial. In this case, in any event, from the initial trial to the third trial there was a 18% decline in terms of accuracy of recognition memory. Hence, it might be expected that there may be some observable electrophysiological differ-

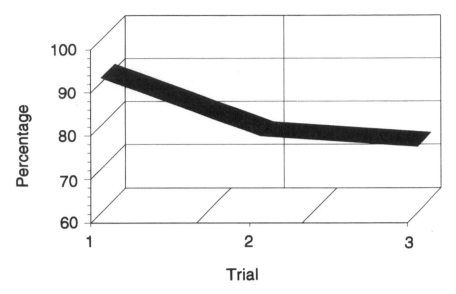

FIGURE 1. Plot of performance data from the proactive interference (PI) task in terms of percentage correct as a function of retrieval trial.

ences between trials 1 and 3 for either or both acquisition or retrieval phases. These differences are explored in Figures 2 to 8.

The electrode arrangement used for recording and the construction of the topographical maps, are schematically shown in Figure 2, overlaid by a sample of the average evoked responses from the first acquisition trial. Note that in all figures positive is up. Close inspection showed that the configuration of the waveforms varied regionally according to the electrode location.

Since previous studies had noted the importance of the centroparietal sites, however, the focus of the analysis was on Pz, which was indeed a critical site to differentially discriminate between the trials. The reason for this is probably due in part to the way the dipoles from the temporal regions sum. Therefore, taking the averaged responses at Pz for the first acquisition trial for illustration, the response was denominated by a large positivity peaking at 230 msec (Figure 3, heavy line). This component did not appear to be uniquely correlated with higher order information processing in that it was also prominent when the subjects were simply watching a series of "scrambled letters" (Figure 3, light line). Since this early positive component was well developed in both instances, it will not be discussed further.

However, there were components which were uniquely correlated with the memory task; that is, not plainly evident in the "scrambled letters" condition. For instance, as shown in Figure 3 for the first acquisi-

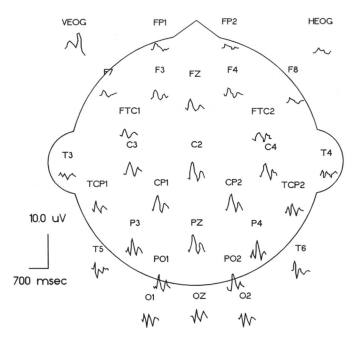

FIGURE 2. Schematic of the electrode placements, with sample of the ERPs from the initial acquisition trial.

tion trial at Pz, there was a negativity which emerged out of the averaging process that was maximal 394 msec following the stimuli. This negative component (N4) was essentially absent in the phase where only mixed-up letters were presented, and it is the main component of interest here. In addition, following the N4 component there was a well-developed Late Positive Component (LPC), which peaked at 472 msec. This component is equivalent to the classic P300. Anticipating the results to be discussed below, differences were seen with respect to the N4 component on both the acquisition and retrieval side for Pz, and for T5 versus T6. There was no significant difference with respect to the latency of the N4 component between trials 1 and 3 for either the acquisition or retrieval trials.

The N4 component was prominent over the parietal vertex, but it was best developed over the left temporal zones (Figure 4). Contrast the event-related potential for the first acquisition phase with that for the "scrambled letters" and note a marked negativity, peaking about 400 msec. Again, the early components (e.g., the sharp positive-going component at 100 msec, and sharp negative component at 150 msec) were common to both conditions, and are part of the elementary visual evoked response. After the visual ERPs, the N4 developed at about 400 msec at this left temporal location.

The spatial distribution of the N4 and LPC are presented for the acquisition phase in Figures 5 and 6, and in Figures 7 and 8 for the retrieval phase. Presentation of the data in topographical maps allows for the easy visualization of regional differences. The distribution of the N4 component for trials 1 and 3 of the acquisition phase is shown in Figure 5. In trial 1, the N4 component occupies a posterior distribution, but with a definite shift toward the left hemisphere. Corresponding to the PI effect, there is a dropout of the N4 component in trial 3 [$F(1, 148) = 7.40$, $p = .018$]. Hence, the N4 diminished in amplitude in the subsequent trials, along with manifesting a left hemisphere bias, greatest over T5. On the other hand, the LPC for the acquisition phase showed a primary centroparietal distribution (Figure 6). We noticed also that the LPC became significantly enhanced over T5 [$F(1, 148) = 10.70$, $p = .002$] in trial 3.

As alluded to above, significant differences between trials 1 and 3

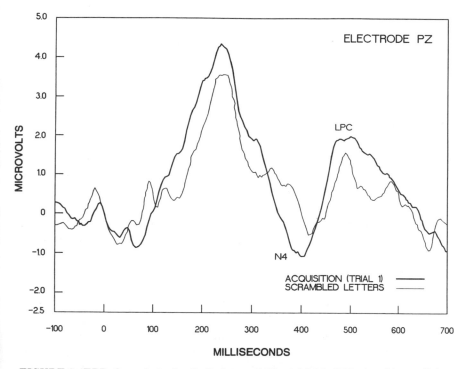

FIGURE 3. ERPs from electrode site Pz for acquisition trial 1 (solid line) and for condition where only scrambled letters were presented (dotted line). The N4 and LPC component of the ERP from the acquisition trial are identified.

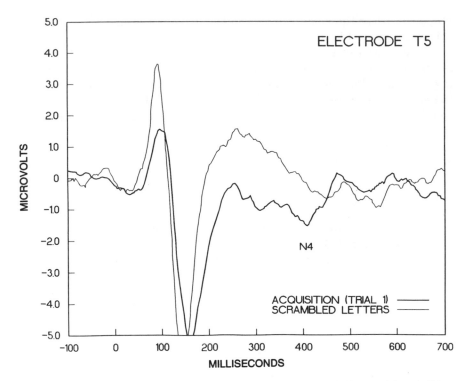

FIGURE 4. ERPs from electrode site T5 for acquisition trial 1 (solid line) and for condition where only scrambled letters were presented (dotted line). The N4 component of the ERP from the acquisition trial is identified.

were also observed for the amplitude of the N4 component in the retrieval phase [F(1, 148) = 44.95, p = .0001]. Again, there was no significant difference in the peak latencies between trials 1 and 3. The spatial distribution of the N4, integrated over the 300 to 400 msec interval is shown in Figure 7. As for the acquisition phase, the N4 component associated with the retrieval phase showed a "flooding" into the left temporoparietal region. The peak latency for the initial retrieval phase was 392 msec. By trial 3, this negativity was much degraded over the posterior temporal zones, especially over the dominant hemisphere. In the retrieval phase, the LPC also shows a decline in amplitude (Figure 8) [F(1, 148) = 12.20, p = .007]. The decline was significant over T5 [F(1, 148) = 12.02, p = .001] as well. This is in contrast to the enhancement of the LPC in the acquisition phase. This double dissociation suggests that the mechanisms for the generation of N4 and the LPC are separable. Furthermore, as was the case for the acquisition trial, there were no significant latency differences between the trials. Hence, the primary changes were with respect to the magnitude of response.

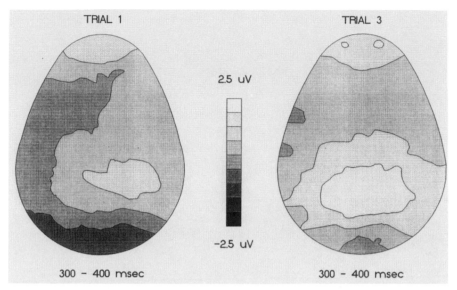

FIGURE 5. Topographical maps from trials 1 and 3 for the acquisition phase to highlight the N4 component. The maps were constructed from voltage changes averaged over the 300 to 400 msec interval following the onset of the stimulus word.

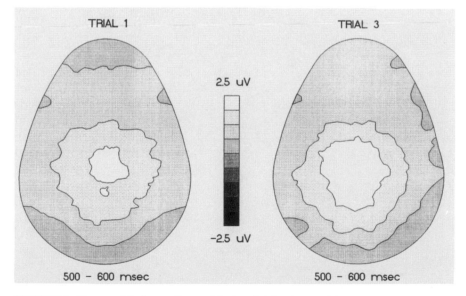

FIGURE 6. Topographical maps from trials 1 and 3 for the acquisition phase to highlight the LPC. The maps were constructed from voltage changes averaged over the 500 to 600 msec interval following the onset of the stimulus word.

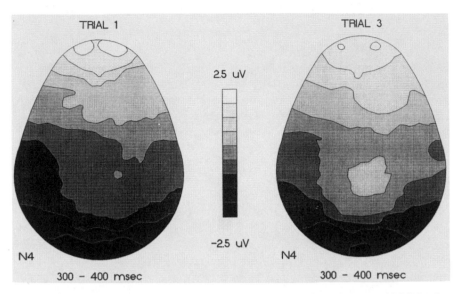

FIGURE 7. Topographical maps from trials 1 and 3 for the retrieval phase to highlight the N4 component. The maps were constructed from voltage changes averaged over the 300 to 400 msec interval following the onset of the stimulus word.

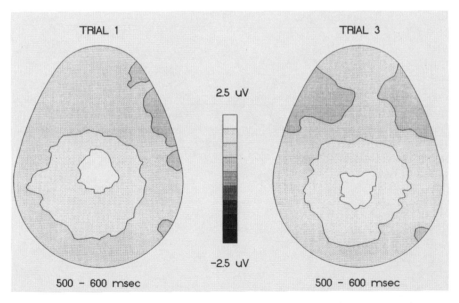

FIGURE 8. Topographical maps from trials 1 and 3 for the retrieval phase to highlight the LPC. The maps were constructed from voltage changes averaged over the 500 to 600 msec interval following the onset of the stimulus word.

DISCUSSION

The use of a specific behavioral probe to provoke electrophysiological changes has an advantage over more conventional EEG analyses by its ability to activate, in a relatively specific manner, those brain pathways most important to a specific type of processing; in this case, memory processing. This is, in a sense, a way of assessing the various stages of information processing. This is not a way to assess specific content, but rather the efficacy of the processing of general categories of information.

With this in mind, this investigation found that associated with the development of the PI effect, was a decline in the magnitude of the N4 component in the retrieval phase. There was a like deterioration in the N4 in the acquisition phase and the LPC in the retrieval phase. There was also a definite left hemisphere bias to the N4 component, which is consistent with the known role of the left hemisphere in language processing. With respect to this paradigm, this implies that as the N4 varies so does memory performance, and that N4 is a reflection of the strength of associative processing. Again, according to the argument of Halgren and Smith (1987), the N4 component reflects activation of the medial portions of the temporal lobe and appears vital to the modulation of the N4 component, although not necessarily its presence or absence (Halgren & Smith, 1987). Hence, the N4 diminution seen in our study, and the N4 decrease with repetition shown by theirs (Smith, Stapleton, & Halgren, 1986), likely reflects lessening contribution of processing in the associative cortex.

Furthermore, the fact that there is a decrease in the N4 component during both the acquisition and retrieval phases, implies that there is a deterioration in some antecedent processing stage, common to both the encoding and retrieval of semantic material. It is possible that this common factor involves frontal lobe pathways. Anatomically, clinical studies have tended to focus on frontal lobe function in the PI effect (Beatty & Butters, 1986; Freedman & Cremack, 1986; Stuss et al., 1982). Moreover, Squire (1982) demonstrated that the failure to release from PI was a unique deficit within Korskakoff patients among the various amnesiac disorders. He also suggested that the frontal lobes may be involved in this inability to release from PI. Hence, it is worth considering that a loss of modulatory function along the prefrontal–temporal lobe axis plays an important role in the accelerated development of the PI effect.

In any event, the processes through which our thoughts and memories are "stamped" into consciousness represents one of the most fascinating questions of modern neuroscience, and one which will require an integrated approach to accrue reasonable answers. It is the authors' hope that this study shows the value of utilizing a combined behavioral and electrophysiological approach. Moreover, while validity and reliability issues are important, the central issue when developing new ways of assessing higher cognitive function is one of sensitivity. By using a multi-faceted approach, anchored in behavior, it should be possible to develop more sensitive strategies to explore higher cognitive function, and to develop better diagnostic approaches in the search for their deficits.

REFERENCES

Battig, F., & Montague, W. E. (1969). Category norms for verbal items in 56 categories: A replication and extension of the Connecticut category norms. *Journal of Experimental Psychology, 80*, 1–46.

Beatty, W. W., & Butters, N. (1986). Further analysis of encoding in patients with Huntington's disease. *Brain and Cognition, 5*, 387–398.

Buchsbaum, M. S., Rigal, F., Coppola, R., Cappelletti, J., King, C., & Johnson, J. (1982). A new system for gray-level surface distribution maps of electrical activity. *Electroencephalography and Clinical Neurophysiology, 53*, 237–242.

Corby, J. C., & Kopell, B. S. (1972). Differential contributions of blink and vertical eye movements as artifacts in EEG recordings. *Psychophysiology, 9*, 640–644.

Craik, F., & Birstwistle, J. (1971). Proactive inhibition in free recall. *Journal of Experimental Psychology, 91*, 120–123.

Cremak, L. S., & Butters, N. (1972). The role of interference and encoding in the short-term memory deficits of Korsakoff patients. *Neuropsychologia, 10*, 89–95.

Cremak, L. S., Butters, N. S., & Moreines, J. (1974). Some analyses of the verbal encoding deficit of alcoholic Korsakoff patients. *Brain and Language, 1*, 41–150.

Donchin, E., Ritter, W., & McCallum, W. C. (1978). Cognitive psychophysiology. In E. S. Callaway, P. Tueting, and S. H. Koslow (Eds.), *Event-related brain potentials in man* (pp. 349–441). New York: Academic Press.

Freedman, M., & Cermak, L. S. (1986). Semantic encoding deficits in frontal lobe disease and amnesia. *Brain and Cognition, 5*, 108–114.

Gardiner, J. M., Craik, F. I., & Birtwistle, J. (1972). Retrieval cues and release from proactive inhibition. *Journal of Verbal Learning and Verbal Behavior, 11*, 778–783.

Halgren, E., & Smith, M. E. (1987). Cognitive evoked potentials as modulatory processes in human memory formation and retrieval. *Human Neurobiology, 6*, 129–139.

Halgren, E., Squires, N. K., Wilson, C. L., Rohrbaugh, J. W., Babb, T. L., & Crandall, P. H. (1980). Endogenous potentials generated in the human hippocampal formation and amygdala by infrequent events. *Science, 210*, 803.

Hillyard, S. A. (1985). Electrophysiology of human selective attention. *Trends In Neuroscience, 8*, 400–405.

Hillyard, S. A., & Galambos, R. (1970). Eye movement artifacts in the CNV. *Electroencephalography and Clinical Neurophysiology, 28*, 173–182.

Hillyard, S. A., & Kutas, M. (1983). Electrophysiology of cognitive processing. *Annual Review of Psychology, 34*, 33–61.

Jacoby, L. L. (1983). Perceptual enhancement: persistent effects of an experience. *Journal of Experimental Psychology, 9*, 21–38.

Jasper, H. H. (1958). Report to the committee on methods of clinical examination in electroencephalography. Appendix: The ten-twenty system of the International Federation. *Electroencephalography and Clinical Neurophysiology, 10*, 371–375.

Kutas, M., & Hillyard, S. A. (1984). Brain potentials during reading reflect word expectancy and semantic associations. *Nature (London), 307*, 161–163.

Picton, T. W., & Stuss, D. T. (1980). The component structure of the human event-related potentials. In H. H. Kornhuber and L. Deecke (Eds.), *Motivation, Motor and Sensory Processes of the Brain: Electrical Potentials, Behavior and Clinical Use. Progress in Brain Research* (pp. 17–49). New York: Elsevier.

Polich, J. (1985). Semantic Categorization and Event-Related Potentials. *Brain and Language, 26*, 304–321.

Semlitsch, H. V., Anderer, P., Schuster, P., & Presslich, O. A. (1986). Solution for reliable and valid reduction of ocular artifacts, applied to the P300 ERP. *Psychophysiology, 23*, 695–703.

Smith, M. E., Stapleton, J. M., & Halgren, E. (1986). Human medial temporal lobe potentials evoked in memory and language tasks. *Electroencephalography and Clinical Neurophysiology, 63*, 145–163.

Smith, M. E., Stapleton, J. M., Moreno, K. A., & Halgren, E. (1985). The effects of anterior temporal lobectomy on endogenous EPs recorded during verbal recognition memory testing. *Society For Neuroscience, Abstracts, 11*, 527.

Squire, L. R. (1982). Comparison between forms of amnesics: Some deficits are unique to Korsakoffs syndrome. *Journal of Experimental Psychology: Learning, Memory, and Cognition, 8*, 560–571.

Stuss, D. T., Kaplan, E. F., Benson, D. F., Weir, W. S., Chiulli, S., & Srarzin, F. F. (1982). Evidence for the involvement of orbitofrontal cortex in memory functions: An interference effect. *Journal of Comparative Physiological Psychology, 96*, 913–925.

Sutton, S., Braren, M., Zubin, J., & John, E. R. (1965). Evoked potential correlates of stimulus uncertainty. *Science, 150*, 1187–1188.

Thomson, D. M., & Tulving, E. (1970). Associatative encoding and retrieval: Weak and strong cues. *Journal of Experimental Psychology, 86*, 255–262.

Underwood, B. J. (1957). Interference and forgetting. *Psychological Review, 64*, 49–60.

Verleger, R., Gasser, T., & Möcks, J. (1982). Correction of EOG artifacts in event-related potentials of the EEG: Aspects of reliability and validity. *Psychophysiology, 19*, 472–480.

Wickens, D. D. (1970). Encoding categories of words: An empirical approach to meaning. *Psychological Review, 77*, 1–15.

Wickens, D. D. (1973). Some characteristics of word encoding. *Memory and Cognition, 1*, 485–490.

Wickens, D. D., Born, D. G., & Allen, C. K. (1963). Proactive inhibition and item similarity in short-term memory. *Journal of Verbal Learning and Verbal Behavior, 2*, 362–368.

Wilson, R. S., Como, P. G., Garron, D. C., Klawans, H. L., Barr, A., & Klawan, D. (1987). Memory failure on Huntington's disease. *Journal of Clinical and Experimental Psychology, 9*, 147–154.

CHAPTER FOUR

A Model for Contextual Interference Effects in Motor Learning

JOHN B. SHEA AND ROBERT C. GRAF

There exists substantial evidence that practice under conditions of high contextual interference can facilitate retention and transfer performance (Magill & Hall, 1990). Contextual interference refers to the situation in which there is interference among different tasks being learned across practice trials. Practice under a condition of high contextual interference (e.g., when multiple tasks are practiced in a random order) typically results in less proficient performance than practice under a condition of low contextual interference (e.g., when multiple tasks are practiced in a blocked order). These findings are reversed for retention and transfer tests, however, with performance being more proficient for the high contextual interference practice condition than for the low contextual interference practice condition. This phenomenon has attracted wide interest among motor skill researchers because it is counter to the common assumption that practice in situations with little or no interference is most advantageous for learning. We describe a contextual interference experiment and prevailing explanations for its findings. We then describe a hybrid connectionist model for contextual interference that has been successful in predicting empirical findings.

JOHN B. SHEA • College of Human Sciences, Florida State University, Tallahassee, Florida 32306-2033. ROBERT C. GRAF • Pennsylvania State University Motor Behavior Laboratory, University Park, PA 16802.

Cognitive Assessment: A Multidisciplinary Perspective, edited by Cecil R. Reynolds. Plenum Press, New York, 1994.

CONTEXTUAL INTERFERENCE EXPERIMENT

An experiment (Titzer, 1991) recently conducted in our laboratory will be briefly described because it closely parallels other experiments which have been conducted to investigate contextual interference effects on the acquisition of motor skills. In this experiment the primary performance measures were movement time and reaction time. Reaction time was the time between the onset of a stimulus light and the initiation of movement. Movement time was the time necessary to perform the desired task.

Figure 1 depicts the apparatus used in this experiment. All subjects initially learned three similar tasks, each requiring that three of six barriers be knocked down in a specified sequence as quickly as possible in response to an appropriate stimulus light. During acquisition subjects

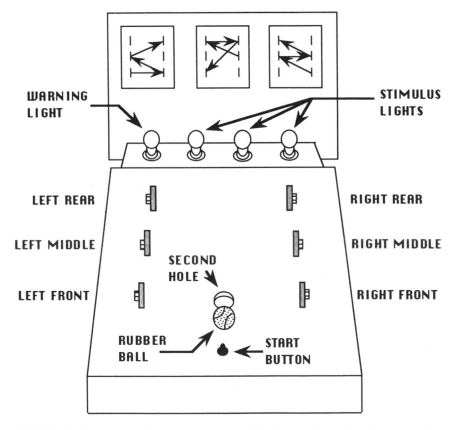

FIGURE 1. Diagram showing the apparatus used in the experiment from the perspective of the subject.

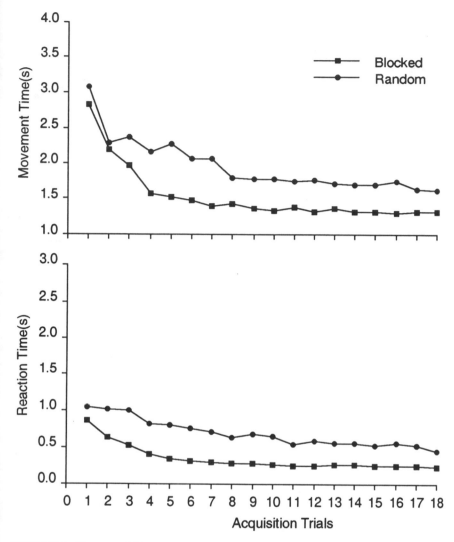

FIGURE 2. Mean acquisition movement time (top panel) and reaction time (bottom panel) measures for blocked and random groups (Titzer, 1991).

received 18 trials for each task (54 acquisition trials). Under high contextual interference or *random* condition, these three tasks were interchanged in an unsystematic order across trials. Under low contextual interference or *blocked* conditions, all trials on one task were completed before the next task was first introduced. Figure 2 shows mean acquisition movement and reaction times collapsed across tasks for the random and blocked conditions. It can be seen that movement and reaction times

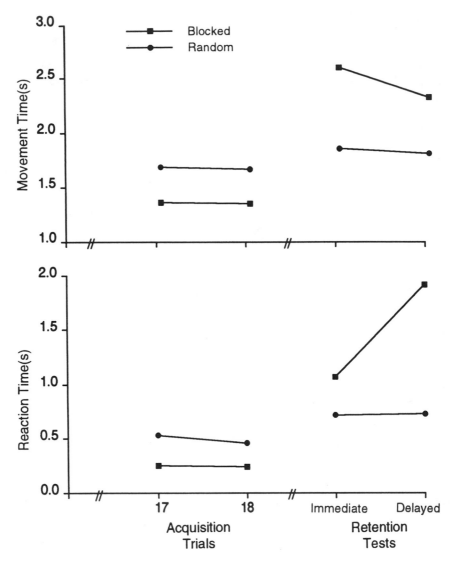

FIGURE 3. Mean retention movement time (top panel) and reaction time (bottom panel) measures for blocked and random groups (Titzer, 1991).

were faster for the blocked than for the random condition across all acquisition trials. Retention was tested after either a 15-second (immediate) or a 10-minute (delayed) retention interval. Subjects performed three trials for each task in a serial order for this test. Figure 3 shows mean retention movement and reaction times collapsed across tasks and trials. It can be seen that the performance of the conditions was now reversed with mean movement and reaction times being faster for the random than for the blocked condition.

EXPLANATIONS

Three explanations have been offered for contextual interference findings. Shea and Zimny (1983, 1988) have offered an elaboration explanation in which practice in a random schedule is more likely to result in the concurrent presence of multiple tasks in working memory than practice in a blocked schedule. This concurrent presence of multiple tasks in working memory is thought to facilitate intertask elaborative processing which enhances retention by providing multiple retrieval routes for the tasks. Both the blocked and random practice schedules have the opportunity to perform intratask elaborative processing because this processing necessitates the presence of only one task in working memory. Presumably intratask processing facilitates the acquisition of individual task characteristics.

Lee and Magill (1985) have proposed a reconstruction explanation in which an action plan for a particular task is forgotten in a random practice schedule as a result of intervening trials on other tasks. The learner is therefore forced to engage in more effortful reconstructive processing to generate the action plan for subsequent performance of the task. In contrast, there is little opportunity for forgetting in a blocked practice schedule because the action plan is present in working memory and can be executed on successive trials with little or no reconstructive activity. The consequence of the more effortful processing performed in a random practice schedule is a stronger task representation and greater retention relative to practice in a blocked practice schedule (Magill & Hall, 1990). A close association between reconstructive and elaborative processing has recently been demonstrated in an experiment by Shea and Wright (1991) in which reconstructive processing was facilitated by the presence of a similar task in working memory. It was reasoned that having a similar task in working memory at the time of reconstruction provided the necessary context for more complete and distinctive processing of the criterion task.

Finally, contextual interference effects have been attributed to the sequencing of tasks in the blocked practice schedule (Magill & Hall, 1990). According to this explanation, the blocked practice schedule may be affected by retroactive interference, which refers to the common finding of poorer retention when an activity is interpolated between learning and a retention test when compared to an equivalent rest interval. The blocked practice schedule can be thought of as a manipulation of retroactive interference because with the exception of the last task practiced, successive trials for different tasks occur between the learning and retention test for each task. It is worth noting that the blocked practice schedule is susceptible to the influence of proactive interference as well as retroactive interference. Retroactive interference has been found to influence the retention of motor skills more than proactive interference (Dickinson & Higgins, 1977; Lewis, McAllister, & Adams, 1951; Mandler & Kuhlman, 1961). In contrast to the blocked practice schedule, retroactive interference would not have as great an influence on retention performance for the random practice schedule. This is because it is likely that only a limited number of trials for different tasks occur between practice of each task and the retention test.

THE MODEL

The model which we describe for contextual interference effects on motor skill acquisition was inspired by the elaboration explanation proposed by Shea and Zimny (1983, 1988), although it has generated predications consistent with both the reconstruction (Lee & Magill, 1985) and retroactive interference (Magill & Hall, 1990) explanations. The model is a hybrid in which a multiple level processing algorithm is implemented in a computer based connectionist architecture.

The multiple level processing algorithm is based upon the general assumptions that subjects utilize a minimum amount of processing to execute a movement task, and utilize higher levels of processing only as required to complete the task in a satisfactory manner. More specifically, it is assumed that higher levels of processing slow task planning and execution. Higher levels of processing can modify lower levels of control. Lower levels of control can act independently of the higher levels, but the higher levels of control act in parallel with the lower levels.

Three levels of processing are hypothesized. These are an execution level, a program level, and a planning level. These levels are named for conceptual clarity, and they could have been identified simply as level 1, level 2, and level 3. The execution level is the lowest level. It is the fastest and most automatic processing level. It receives input and produces output. The program level is the next highest level. It performs additional processing on the input and modifies the behavior of the execution level. The planning level is the highest level. It receives input and modifies the behavior of the program level.

These three levels interact in a dynamic way. Task input is received by the system and the execution level attempts to produce a satisfactory solution as determined by an internal criterion. This criterion is error based with a larger tolerance for error as a trade-off for speed. Output is generated if a satisfactory solution is achieved. Otherwise, the program level of processing is brought to bear on the task and works in parallel with the execution level to achieve a satisfactory solution. If a satisfactory solution is achieved, output is generated. Otherwise, the planning level contributes its influence in parallel with the first two levels and output is generated.

BACKGROUND

In order to explain the behavior of the multilevel processing model, the basic terms and operations of a connectionist model must be made clear. A unit is a simplest processing element of a connectionist network. It is linked to other units by lines of communications called connections. A unit receives input along a connection, alters its state of activation as a function of that input, and communicates this activation to other units via an output connection. The activation is a measure of the excitation of a unit. Activation is usually a monotonic function of a unit's total input. In linear systems activation is unbounded. In the more powerful nonlinear systems activation typically varies between 0 and 1.

A layer of a connectionist network consists of a group of units that receive input from a common set of units and provide output to a different common set of units. The input layer receives its input from outside the network. The output layer makes its outputs accessible to an observer outside of the network. Hidden layers are those whose inputs and outputs are not directly accessible from outside the network.

An input vector is the ordered set of inputs imposed upon the input layer. The output vector is the ordered set of activations produced at the output layer in response to the input vector. The target vector is the desired set of output activations that the network is expected to learn as a response to a paired input vector.

Learning occurs in the network by a process of modifying the connection weights so the desired set of output activations are produced; that is, the target vector. A connection weight is a multiplicative factor that modifies the amount of input that a unit receives along a connection. The connection weight can be conceptualized as a measure of strength of the connection between two units. The back propagation learning algorithm computes the difference between the output vector and the target vector and propagates this error backwards through the network modifying connection weights to minimize this error.

Figure 4 shows a simple single-level three-layer fully connected model. "Fully connected" means that every unit of a given layer is connected to every unit of its target layer. Figure 5 is a simplified schematic of the same network. Instead of drawing each unit in a layer, a vertical line is used to represent the entire layer. The number of units in a layer is indicated by the attached notation; for example, $n = 4$ for the single

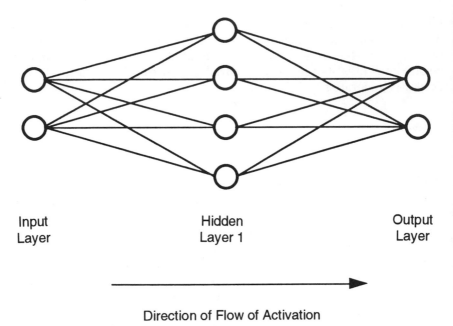

Input Layer — Hidden Layer 1 — Output Layer

Direction of Flow of Activation

FIGURE 4. A simple single-level three-layer fully connected model.

hidden layer. Connections are abbreviated with a single horizontal line. Hidden layers are denoted with an h followed by a unique identification number.

A learning cycle or trial is composed of several steps. First, an input vector is presented to the network. The individual units in the input layer become activated and communicate their activation to the next layer via the connections between units. The amount of activation experienced by the target units is proportional to the connection weights on the link between these units. Activation is propagated forward through the network until a pattern of activations appears at the output layer. The error between the output vector and the target vector is computed. This error is back propagated through the network and the connection weights adjusted to minimize this error.

MODEL DESCRIPTION

The present model for contextual interference is a three-level five-layer model (Figure 6). It expands upon the fundamental operational elements of a fully connected back propagation network and extends the dynamics of the system to include the principles of the multiple level processing learning algorithm. It is critical to the understanding of this hybrid model to clearly distinguish between a layer and a level. A layer is a set of processing units receiving activation from a common source and sending activation to a common target. The source or target can be a single unit or another layer. A level is a set of all layers involved in the processing of a single input vector. The definition of level is original to this research.

The execution level (level 1) consists of the input layer, h3 (the third hidden layer), and the output layer. Activation is propagated from the input layer to h3, and from h3 to the output layer. The program level (level 2) consists of the input layer, h2, h3, and the output layer. Activation is propagated from the input layer to h2 and h3, from h2 to h3, and from h3 to the output layer. Notice that the program level expands upon and modifies the behavior of the execution level. This is implementation of one of the specific assumptions of the multiple level algorithm. The planning level (level 3) consists of all layers of the model. Activation is spread through the network from the input layer to h1, h2, and h3, from h1 to h2, from h2 to h3, and from h3 to the output layer. Again, notice that level 3 encompasses and modifies the behavior of both level 2 and level 1.

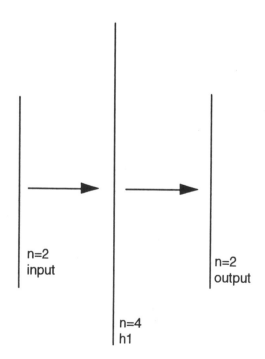

FIGURE 5. A simplified schematic of the single-level three level fully connected model depicted in Figure 4.

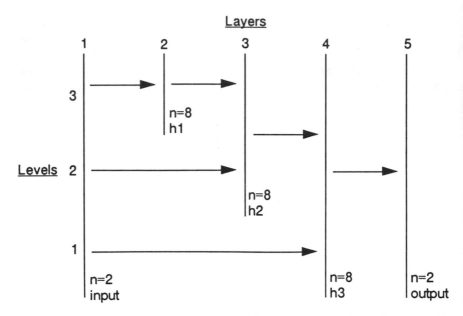

FIGURE 6. Schematic showing the three-level five-layer contextual interference model.

Some additional original network parameters were developed and implemented in this model to facilitate its operation and make it more consistent with motor learning concepts. Two learning rates are used, a global learning rate and an internal learning factor. The global learning rate is a multiplicative factor used to scale the connection weight change during the learning phase when knowledge of results (KR) is provided in the form of the target vector. This is the usual learning rate expected in a standard single level back propagation model. The internal learning factor is unique to this model and consists of a decimal fraction used to scale the global learning rate whenever learning occurs in the absence of KR. This learning factor is used whenever the network trains itself based upon its own best estimate of the target vector.

An internal error criterion was utilized to operationalize the concept that a subject produces output whenever an internally satisfactory solution to the task is attained. This internal error criterion represents the greatest magnitude of internal error that the system can tolerate before processing is switched to a higher level. A mechanism is required to provide the system with a self-generated estimate of the target. This best estimate comes from two sources of information available to the system. These are (1) KR from the last trial (if KR was provided); and (2) the activations generated by the previous level of processing (if any).

Finally, a small amount of noise was added to the network's input and target vectors to simulate the noise in an organic system and to reduce the probability that the network would get stuck in a local error minima.

The present multiple-level multiple-layer model has several advantages over a single-level multiple-layer model like the one described by Masson (1990). First, it can account for processing time behavior during acquisition and retention for blocked and random groups. Second, it can learn in the absence of KR. Third, it can modify behavior and output based upon higher level influences and thus simulate the increase in error and processing time observed when automated skills are brought under higher level conscious control.

Simulated Experiment

The model was tested by simulating a contextual interference experiment. The task is depicted in Figure 7 and consisted of a simple two-dimensional arm movement. Given an xy coordinate pair as input, the model was to move from a common starting point and produce a normalized joint angle output that located the hand at the desired point in space based on the geometry of the simulated arm. The scale of the xy coordinate system was unspecified. The network had to learn both the scale of the coordinate system and the correct joint angles. This is not a trivial task. The transformation from xy coordinates to normalized joint angles are described by the following equations:

$$\alpha = \left[\pi - \tan^{-1}\left(\frac{y}{1 - \chi} \right) - \cos^{-1}\left(\frac{\sqrt{(1 - \chi)^2 + y^2}}{\sqrt{2}} \right) \right] \cdot \frac{1}{\pi}$$

$$\beta = \cos^{-1}[(1 - \chi)^2 + y^2 - 1] \cdot \frac{1}{\pi}$$

where α and β are normalized joint angles, and x and y are the xy coordinates of the hand location.

It is remarkable that the network can learn to make this transformation without explicit rules and given only three different examples.

Subjects consisted of a random set of connection weights created by the network upon startup. Each subject was initialized to the network by preliminary training to the center point of the xy coordinate system (.5, .5) and $\alpha\beta$ joint angles (.41, .66). The internal error criterion was set to .2 and the network was trained until the maximum joint angle error was less than or equal to .33. Each initialized subject's connections weights were saved for future retrieval prior to acquisition training. This procedure completely eliminates individual differences between groups.

Specifically, the network was trained with three tasks consisting of

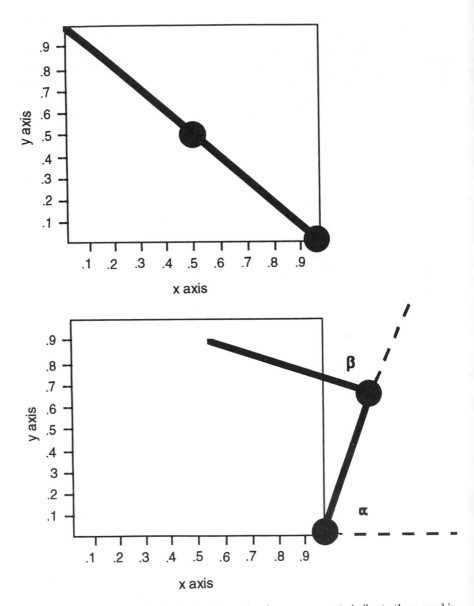

FIGURE 7. Depiction of a simple two-dimensional arm movement similar to those used in the simulated experiment. The top panel shows the basic geometry of the arm relative to the coordinate system. The bottom panel shows an example with the hand at point $x = .5$, $y = .9$.

xy coordinate inputs and paired normalized joint angles. Two training schedule groups were formed. A blocked group received 36 acquisition trials of each task in a blocked schedule. Tasks were counterbalanced for the 12 experimental subjects in this group. A random group of 12 subjects received 36 acquisition trials of each task in a random presentation order. Retention was assessed by presenting each task without KR one time after the acquisition stage and recording RMS error and level. Measures of performance were RMS error of the $\alpha\beta$ joint angles and the numerical value (1, 2, or 3) of the highest processing level utilized by the network during a trial.

Figure 8 shows mean RMS error and level measures for acquisition trials, as well as for each task for the retention test. The findings for RMS error measures were consistent with those for contextual interference experiments (see Figures 2 and 3). While performance was better (more accurate) for the blocked group than for the random group during acquisition, performance was better (more accurate) for the random group than for the blocked group for the retention test. The findings for level measures showed that the random group had a higher level of processing during both acquisition and retention than the blocked group.

DISCUSSION

We have presented a connectionist model which is capable of simulating contextual interference effects on motor skill acquisition and retention. This model has been useful for testing predictions derived from different theoretical explanations for contextual interference, as well as for generating predictions of its own. For example, the model has provided a measure for the level of cognitive processing brought to bear on the learning of a motor task. This invokes questions concerned with the investigation of variables thought to affect the processing resources necessary for task performance. In the demonstration experiment the random group had a greater number of levels for processing than the blocked group. It would be interesting, however, to investigate if extended practice would reduce the number of levels necessary for the random group to perform the task (Logan, 1988). The success of the present model in replicating contextual interference findings has been encouraging, and even its failures have often proven to be informative. In these cases we have either redesigned and modified the model, or reconceptualized our thoughts of the processing activities performed during learning. In these cases we have found that data obtained in an actual experiment did not conform with data generated by the model because of constraints imposed by our experimental procedures, or by strategies engaged in by subjects which are not encompassed by the model (e.g., guessing). The

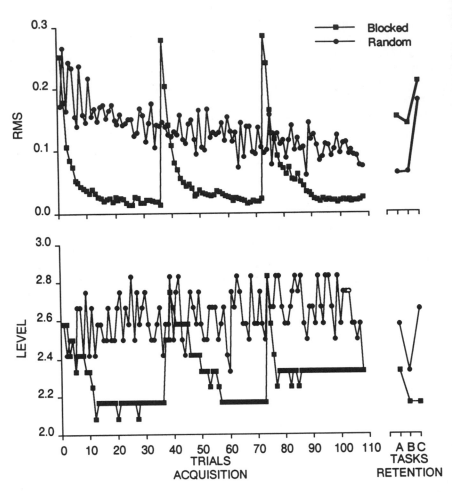

FIGURE 8. Simulated experiment means RMS error (top panel) and level (bottom panel) measures for acquisition trials, and for each task for the retention test.

success of the model has not been limited to simulating the effects of contextual interference on the acquisition, retention, and transfer. It has also successfully demonstrated retroactive interference effects, learning in the absence of knowledge of results, the speed–accuracy trade-off and the speed-up with learning effect.

REFERENCES

Dickinson, J., & Higgins, N. (1977). Release from practive and retroactive interference in short-term memory. *Journal of Motor Behavior, 9,* 61–66.

Lee, T. D., & Magill, R. A. (1985). Can forgetting facilitate skill acquisition? In D. Goodman, R. B. Wilberg, & I. M. Franks (Eds.), *Differing perspectives in motor learning, memory, and control* (pp. 3–22). Amsterdam: North-Holland.

Lewis, D., McAllister, D. E., & Adams, J. A. (1951). Facilitation and interference in performance on the modified Mashburn apparatus: I. The effects of varying the amount of original learning. *Journal of Experimental Psychology, 41*, 247–260.

Logan, G. D. (1988). Toward an instance theory of automatization. *Psychological Review, 95*, 492–527.

Mandler, G., & Kuhlman, C. K. (1961). Proactive and retroactive effects of overlearning. *Journal of Experimental Psychology, 61*, 76–81.

Magill, R. A., & Hall, K. (1990). A review of the contextual interference effect in motor skill acquisition. *Human Movement Science, 9*, 241–289.

Masson, M. E. J. (1990). Cognitive theories of skill acquisition. *Human Movement Science, 9*, 231–239.

Shea, J. B., & Wright, D. L. (1991). When forgetting benefits motor retention. *Research Quarterly for Exercise and Sport, 62*, 293–301.

Shea, J. B., & Zimny, S. T. (1983). Context effects in memory and learning movement information. In R. A. Magill (Ed.), *Memory and control of action* (pp. 345–366). Amsterdam: North-Holland.

Shea, J. B., & Zimny, S. T. (1988). Knowledge of incorporation in motor representation. In O. G. Meijer & K. Roth (Eds.), *Complex movement behavior: The motor-action controversy* (pp. 289–314). Amsterdam: North-Holland.

Titzer, R. C. (1991). *The influence of a reminder on the contextual interference effect.* Unpublished master's thesis, The Pennsylvania State University, University Park, PA.

CHAPTER FIVE

Cognition and Motor Skill Acquisition: Contextual Dependencies

David L. Wright and Charles H. Shea

Every day we perform skilled activities in environments that are comprised of a wide variety of stimuli that we do not explicitly identify as important to successful completion of an intended action. Nevertheless, it appears that the environmental contexts in which we perform can exert powerful influences on our ability to retrieve and process information. For example, the seemingly "absent-minded" professor is sometimes caught off-guard when outside of the classroom setting he or she is confronted by a student in his or her class. In this situation it is not unusual for the professor to appear embarrassed by his or her inability to recall the student's name or even recognize the student. Upon the professor's return to class, however, the student's name is easily recalled. In this case, reinstating the context associated with the student (the classroom) facilitated the retrieval of a specific memory (the student's name).

Magill (1988) offers an example of how the context can influence motor performance. He cites the following comment that is often heard

Acknowledgements: The authors wish to thank Chad Whitacre and Yuhua Li for their assistance in the data collection. Parts of the research reported in this chapter were supported by a research incentive grant from the College of Education, Texas A&M University, awarded to the first author.

David L. Wright and Charles H. Shea • Human Performance Laboratories, Texas A&M University, College Station, Texas 77843-4243.
Cognitive Assessment: A Multidisciplinary Perspective, edited by Cecil R. Reynolds. Plenum Press, New York, 1994.

from baseball players, "I have never seen a curve thrown like that before" (p. 374). The flight characteristics of the curve ball probably were not different from that of any other curve ball. A unique throwing motion or other distracting stimuli might, however, have caused the pitch to appear to be quite different from that of other pitchers. In essence, the curve ball was embedded in a new context. Thus, the batter experiences more difficulty in successfully hitting this pitch because processing the cues for selecting an appropriate response was influenced by the new context.

There are many other anecdotal examples, such as spontaneous memories at a 25-year high school reunion or as a result of hearing an old song on the radio, which support the notion that contextual stimuli influence memory (see Bjork & Richardson-Klavehn, 1989; Smith, 1988, for other examples). Such effects have been the focus of close examination under the rubric of context-dependent memory. More specifically, this refers to the situation in which cognitive processing is influenced by subtle changes in the contextual environment in which a task is initially encoded and subsequently retrieved (Smith, 1988).

CONTEXT AND HUMAN VERBAL LEARNING

Davies and Thomson (1988a) stated that the effect of the context in the learning environment is "sufficiently powerful and pervasive as to form an essential feature of any theory of memory" (p. 336). Whether or not one agrees with Davies and Thomson's (1988a) statement most would certainly agree that this area of research has commanded a great deal of experimental attention in recent years (see Davies & Thomson, 1988b). Contextual influences during verbal skill learning have been well documented for a wide variety of activities including word recall tasks (Smith, 1988; Tulving & Thomson, 1973), problem-solving tasks (Luchins, 1942), reading tasks (Stanovich & West, 1983), and simulated eyewitness testimonies (Geiselman, 1988).

The investigations examining the role of the context during verbal learning have made use of an assortment of contexts. The list includes input modality (Geiselman & Bjork, 1980), physical setting (Gooden & Baddeley, 1975, 1980), and physiological state of the learner (Eich, 1980; Eich & Birnbaum, 1988), to name but a few. Some of these investigations have reported that performance is greatly facilitated through contextual reinstatement (Smith, 1988), while others have identified relatively modest (Watkins, Ho, & Tulving, 1976) or no effects (Fernandez & Glenberg, 1985) of reinstating the context. In many cases, the magnitude of the effect is mediated by the type of test used to examine the influence of the contextual manipulation. For example, a meta-analysis examining the role of environmental contextual factors during verbal learning revealed that free recall was more sensitive to context manipulations than recognition or cued-recall tests (see Vela & Smith, 1991). In addition, an interference reduction or multiple input context paradigms appear to display greater context effects than the more traditional reinstatement paradigm (Bjork & Richardson-Klavehn, 1989).

Despite some of the problems inherent in examining context-dependent memory phenomena, ample evidence appears to have accrued to support the contention that contextual factors do exert an important influence during verbal skill learning. Current research efforts are now focused on identifying the underlying mechanisms contributing to the context effects that are typically exhibited. For example, the display of environmental-context dependencies have been interpreted both as a function of encoding (encoding hypothesis) and retrieval (outshining hypothesis) processes (Smith, 1988; Vela & Smith, 1991), or based on an individual's ability to mentally reinstate the context at the time of test (mental reinstatement hypothesis; Bjork & Richardson-Klavehn, 1989). In contrast, Eich and Birnbaum (1988) has proposed that environmental-context dependent memory phenomena may just be a special case of mood-dependent memory. From this perspective, successful transfer from one environment to an alternative environment depends on the extent to which the two situations afford similar affective states as opposed to perceptual characteristics.

In addition to the specific pursuits to address context-dependent memory per se, contextual factors are also currently being entertained as integral components of a number of contemporary theories of memory and skill acquisition. Murdock's (1989) theory of distributive associative memory (TODAM), Raaijmakers and Shiffrin's (1981) search for associative memory (SAM), Hintzman's (1984) multiple trace model (Minerva 2), Anderson's ACT* (1983), and Schneider and Detweiler's (1987) connectionist architecture are some examples. It appears, therefore, that Davies and Thomson's (1988a) appeal to include context as a part of a more general memory framework addressing skill acquisition is becoming reality and highlights the importance of this component in the verbal learning environment.

CONTEXT IN THE MOTOR DOMAIN

From a brief description of the work on context and memory with respect to verbal learning, one can see that this phenomenon has been systematically examined in recent years. Unfortunately, the same cannot be said about context effects developed as a result of practice on motor skills. While some investigators (Bjork & Richardson-Klavehn, 1989; Smith et al., 1978) have alluded to the potential influence of environmental context on motor skill learning, little experimental rigor has been focused in this direction. Nevertheless, there are some examples in the motor domain that suggest that reinstatement of the original learning environment can facilitate the accuracy of subsequent movement reproduction. The work of Lee and his colleagues (Lee & Hirota, 1980; Lee & Magill, 1985), in which they applied the encoding specificity principle (Tulving & Thomson, 1973) in an attempt to gain insight into the underlying structure of the memory representation for movement, emphasizes the importance of reinstating movement context in order to facilitate recall performance.

Lee and Hirota (1980), using a short-term memory paradigm, had subjects either actively or passively practice a 30 cm movement on a linear slide. Subsequent recall was performed either actively or passively. This resulted in four experimental conditions, two congruent conditions (active-active, passive-passive) and two incongruent conditions (active-passive, passive-active). The results demonstrated that when the encoding and retrieval operations were incongruent at recall, movement accuracy was considerably poorer than when encoding and retrieval operations were congruent. These data were later replicated in a learning paradigm by Lee and Magill (1985, Exp. 1). A subsequent manipulation made by Lee and Magill (1985, Exp. 2) further emphasized the importance of reinstating the original acquisition context in order to facilitate accurate movement reproduction. Subjects were administered 16 practice trials of a 30 cm movement on a linear slide. These trials were executed with either their right or left hand. Movement reproduction was performed with either the same hand (right-right, left-left), or opposite hand (right-left, left-right) used in acquisition. Consistent with earlier findings, reinstatement of the learning context resulted in less error in movement reproduction than in the switched condition. It should be noted, however, that the changes in context were confounded with changes in the mechanism for movement control. Thus, it was impossible to determine the relative influence, if any, of the context.

Contextual influences have also been demonstrated using a somewhat different approach by Lintern (1985). She demonstrated that enriching the learning context via the presentation of additional visual cues during a simulated aircraft landing task facilitated task acquisition and transfer. The study revealed that extended exposure to the supplemental visual cues throughout practice resulted in performance becoming dependent on the continued presence of these cues. Therefore, if practice is extensive enough to lead to the development of a dependency, the usefulness of enriching the context to increase the rate of task acquisition would be negated by the detrimental effect of the dependency that evolved.

The work of Lee and colleagues (Lee, 1982; Lee & Hirota, 1980; Lee & Magill, 1985), and Lintern (1985) offers some preliminary evidence that there is a subtle influence exerted by the learning context during motor skill acquisition and retention. The purpose of this chapter is to provide a closer examination of the context dependency phenomenon and its potential implications for motor skill acquisition. To accomplish this purpose a taxonomy of contextual stimuli will be presented followed by a discussion of a series of recent experiments that investigated the influence of context on the accuracy and latency of motor performance.

How Should the Contexts in Which Motor Skill Acquisition Occurs Be Categorized?

It would seem important at the outset to clearly delineate the composition of the environment in which skill acquisition is assumed to occur. There appears to be some consensus, at least in the verbal domain, that the notion of context implies a distinction between an imperative stimulus and its setting, with the latter being assumed to constitute the context (Davies & Thomson, 1988a). Distinguishing between the numerous definitions of the term *context* is a difficult task. In some cases context has assumed an "internal" connotation such as the emotional or physiological state of the learner (Eich, 1980; Eich & Birnbaum, 1988). In contrast, the physical setting or some other "external" attribute might be considered an appropriate dimension on which to base a definition of context (Gooden & Baddeley, 1975, 1980; Smith, 1988). It is not surprising, therefore, that Thomson and Davies (1988) conclude that the current status of understanding of the context effects on memory, at least in the verbal domain, provides a "confused and confusing" (p. 4) picture.

The clarity of the definition of context within the motor domain is no less cloudy than in the verbal domain. Lee (1982) intimated that the memory representation for movement is multidimensional in nature (see also Reeve & Mainor, 1985). More specifically, he considers the core of the movement memory trace to consist of a "functional movement code." This, for example, may be comprised of location or timing information when attempting to encode movement extent (Diewert & Roy, 1978; Lee, 1982). More important, for the present discussion, is Lee's contention that the functional movement code is "viewed as being embedded within a particular context, defined in terms of the particular sensory and motor information derived from the production of the criterion movement" (p. 86). Such contextual information has been manipulated through changes in feedback modalities at encoding and retrieval (Martenuik & Rodney, 1979; Newell, Shapiro, & Carlton, 1979) and within a switched-limb paradigm (Wallace, 1977).

A quite different classification of context was put forward by Wright and Shea (1991). They classified the environmental context in which the learning of motor skills occurs along two stimulus dimensions: intentional and incidental. Intentional stimuli were defined as stimuli essential for acquisition of the tasks being learned. The information these stimuli convey is often emphasized in the instructions the learner receives prior to engaging in a period of practice. In contrast, the incidental stimuli are those that can become associated with a particular response because of their discriminate presence in the learning environment. Intentional and incidental stimuli are distinguished from ambient stimuli that are present throughout acquisition and/or retention (e.g., room color, lighting, noise) which have been the focus of a number of studies in the verbal domain (Dulsky, 1935; Smith, 1988).

Wright and Shea (1991) proposed that an associational memory network can develop as a result of practice that links the intentional stimuli, incidental stimuli, and the tasks (see Figure 1). The development of the proposed memory network begins with the initial instructions that lead the learner to associate the intentional stimuli with the tasks being acquired. After a period of practice, an association develops between the intentional and incidental stimuli. Further practice experience can result in the emergence of a direct association between the incidental stimuli and the tasks. If this occurs, contextual dependencies should be diminished because either intentional or incidental stimuli alone or in combination would be sufficient to sustain performance. This perspective suggests that both intentional and incidental stimuli are maintained in memory as part of the internal representation of the tasks. If this were the case, both types of stimuli could be used independently as effective retrieval cues. Therefore, if the associational network is well developed performance should be relatively context independent. Should the asso-

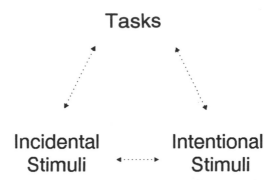

FIGURE 1. Simplified diagram illustrating the associations proposed by Wright and Shea (1991) that develop as a result of acquisition experiences with intentional and incidental stimuli.

ciational network be weak or incomplete, however, contextual reinstatement becomes more important in order to maintain performance. Thus, task or practice factors that inhibit or delay the development of the associational network should result in performance that is more susceptible to contextual dependencies.

DOES TASK DIFFICULTY MEDIATE THE INFLUENCE OF THE CONTEXT DURING MOTOR SKILL ACQUISITION?

In a series of experiments Wright and Shea (1991) investigated the extent to which task difficulty was an important mediator of the development of contextual dependencies arising during motor skill acquisition. They required subjects to practice three sequences involving either three-key presses (low difficulty) or four-key presses (high difficulty). Subjects were told that a sequence of key presses would be governed by the presentation of the numbers 1 through 3 or 4 (depending on the level of manipulation to which the subject was assigned) on the screen at the beginning of a trial (see Figure 2).

The numbers representing a to-be-executed sequence were defined as the intentional stimuli. In addition, each sequence used in the low or high difficulty conditions was consistently paired with a set of incidental stimuli throughout acquisition. The subjects were never explicitly informed that the incidental stimuli were paired with specific sequences.

When the individuals who had acquired the difficult sequences experienced a disruption in the learning context established during acquisition at retention, response error increased beyond that evident when the acquisition context was reinstated at the time of retention (see Figure 3). This was not the case for the less difficult three-key sequences. It appeared the retrieval and/or execution of the less difficult tasks were relatively context independent.

Insight into the mechanism by which difficulty mediates the display of contextual dependencies was obtained from the subject's verbal reports provided at the conclusion of testing. Individuals who attempted to acquire the relatively difficult four-key sequences revealed very poor knowledge of the relationship between each of the sequences, the intentional stimuli, and the incidental stimuli. Wright and Shea (1991) concluded that the associative memory network that had developed to support retrieval of task-specific information for the four-key tasks was rather impoverished.

Verbal report data obtained from those individuals acquiring the three-key sequences revealed a very rich memorial structure for the sequence information. More specifically, almost every individual could provide an accurate description of each of the intentional and incidental

96

CHAPTER FIVE

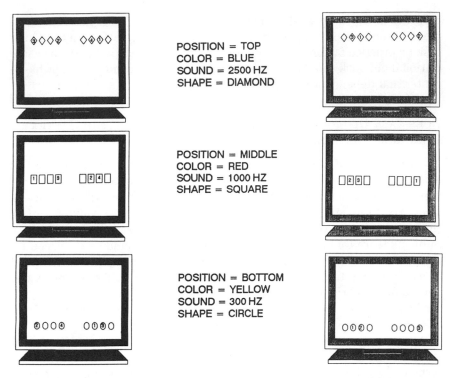

FIGURE 2. Graphics screen displays for the four key (left) and three key (right) sequences in Wright and Shea (1991). Note that each sequence was accompanied by a set of incidental stimuli (center).

stimuli, and their appropriate relationships with each of the three-key sequences. This data, in conjunction with the retention performance data, suggests that very specific contextual information accompanied the necessary task-specific information in the memory trace for each of the three-key sequences. More importantly, each component of the memory trace, including the incidental information, could be used independently to generate a successful response.

These data suggest that increased task difficulty restricts the extent to which the learner has the opportunity to survey the task environment to adequately identify potential contingencies between the to-be-learned task(s) and alternate sources of information. This is consistent with the finding that the individuals learning the relatively difficult four-key sequences were unable to elicit a correct sequence in response to the presentation of the incidental stimuli alone (Wright & Shea, 1991, Exp. 1). It appears, therefore, that the associative memory network for these individuals did not include a direct relationship between the incidental information and the task sequences. As the difficulty of the task-to-be-learned

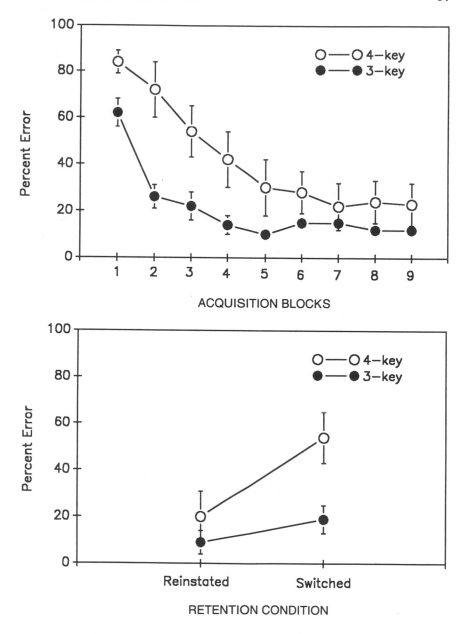

FIGURE 3. Acquisition (top) and retention (bottom) performance for the four and three key sequences in Wright and Shea (1991). Note that acquisition performance has been collapsed across retention conditions. Acquisition blocks represent an average of 12 trials with the retention blocks an average of 3 trials.

is decreased, the processing of the stimuli in the learning environment is broadened. This results in the incorporation of additional sources of information and the embellishment of stimuli–task relationships within the extant memory structure. This conclusion is substantiated by the finding that the individuals learning the less difficult sequences exhibited successful production of the sequences even in circumstances in which only partial contextual information was made available to them (Wright & Shea, 1991, Exp. 2).

CAN RESPONSE LATENCIES REVEAL ADDITIONAL INSIGHT INTO THE CONTEXTUAL DEPENDENCY PHENOMENON?

Wright and Shea (1991) did not find evidence supporting the development of contextual dependencies in tasks involving three-key presses. This conclusion was based on the finding that the percent correct responses at retention did not decrease when the context was changed from that experienced during acquisition. There was, however, an indication that changing the contextual environment at retention resulted in delays in responding. These delays were not examined because the instructions to the subjects simply indicated they should produce the sequences within a fixed time limit with no premium placed on producing the sequences as quickly as possible.

In a subsequent experiment Shea and Wright (1991, Exp. 1) addressed the issue of response latency by assessing the impact of altering the context on the reaction time of subjects performing simple one-key tasks. Based on the response error data of Wright and Shea (1991), contextual dependencies would not be predicted because it is assumed that a relatively complete associational network would develop for this simple task with relatively little practice experience. An associational network linking the intentional stimuli, incidental stimuli, and tasks would be expected to decrease dependencies on particular contextual stimuli. Based on a post hoc examination of data from Wright and Shea (1991), using response latency as a more sensitive index of memory performance (Sternberg, 1966), one might expect an increase in response latency when the contextual environment is altered from that experienced during practice. That is, the utilization of the associational network to resolve conflicting or account for missing contextual information requires additional time beyond that necessary during contextual reinstatement.

Subjects were asked to respond by depressing a response key as quickly as possible when one of two circles displayed on a computer monitor was illuminated. If the left circle was illuminated the subject was required to press the left key with the left index finger. When the right circle was illuminated the subject was to depress the right key with the right index finger. A tone was presented simultaneously with the illumination of the circles. A low tone (500 hz) was always presented simultaneously with the illumination of the left circle and a high tone (1500 hz) with the right circle. The subject was never informed that a tone would be presented or that it was associated with a specific circle/response key.

The findings, in terms of percentage of correct responses, were consistent with the findings of Wright and Shea (1991) for the three-key sequences. Switching or withdrawing the incidental stimulus from that present in the original practice environment had little effect on the subject's ability to execute the correct response. Indeed, no incorrect responses were executed during test trials. RT increased, however, when the intentional–incidental stimuli association was changed from that presented during practice (see Figure 4). More specifically, removing the incidental stimulus and requiring the subjects to perform the response in the presence of the intentional stimulus alone resulted in increased response latencies. Further response delays were experienced when the incidental stimulus was switched from that established during practice.

While no response errors were produced, response latencies were increased in an incongruent context. This constitutes a more subtle form of contextual dependency. Thus, contrary to the conclusion of Wright and Shea (1991), it appears that contextual dependencies do develop during practice even for extremely simple motor responses. It is apparent,

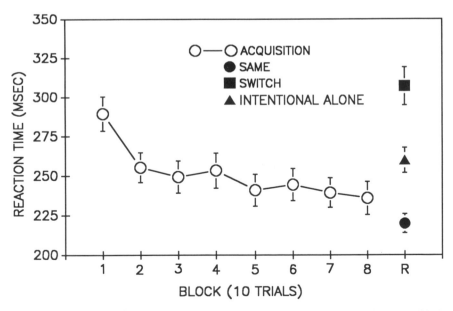

FIGURE 4. Practice and test performance for the eight practice blocks and one test block in Experiment 1 of Shea and Wright (1991). Note that practice blocks have been collapsed across retention conditions.

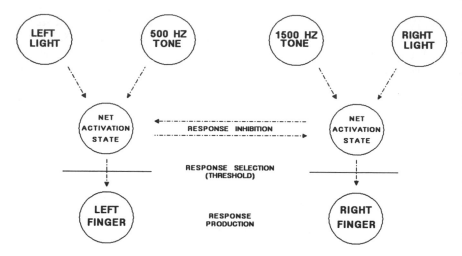

FIGURE 5. Framework illustrating the activation states incremented by the associations developed between the intentional stimuli, incidental stimuli, and the specific tasks.

therefore, that merely reducing task demands is not sufficient to eliminate the occurrence of contextual dependencies.

As a result of these findings, Shea and Wright (1991) proposed a framework characterizing the interplay of the incidental and intentional stimuli (see Figure 5). The framework proposes that stimulation of a visual (intentional stimulus) and/or auditory (incidental stimulus) state can facilitate or attenuate a net activation state for a response depending on whether the associations developed over practice are reinstated or changed at the time of the test. They proposed that the extent to which these stimuli mediate response latency is dependent on the strength of the associations that have been developed between the stimuli (intentional and incidental) and specific responses.

The association between an intentional stimulus and a response is enhanced via practice, instructions, and, in the present experiment, by the spatial correspondence between an intentional stimulus and the response (Fitts & Seeger, 1953; Simon & Wolf, 1963). The association between the incidental stimulus and the response is incremented solely by practice. Thus, the strength of the intentional stimulus–response association is assumed to be stronger than the incidental stimulus–response association.

When the original practice context is reinstated during a test trial, the net activation state for a particular response is incremented by both incidental and intentional stimuli resulting in a relatively rapid RT. If the incidental stimuli is eliminated, however, the net activation state is reduced since the increment arising from the incidental stimuli is removed. Thus, RT increases when the incidental stimulus is removed. In the switched condition, an incidental stimulus previously presented simultaneously with one intentional stimulus is now presented with the alternative intentional stimulus. In this case, the intentional stimulus is associated with one response and the incidental stimulus is related to another response. The incongruence in the intentional–incidental relationship in this situation results in a form of response competition. More specifically, the net activation state for a particular response is not only reduced because the associated incidental stimulus is not present, but also because the presence of an incidental stimulus associated with a different response exerts an inhibitory influence on that response. The consequence of this response competition is reflected in a relatively slow RT.

Finally, when the incidental stimulus is presented alone, subjects did not respond. These data suggest a threshold level of activation is required in order for a response to be initiated. It would appear that the net activation state when an incidental stimulus is presented alone is insufficient to evoke a response. This suggests that the incidental stimulus–response relationship was relatively weak.

DOES INCREASING OR DECREASING THE ASSOCIATION BETWEEN THE INCIDENTAL STIMULI AND THE TASKS INFLUENCE THE CONTEXTUAL DEPENDENCY EFFECT?

The framework outlined by Shea and Wright (1991) suggests that if the relationships between the incidental stimuli and the responses were systematically reduced or incremented, contextual dependencies would be reduced or enhanced accordingly. More specifically, the extent to which the net activation state would be incremented or inhibited by an incidental stimulus is dependent on the strength of the relationship between this stimulus and a response. A weak relationship between the incidental stimulus and a response should therefore translate into a smaller facilitory or inhibitory influence. This, in turn, should lead to less change in RT as a result of reinstating or switching the incidental stimulus.

In two experiments (Shea & Wright, 1991, Exp. 2 & 3) an attempt was made to systematically manipulate the strength of the relationship between the incidental stimuli and the tasks. The strength of this relationship was weakened by reducing the difference (and thus the discriminability) between the incidental stimuli that could be associated with particular responses. For example, one incidental stimulus condition involved the simultaneous presentation of a 1000 Hz tone with both the left and right finger responses in a choice reaction time task. Thus, the subjects were unable to develop distinct associations between the incidental stimulus and the responses because the same incidental stimulus was presented on every trial. In other incidental stimuli conditions (500–1500, 750–1250, 900–1100 Hz) the tones were assumed to be more readily discriminable, and therefore easier to associate with a response. In contrast,

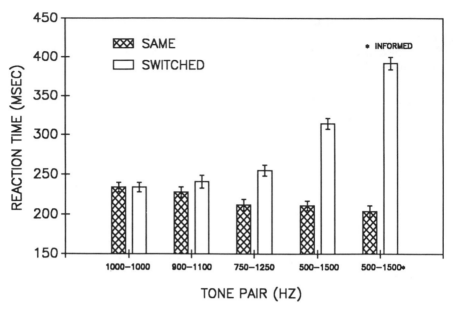

FIGURE 6. Test performance for the ten conditions in Experiments 2 and 3 of Shea and Wright (1991).

an increase in the relationship between the incidental stimuli and the responses was achieved by informing the subjects of the contingencies between the incidental stimuli and the tasks that existed during practice.

In general, the magnitude of the facilitory and inhibitory influences exerted by the incidental stimuli were consistent with that predicted by the proposed framework (see Figure 6). When the incidental stimuli were distinct enough to be clearly associated with a specific response, a faster RT resulted when a congruent incidental stimulus was reinstated. In contrast, an increase in RT occurred when the incidental stimulus was switched during the test trials. These effects (facilitory and inhibitory) were reduced when the incidental stimuli were difficult to discriminate and, presumably, difficult to associate with particular responses.

An additional finding that is particularly noteworthy was that 5 of the 12 (42%) subjects informed of the associations between the incidental stimuli and the responses in the switched condition did not respond on the first test trial. The proposed framework predicts that when the association between the incidental stimulus and the response is sufficiently strong, the incidental stimulus can inhibit the production of a response. The informed manipulation apparently increased the incidental stimulus–response relationship to the appropriate level for some of the subjects. In comparison, it should be noted that no subject in the uninformed condition failed to respond correctly during the test trials.

The present data lend support to two key features of the framework advanced by Shea and Wright (1991): a facilitory effect when the context is reinstated and an inhibitory effect when the context is changed. It appears, however, that contextual reinstatement leads to moderate decreases in response latency at best. This finding is not entirely in concert with the framework of Shea and Wright which assumes the magnitude of the facilitory component should be equivalent to that of the inhibitory effect (which is quite large). This was obviously not the case. This may be due, at least in part, to a floor effect that limits the production of RTs more consistent with those predicted by the framework.

Since the intentional and incidental stimuli were presented in visual and auditory modalities respectively, the facilitory component may be likened to the phenomenon called intersensory facilitation (e.g., Nickerson, 1973; Todd, 1912). Intersensory facilitation is said to occur when stimulus pairs presented together elicit a faster RT than when either of the stimuli is presented alone. A number of explanations have been offered for this phenomenon; however, none appears to adequately account for the present data. For example, intersensory facilitation should not have been enhanced by practice or influenced by the changes in incidental stimuli pairs as long as the intensity of the stimuli were not changed. Thus, we are left with a relatively meager but stable facilitation under contextual reinstatement which is not easily reconciled with mechanisms advanced for intersensory facilitation.

In contrast to the small benefit gained when experiencing contextual reinstatement, it appears that being exposed to a contextual change can lead to a severe disruption in performance. This is clearly evident in the substantial increase in response latencies (Shea & Wright, 1991, Exp. 2) and response errors (Shea & Wright, 1991, Exp. 3) that were elicited when the context was switched from that present during practice. The model forwarded by Shea and Wright attributes the detrimental effect of contextual change to the response competition that exists between the incongruent intentional and incidental stimuli that were presented. Since the intentional and incidental stimuli are assumed to contend for response production, the inhibitory effect may be considered a form of the classic Stroop phenomenon (see MacLeod, 1991, for review). Indeed, both the data and the proposed framework appear consistent with explanations forwarded for increased response latencies demonstrated with Stoop tasks.

SUMMARY

The data examined herein support the contention of Smith et al. (1978) and Bjork and Richardson-Klavehn (1989) that contextual factors can exert an influence on motor skill learning and performance. The mechanism by which this occurs is poorly specified at this time. Recent experimental efforts (Shea & Wright, 1991; Wright & Shea, 1991) have focused on the incorporation of incidental information within the memorial structure that develops to enable task recall. Inclusion of incidental information within the memorial network appears to be dictated to some extent by the difficulty of the task being acquired. This may be due to the reduced opportunity to survey the available incidental information when task acquisition is particularly challenging. Even if the task demands are reduced and the learner has the opportunity to process incidental stimulus-task contingencies, however, the incidental stimuli needs to be clearly discriminable in order to become associated with the appropriate response and subsequently incorporated as part of the extant memorial network. As this component of the network is embellished, both the facilitory effect of the incidental stimuli during contextual reinstatement and the inhibitory influence during contextual change are accentuated.

The present data highlight not only the importance of the intentional stimulus–task association but also the relationship that develops between the incidental stimulus and the task in determining the occurrence of contextual dependencies. This finding appears important since much of the teaching that occurs in many skill acquisition environments places heavy emphasis on intentional sources of information. This is particularly true with respect to instructions, feedback, and cues highlighted during demonstrations. The present data suggest that other sources of information are contained in the higher order cognitive representation of a task which exert a subtle influence on performance. Information sources such as those defined herein as incidental should not continue to be ignored and deserve future experimental attention.

REFERENCES

Anderson, J. R. (1983). *The Architecture of Cognition*. Cambridge, MA: Harvard University Press.

Bjork, R. A., & Richardson-Klavehn, A. (1989). On the puzzling relationship between environmental context and human memory. In C. Izawa (Ed.), *Current issues in cognitive processes* (pp. 313–344). Hillsdale, NJ: Lawrence Erlbaum Publishers.

Davies, G. M., & Thomson, D. M. (1988a). Context in context. In G. M. Davies & D. M. Thomson (Eds.), *Memory in context: Context in memory* (pp. 335–345). New York: John Wiley & Sons Ltd.

Davies, G. M., & Thomson, D. M. (Eds.). (1988b). *Memory in context: Context in memory*. New York: John Wiley & Sons Ltd.

Diewert, G. L., & Roy, E. A. (1978). Coding strategy for memory of movement extent information. *Journal of Experimental Psychology: Human Learning and Memory, 4*, 666–675.

Dulsky, S. G. (1935). The effect of a change of background on recall and relearning. *Journal of Experimental Psychology, 18,* 725–740.

Eich, E. (1980). The cue-dependent nature of state-dependent retrieval. *Memory and Cognition, 8,* 157–173.

Eich, E., & Birnbaum, I. M. (1988). On the relationship between the dissociative and affective properties of drugs. In G. M. Davies & D. M. Thomson (Eds.), *Memory in context: Context in memory* (pp. 81–93). New York: John Wiley & Sons Ltd.

Fernandez, A., & Glenberg, A. M. (1985). Changing environmental context does not reliably affect memory. *Memory and Cognition, 13,* 333–345.

Fitts, P. M., & Seeger, C. M. (1953). S-R compatibility: Spatial characteristics of stimulus and response codes. *Journal of Experimental Psychology, 46,* 199–210.

Geiselman, R. E. (1988). Improving eyewitness memory through mental reinstatement of context. In G. M. Davies & D. M. Thomson (Eds.), *Memory in context: Context in memory* (pp. 245–266). New York: John Wiley & Sons Ltd.

Geiselman, R. E., & Bjork, R. A. (1980). Primary and secondary rehearsal in imagined voices: Differential effects on recognition. *Cognitive Psychology, 12,* 188–205.

Gooden, D. R., & Baddeley, A. D. (1975). Context-dependent memory in two natural environments: On land and underwater. *British Journal of Psychology, 66,* 325–332.

Gooden, D. R., & Baddeley, A. D. (1980). When does context influence recognition memory? *British Journal of Psychology, 71,* 99–104.

Hintzman, D. L. (1984). Minerva 2: A simulation of human memory. *Behavior Research Methods, Instrumentation, and Computers, 26,* 96–101.

Lee, T. D. (1982). Encoding specificity: A reply to Crocker (1981). *Journal of Motor Behavior, 14,* 86–90.

Lee, T. D., & Hirota, T. T. (1980). Encoding specificity principle in motor short-term memory for movement extent. *Journal of Motor Behavior, 12,* 63–67.

Lee, T. D., & Magill, R. A. (1985). On the nature of movement representation in memory. *British Journal of Psychology, 76,* 175–182.

Lintern, G. (1985). Context and dependency effects in skill acquisition. In R. Eberts & C. G. Eberts (Eds.), *Trends in ergonomics/human factors II* (pp. 249–256). Amsterdam: Elsevier Science (North Holland).

Luchins, A. S. (1942). Mechanization in problem solving. *Psychological Monographs, 54,* no. 248.

MacLeod, C. M. (1991). Half a century of research on the Stroop effect: An integrative review. *Psychological Bulletin, 109,* 163–203.

Magill, R. A. (1988). Insights into memory and control in motor behavior through the study of context effects: A discussion of Mathews et al. and Shea and Zimny. In R. A. Magill (Ed.), *Memory and control of action* (pp. 367–376). Amsterdam: Elsevier Science (North Holland).

Marteniuk, R. G., & Rodney, M. (1979). Modality and retention effects in intra- and cross-modal judgments of kinaesthetic and visual information. *British Journal of Psychology, 70,* 405–412.

Murdock, B. B. (1989). Learning in a distributed memory model. In C. Izawa (Ed.), *Current issues in cognitive processes* (pp. 69–106). Hillsdale, NJ: Lawrence Erlbaum Publishers.

Newell, K. M., Shapiro, D. C., & Carlton, M. J. (1979). Coordinating visual and kinaesthetic memory codes. *British Journal of Psychology, 70,* 87–96.

Nickerson, R. S. (1973). Intersensory Facilitation of reaction time: Energy summation or preparation enhancement? *Psychological Review, 80,* 489–509.

Raaijmakers, J. G. W., & Shiffrin, R. M. (1981). Search of associative memory. *Psychological Review, 88,* 93–134.

Reeve, T. G., & Mainor, R. (1985). Effects of movement context on the encoding of kinesthetic spatial information. *Research Quarterly for Exercise and Sport, 54*, 352–363.

Schneider, W., & Detweiler, M. (1987). A connectionist/control architecture for working memory. In K. W. Spence (Ed.), *The psychology of learning and motivation* (pp. 53–119). New York: Academic Press.

Shea, C. H., & Wright, D. L. (1991). *Response delays as a function of contextual dependencies*. Paper presented at the North American Society for the Psychology of Sport and Physical Activity. Asilomar, CA.

Simon, J. R., & Wolf, J. D. (1963). Choice reaction time as a function of angular stimulus-response correspondence and age. *Ergonomics, 6*, 99–105.

Smith, S. M. (1988). Environmental context-dependent memory. In G. M. Davies & D. M. Thomson (Eds.), *Memory and context: Context in memory* (pp. 13–34). New York: John Wiley & Sons Ltd.

Smith, S. M., Glenberg, A., & Bjork, R. A. (1978). Environmental context and human memory. *Memory and Cognition, 6*, 342–353.

Stanovich, K. E., & West, R. F. (1983). On priming by a sentence context. *Journal of Experimental Psychology: General, 112*, 1–36.

Sternberg, S. (1966). High speed scanning in human memory. *Science, 153*, 652–654.

Thomson, D. M., & Davies, G. M. (1988). Introduction. In G. M. Davies & D. M. Thomson (Eds.), *Memory in context: Context in memory* (pp. 1–10). New York: John Wiley & Sons Ltd.

Todd, J. W. (1912). Reaction time to multiple stimuli. *Archives of Psychology, 3*, 1–65.

Tulving, E., & Thomson, D. M. (1973). Encoding specificity and retrieval processes in episodic memory. *Psychological Review, 80*, 353–370.

Vela, E., & Smith, S. M. (1991). *Environmental context-dependent memory: A review and meta analysis*. Unpublished manuscript.

Wallace, S. A. (1977). The coding of location: A test of the target hypothesis. *Journal of Motor Behavior, 9*, 157–169.

Watkins, M. J., Ho, E., & Tulving, E. (1976). Context effects in recognition memory for faces. *Journal of Verbal Learning and Verbal Behavior, 15*, 505–517.

Wright, D. L., & Shea, C. H. (1991). Contextual dependencies in motor skills. *Memory and Cognition, 19*, 361–370.

CHAPTER SIX

Applications of Cognitive Design Systems to Test Development

SUSAN EMBRETSON

Until recent times, cognitive testing had been a stagnant field. Carroll and Maxwell (1979), in their *Annual Review of Psychology* paper on testing, pointed out that little had changed since the first author had reviewed the field 25 years earlier. Carroll and Maxwell (1979) pointed out, however, that cognitive psychology was a new force that could substantially change testing. Since their chapter appeared, an extensive foundation of research has been assembled which covers many types of items that appear on cognitive tests (e.g., Bejar, Chaffin & Embretson, 1990; Carpenter, Just, & Shell, 1990; Embretson, 1985; Pellegrino, 1985; Sternberg, 1985).

Cognitive theory has several potential benefits for cognitive testing, if the theory is sufficiently well developed. First, cognitive theory permits construct validity to be anchored to the processes that are involved in item solving. Embretson (1983, 1992a, in press) postulates that the construct representation of a test (i.e., the latent constructs that are involved in item solving) can be understood and manipulated in accordance with a cognitive theory of the task. The theory elaborates how item stimuli influence the processing requirements of the item task, which in turn allows the test developer to influence construct representation. Second, cognitive theory also permits the correlations of test scores to be understood and manipulated. Embretson (1983, in press) postulates that construct representation underlies nomothetic span (i.e., the correlates

SUSAN EMBRETSON • Department of Psychology, University of Kansas, Lawrence, Kansas 66045.
Cognitive Assessment: A Multidisciplinary Perspective, edited by Cecil R. Reynolds. Plenum Press, New York, 1994.

of test scores). Thus, manipulations of the item stimuli should influence the nomothetic span of the test as well as construct representation. Third, item development becomes a scientific process rather than an artistic process. Items are developed to represent explicit specifications that influence processing. The item writer becomes an experimenter who designs tasks to reflect specific aspects of a theory in the task. For some tasks, specifications have become sufficiently explicit for artificial intelligence to be used in item construction (e.g., Bejar, 1990; Hornke & Habon, 1986). Fourth, cognitive theory can improve the efficiency of test development. Better quality items with more precisely targeted difficulties can be expected. Developing items by specifications from theory should yield better discriminating items because the item stimuli that influence irrelevant processes can be eliminated. Consequently, empirical tryouts should result in less item attrition. Further, the empirical tryouts need include only items with the desired difficulty levels because the specifications also yield predictions of item difficulty levels.

Despite these several advantages, however, test developers have been slow to apply cognitive design to testing. One obstacle to applications may be the lack of appropriate test development models. That is, test developers who have employed traditional psychometric principles may not know how cognitive design principles can be incorporated into testing procedures. The current chapter illustrates a conceptual and procedural framework for test design (Embretson, 1992a, in press) by describing the development of a test for complex spatial ability. Prior to presenting the actual applications, the conceptual and procedural framework will be briefly described.

COGNITIVE DESIGN SYSTEMS: CONCEPTUAL AND PROCEDURAL FRAMEWORK

A cognitive design system (Embretson, 1992a, in press) is a framework for utilizing cognitive theory to develop ability tests. The conceptual framework is a reformulation of the construct validity concept to centralize the role of cognitive theory in test development. The procedural framework is a series of stages required to simultaneously achieve optimal cognitive and optimal psychometric properties in the test. The cognitive design system has the following properties: (1) test content is prescribed by explicit principles; (2) score meaning is linked to underlying cognitive processes, rather than just to correlations with other measures; (3) item parameters represent the sources of cognitive complexity in the item; and (4) abilities are linked to the processes that underlie task difficulty.

CONCEPTUAL FRAMEWORK

The classic concept of construct validity places the nomological network as central to test meaning. Accordingly, Cronbach and Meehl (1955) state: "the vague, avowedly incomplete network gives the constructs whatever meaning they do have" (p. 289). The nomological network consists primarily of the empirical relationships of test scores to other variables. Bechtoldt (1958) points out that this conceptualization of construct validity confounds test meaning with test significance. Test meaning, according to Bechtoldt, concerns the constructs that are measured by the test. Test significance, in contrast, concerns the relationships of the test with other measures of individual differences. Since Cronbach and Meehl (1955) conceptualize test meaning as arising from the elaboration of the nomological network, it is clear that test significance determines test meaning.

Embretson (1983) postulated that the theory and methods of cognitive psychology permitted two aspects of construct validity to be distinguished. Construct representation concerns the processes, strategies, and knowledge structures that are involved in responding to test items. The relevant empirical data includes the modeling of task difficulty (accuracy and response time) from systematically varied aspects of the item task. Nomothetic span concerns the relationship of the test to other measures of individual differences. The relevant empirical data includes the correlations of test scores with other tests, criterion measures, and so forth. Embretson (in press) points out that construct representation and nomothetic span correspond roughly to Bechtoldt's meaning and significance, respectively.

Embretson (1992a, in press) suggests that, unlike the classical conceptualization of construct validity, the two-part conceptualization (i.e., construct representation and nomothetic span) permits cognitive theory to have a central role in test design. The classic conceptualization of construct validity permits no clear role for test and item design because test meaning arises from test significance. Thus, the test must already exist. The external correlations of the test scores give little information about how to redesign the items or testing procedures. In the two-part conceptualization of construct validity, however, test meaning arises from data on the processes that are involved in item solving. In turn, test significance follows from test meaning because the latent constructs in performance determine its correlations with other measures.

Notice that the relationship between test meaning and test significance is reversed in the two-part conceptualization as compared to the classic conceptualization. Test meaning precedes, rather than follows, test significance. Since test meaning is prior, manipulations of the item stimuli, item presentation conditions, and preceding task experience can influence construct representation directly, prior to the existence of a fully developed test. Then, in turn, construct representation can influence nomothetic span. Thus, test design can have an explicit role in determining construct validity.

PROCEDURAL FRAMEWORK

The procedural framework is the series of steps required to centralize the role of cognitive theory in test development. One such system is outlined in Table 1. An underlying assumption for the procedural framework is that cognitive theory may be represented by mathematical models which link the test items (item stimuli, presentation conditions or preceding experiences) to performance. Some steps in Table 1, such as developing or evaluating a cognitive model, are unfamiliar to test developers. Other steps, such as evaluating test properties and banking items, are familiar, but the manner in which they are conducted differs substantially when cognitive theory is involved.

To understand better the goals of the procedural framework, it is useful to consider items within the context of a larger task domain. Several subsets appear in the task domain. A psychometric subset would include the items or item bank for a particular test. A cognitive model subset includes items that fit a particular cognitive model. Different cognitive models may be appropriate for various subsets in the domain. The target cognitive subset contains the items that fit a cognitive model that includes only the processes that are specified as the goals of measurement for the test. A successful application of the steps in Table 1 achieves the goal of the psychometric subset being contained within the target cognitive model subset.

Cognitive models are central to the procedures in Table 1 in several ways. First, cognitive models provide a basis for item selection and item specification. The independent variables of the cognitive model provide a means to specify the sources of cognitive complexity in the items. Second, cognitive models are needed to support construct representation; that is, construct representation is supported when a theoretically and empirically plausible cognitive model has been developed for the test. Third, cognitive models provide a basis for evaluating the test with respect to the intended goals of measurement. If the test items are well specified, test item difficulty should be explained by a model that includes only the intended processes according to the goals of measurement. Fourth, cognitive models may be linked to psychometric models. Several item response theory (IRT) models have been postulated explicitly to include sources of cognitive complexity in the measurement model (e.g., Fischer, 1973; Embretson, 1984; Mislevy & Verhelst, 1990; Whitely, 1980). Fifth, cognitive models provide a basis for specific hypotheses about the nomothetic span of the test. If the desired construct representation has been achieved,

TABLE 1. Cognitive Design Systems

Specify General Goals of Measurement
  Construct representation (meaning)
  Nomothetic span (Significance)

Identify Design Features in Task Domain
  Task-general features (mode, format, conditions)
  Task-specific features

Develop a Cognitive Model
  Review theories
  Select or develop model for psychometric domain
  Revise model
  Test model

Evaluate Cognitive Model for Psychometric Potential
  Evaluate cognitive model plausibility on current test
  Evaluate impact of complexity factors on psychometric properties
  Anticipate properties of new test

Specify Item Distributions on Cognitive Complexity
  Distribution of item complexity parameters
  Distribution of item features

Generate Items to Fit Specifications
  Artifical intelligence?

Evaluate Cognitive and Psychometric Properties for Revised Test
    Domain
  Estimate component latent trait model parameters
  Evaluate plausibility of cognitive model
  Evaluate impact of complexity factors on psychometric properties
  Evaluate plausibility of the psychometric model
Calibrate final item parameters and ability distributions

Bank Items by Cognitive Complexity Parameters
  $\eta_m q_{im}$ (weight $\times$ item score)
  b_{ik} (component subtask difficulty)
  $P_{strategy}$

Assemble Test Forms to Represent Specifications
  Fixed content test
  Adaptive test

Validate

---

then specific patterns of correlations with other measures can be expected.

COGNITIVE DESIGN APPROACH TO SPATIAL ABILITY

This section describes the application of the cognitive design system approach to developing a test of complex spatial ability. Three forms were developed for the Spatial Learning Ability Test (SLAT), which measures initial spatial ability and the modifiability of spatial ability following standardized instruction. Only the role of the cognitive design system in the construct validity of initial ability will be considered below. It should be noted, however, that construct validity, especially construct representation, is crucial to interpreting the meaning of performance modifiability. A major goal in the development of the SLAT was to clearly specify construct representation.

SPECIFYING THE GENERAL GOALS OF MEASUREMENT

The measurement goals for both construct representation and nomothetic span need to be specified. For construct representation, the goal for the SLAT was to develop items that are solved by the mental manipulation of complex objects in space. The role of verbal processing in solving the items was to be minimized. For nomothetic span, the goal for the SLAT was to represent spatial ability rather than verbal reasoning. If achieved, the SLAT should have low correlations with verbal ability and also have incremental validity over verbal ability in predicting criteria that involve complex spatial processing.

IDENTIFYING DESIGN FEATURES IN THE TASK DOMAIN

Design features may be general or specific. General features apply to many task domains, while specific design features apply only to particular or related task domains. Since accomplishing the goals of measurement in the design system depends on the design features, this stage of initial identification is quite important.

General design features include variables such as item presentation mode, item format, and item presentation conditions. The general features of the SLAT were driven by the requirements for modifiability measurement. Static item displays and multiple choice formats were indirectly entailed by optimizing the modifiability measurement. Adequately measuring modifiability requires optimal precision for each repeated measurement which is best obtained by computerized adaptive testing (see Embretson, in press). Computerized adaptive testing, however, requires special programs for item presentation and calibration. The currently available programs, such as the MICROCAT program, (Assessment Systems, 1989) require static item displays and multiple choice formats. Item presentation conditions were also influenced by the modifiability measurement. Since modifiability is to be measured after instruction, the initial ability should not be preceded by extensive practical or instructions.

Specific design features vary across task domains. For the SLAT, the spatial folding task was selected because it involves complex spatial manipulations. Furthermore, the task has some psychometric history in that it appears on the Space Relations Test of the Differential Aptitude Test (DAT). Figure 1 shows two spatial folding items, which consist of an unfolded stem and four folded alternatives. The task is to select the folded alternative that results from folding down the unfolded stem. The top item in Figure 1 contains sides with directed markings that appear differently in different orientations. The bottom line in Figure 1 contains two sides with undirected markings. The shaded sides (i.e., the black and the white sides) appear the same in every orientation.

Some obvious design features include (1) directed versus undirected markings; (2) stem shape; (3) relationship of the markings on the key to the markings on the stem; and (4) the relationship of the distractors to the stem. Although these specific design features could be used to develop items, their impact on cognitive processing is unclear. They may indeed influence processing directly, or they may set limits on processing or, they may influence the variables that have a direct influence on processing.

Adequate selection of specific design features requires that a cognitive model of the task be developed. If construct representation is to be understood, design features should influence processing directly, not through other variables. Although traditional test development rarely continues beyond the identification of design features that (may) predict item difficulty, the cognitive design approach requires some additional stages to optimize design features.

DEVELOPING A COGNITIVE MODEL

A cognitive model needs to be developed for the selected task domain. Developing the cognitive model requires reviewing the experimental literature on the task or related tasks, selecting or formulating appropriate models, revising models, and testing models. This aspect of cognitive design systems is relatively unfamiliar to test developers but forms a major basis for construct validity.

Although the spatial folding task has not been studied extensively, cognitive models have been developed for several other complex spatial tasks. For example, processing difficulty on tasks that require two-dimensional or three-dimensional rotation between pairs of objects (Bejar, 1990; Cooper & Shephard, 1973; Just & Carpenter, 1985) are well described by cognitive models. Degrees of rotation between target and object typically has a linear relationship to response time, which supports the theory that mental rotation is a physical analogue process. A study of the spatial folding task (Shephard & Feng, 1971) indicated that the number of surfaces carried influences processing difficulty as well.

Embretson and Waxman (1989) developed several models of the spa-

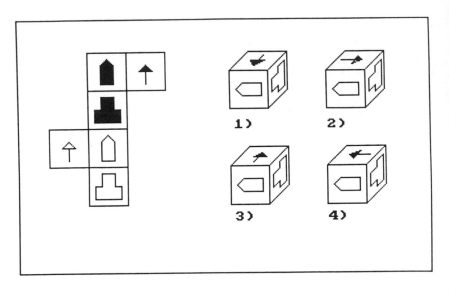

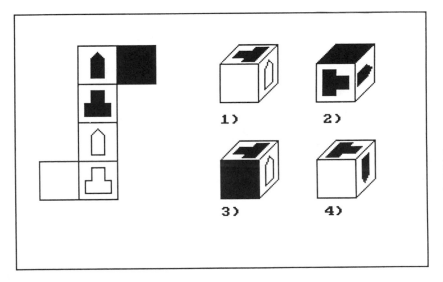

FIGURE 1. Two spatial folding items.

tial folding task. An attached folding model, which is applicable to both SLAT and DAT items is shown on Figure 2. A series of spatial manipulations are postulated in the model. The model begins with the encoding of the stem, and then the alternatives. Next, a search process for an anchoring point (pairs of sides with the same markings) between the stem and

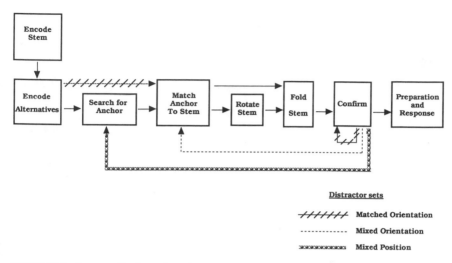

FIGURE 2. A generalized version of the attached folding model. (From S. E. Embretson [in press]. "Developments toward a Cognitive Design System for psychological tests." In R. Dawis & D. Lupinsky [Eds.] *Assessing Individual Differences in Human Behavior.* Minneapolis: University of Minnesota Press)

alternative is undertaken. If needed, the stem is mentally rotated to align the anchoring points. Then, the stem is mentally overlaid on the alternative and folded. Figure 3 presents a schematic diagram to show the attached folding process, as postulated by Embretson and Waxman (1989).

Figure 4 shows how the difficulty of the rotation and folding process can be varied systematically between items. In Figure 4, a stem and six different keys are shown. The keys in the top row vary the difficulty of the attaching process. The degrees of rotation required to anchor the stem differ between the three keys. The keys in the bottom row vary in the difficulty of the folding process. All keys in the bottom row have zero degrees of rotation, but they vary in the number of surfaces carried in folding.

In a series of studies, Embretson and Waxman (1989) found that cognitive models that included the degrees of rotation and the number of surfaces carried gave good prediction of item difficulty and response time. Some inconsistencies in the model were found, however, when the task contained undirected markings on the sides of the cube. Embretson and Waxman (1989) found that if items had only undirected markings on the sides, three surface problems at zero degrees of rotation were processed more quickly than predicted by the model, as shown in the top of Figure 5. In contrast, if items had only directed markings on the sides, both two and three surface problems at zero degrees of rotation were processed much more slowly than one surface problem, as shown in the bottom of Figure 5.

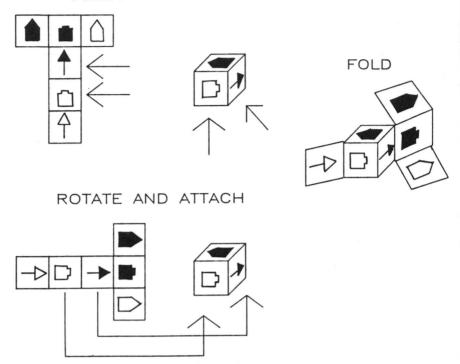

FIGURE 3. An illustration of attaching and folding. (From "Psychometric models for learning and cognitive processes" by S. E. Embretson [1992]. In N. Frederiksen, R. Mislevy, & I. Bejar [Eds.], *Theory for a New Generation of Tests*, Hillsdale, NJ: Lawrence Erlbaum)

To understand these results, consider the bottom item in Figure 1, which contains some undirected markings. A complete folding is not required to confirm that it is correct. If the stem is anchored to the two sides with directed markings, determining that the right side of the folded alternative should be shaded black (and the left side is white) is sufficient to solve the item without actually folding the shaded sides in place. Since the number of surfaces carried is postulated to manipulate the folding process, these results suggest that the folding process may be omitted if the items contained undirected markings.

To accommodate these results, among others, the generalized Embretson and Waxman (1989) model, as shown in Figure 2, includes both rotation and folding as optional processes, depending on the item. The rotation process can be omitted if the search process results in an anchoring point that is aligned between stem and alternative. The folding process can be omitted if the orientation of the markings on the third side is not relevant (e.g., for undirected markings). That is, after overlaying the stem, the examinee can confirm the position of the third side without checking the alignment (e.g., in the bottom item of Figure 2).

Embretson and Waxman (1989) also examined the impact of distractor type on processing. The distractor type can define different cognitive models, as shown in Figure 2 for three types (i.e., distractors with mixed positions, matched orientations and mixed orientations). If each alternative shows different markings (mixed positions), Embretson and Waxman (1989) postulated that attached folding process would have to be applied separately to each alternative. On the other hand, if all alternatives show the same markings, a single attached folding process could suffice. The results indicated that items with distractors of mixed positions involved greater response time and less accuracy. For items with uniform positions, the distractors could still vary in the orientation of the markings. For example, the top item in Figure 1 shows distractors with matched orientations for the anchoring point. Distractors with mixed rotations would display the same markings, but in different orientations. Embretson and Waxman (1989) postulated that items with mixed orientations for distractors would be more difficult. In fact, the orientation of the distractors had no impact on response time or accuracy.

It should be noted that a more general attached folding model is required in order to include the distractor types that appear on the DAT Space Relations Test. Some DAT items contain distractors in which the markings on the sides do not correspond to any markings in the stem.

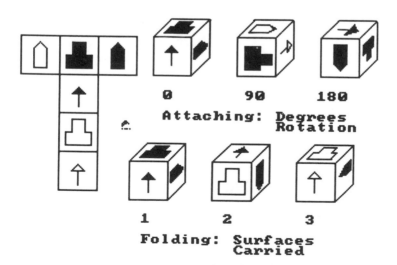

FIGURE 4. A stem and six correct answers that vary in attaching and folding difficulty (From S. E. Embretson & M. Waxman [1989]. *Cognitive models of a three-dimensional task*. Psychonomic Society, Atlanta, GA)

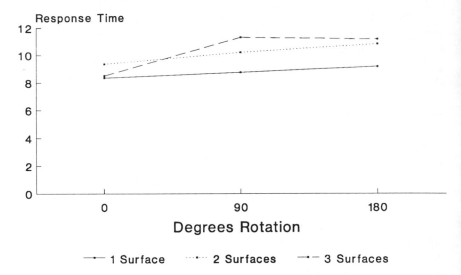

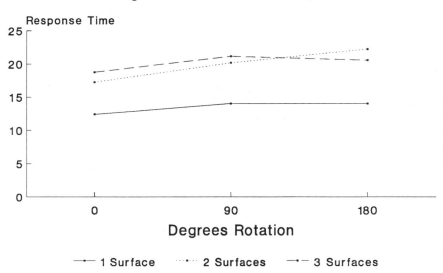

FIGURE 5. The impact of surfaces carried and degrees of rotation on response time. (From S. E. Embretson & M. Waxman [1989]. *Cognitive models of a three-dimensional task*. Psychonomic Society, Atlanta, GA)

These perceptually mismatched sides can be processed without either rotation or folding. The search process for an anchor in Figure 2 would reveal perceptually mismatched markings on the alternative, so then the examinee immediately can confirm the distractors (as false) without rotation or folding.

Another finding that is relevant to cognitive design concerns stem shape, which had no role in prediction once the effects of degrees of rotation and number of surfaces were removed. Although stem shape was corrected with item processing difficulty, it apparently exerts its influence through other variables.

Several implications about design features can be drawn from these studies. First, degrees of rotation and number of surfaces carried are good design variables. Not only do they operationalize the independent variables of a theoretically plausible model of the task, but they have strong impact on overall processing difficulty. Second, stem shape is not a relevant design variable. Stem shape can vary between items without influencing processing if degrees of rotation and number of surfaces carried are controlled. Third, distractor type could be a design variable, but the effects depend on the specific types of distractors. Fourth, the cognitive model for the target domain should reflect both rotation and folding, but not alternative processes. Since the goals of measurement specify spatial processes, items that can be solved without either rotation or folding should not be included (e.g., distractors with perceptually mismatched sides). Fifth, items with mostly undirected markings probably should be excluded from the target task domain. The results suggest that a major spatial process is more clearly involved only when directed markings are included on the sides of the figures.

SPECIFYING ITEM DISTRIBUTIONS ON COGNITIVE COMPLEXITY

Consistent with the considerations above, it was decided that SLAT items should include only stems with directed markings on most sides. Furthermore, to better control processing strategies, it was decided that all distractors should display only the same markings as the key; then the item may be solved with a single attached folding process. If the markings on the distractors differ from the key, the examinee may need to fold or to orient the stem separately to falsify for each one. Processing becomes more poorly specified by the item stimuli in this case because the examinee may apply either a self-terminating or exhaustive strategy in processing the distractors. For the self-terminating strategy, processing stops when the key is encountered. Thus, key position becomes a very salient factor in determining the number of attached foldings in the self-terminating strategy.

Two types of items were specified for the task domain. The spatial items were specified to maximize the impact of attaching and folding. Thus, all spatial items had only directed markings on the sides, as shown in the top item in Figure 2. The position items were specified so as to be solvable without folding. All position items contained two sides with undirected markings, which were the sides that were folded as shown in the bottom item in Figure 2.

For the spatial items, the item specifications resulted from crossing Degrees (0,90,180) by Surfaces (1,2,3) by Distractor Type (matched versus mixed orientations), which yields 18 item frames. These specifications were implemented on items that varied in shape (three types) and marker configurations (two types), which were counterbalanced with Degrees and Surfaces. A total of 54 items were specified. For the position items, Degrees (0,90,180) by Distractor Type (matched vs. mixed) yielded 6 item frames. As for spatial items, these specifications were counterbalanced with stem shape and marker configuration for a total of 18 items.

In summary, the SLAT specifications were explicitly designed to maximize the role of spatial processes in the items, particularly as defined by the stem to key relationship. It is interesting to compare the SLAT specifications to the implicit specifications in the traditionally designed DAT Space Relations Test that are shown on Table 2 and in Figure 6. In general, these data show that the SLAT contains more items that involve difficult spatial processes to confirm the key than the DAT.

Table 2 shows the proportion of items within each combination of the degrees of rotation and the number of surfaces carried for the SLAT and Form V of the DAT Space Relations Test. In Table 2, only the stem to key relationships are considered. For the SLAT, the various combinations are balanced except that two surface problems are more frequent. Two sur-

TABLE 2. Proportions of Items in Categories
of Stem to Key Relations for the SLAT and the DAT

| Variable | Degrees of Rotation | | | |
	0	90	180	Marginal
SLAT				
1 surface	.083	.083	.083	.250
2 surfaces	.167	.167	.167	.500
3 surfaces	.083	.083	.083	.250
Marginal	.333	.333	.333	1.000
DAT				
1 surface	.283	.150	.066	.500
2 surfaces	.167	.033	.033	.233
3 surfaces +	.100	.150	.167	.266
Marginal	.497	.333	.266	1.000

face problems are overrepresented because all position problems had a key that would involve two surfaces carried if the stem were folded. For the DAT Space Relations Test, problems at 0 degrees rotation and problems with one surface carried are clearly overrepresented. The most frequent combination is 0 degrees rotation with one surface carried. Thus, in general, the implicit item specifications on the DAT Space Relations Test minimize the role of the attaching and folding process in the stem to key relationships.

Figure 6 compares the relative frequencies of distractor types on the SLAT and the DAT Space Relations Test. The distractors were compared to the key for the amount of spatial processing required for falsification. If the distractors require less spatial processing than the key, the examinee can falsify the distractors and accept the key without performing the more difficult stem to key spatial processes. Thus, the degrees of rotation and the number of surfaces carried were scored for the maximum distractor and then compared to the key. In Figure 6, processing on the maximum distractor is classified as either less than, equal to, or greater than the key. It can be seen that while about .20 of the DAT Space Relations items have a maximum distractor with fewer degrees of rotation than the key, the SLAT has none. A large proportion of SLAT items have a distractor that requires greater degrees of rotation than the key for falsification. Similarly, for the number of surfaces carried, the SLAT items are uniformly equal to the key, while the largest proportion of DAT Space Relations items require fewer surfaces carried than the key. Last, the proportion of SLAT and DAT Space Relations items that have distractors that do not match the key (due to incompatible markings, noncongruent sides, etc.) are shown under the label "none." The examinee can falsify these distractors without any spatial processing by a perceptual comparison process. Although the SLAT has no such items, the DAT Space Relations Test has several.

The results shown on Figure 6 suggest that the DAT Space Relations Test contains a large proportion of items with distractors that require less spatial processing than the key as compared to the SLAT. Thus, if an examinee applies a falsification strategy when appropriate, the burden on spatial processing can be minimized in the DAT. Coupled with less difficult stem to key relationships on the DAT, it is clear that the burden on spatial processing resources is less in the DAT than in the SLAT.

GENERATING ITEMS TO FIT SPECIFICATIONS

Items were drawn according to specifications in the MICROCAT program. It should be noted, however, that given the explicit item specifications, artificial intelligence could easily be applied to generate items. The 72 items were placed in three forms, consisting of 24 frames each.

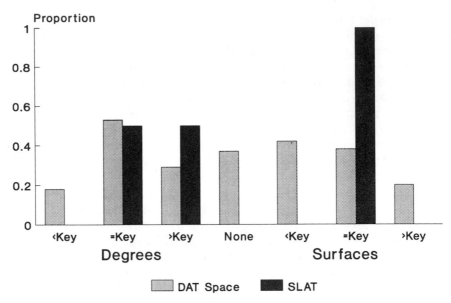

FIGURE 6. Distractor characteristics in the SLAT and the DAT.

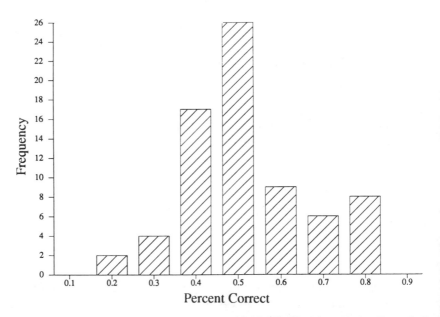

FIGURE 7. Frequencies of item difficulties in the SLAT calibration sample. (From S. E. Embretson [1992c]. "Technical manual for the Spatial Learning Ability Test")

The forms were structurally equivalent because the 24-item frames were replicated on each form (the exact stem shape and marker configuration of the replications varied between forms). An additional 4 items were created to link calibration results across forms. The linking items were matched to 4 items of moderate difficulty in specifications, except that different marker configurations were used.

EVALUATING THE COGNITIVE AND PSYCHOMETRIC PROPERTIES OF ITEMS

Psychometric Properties

The three forms of the SLAT were administered to a sample of 582 Air Force recruits for calibration (see Embretson, 1992b,c). Each SLAT form was administered in the pretest condition, along with the linking items, to roughly one-third of the subjects.

Figure 7 presents the percentages correct (p-value) for the SLAT items. It can be seen that although the items as a whole were somewhat easy for the sample (too many p-values above .50), the item specifications resulted in a wide range of difficulties. Figure 8 presents the biserial correlations of items with total scores. It can be seen that the biserial correlations were generally high and that even the item with the lowest

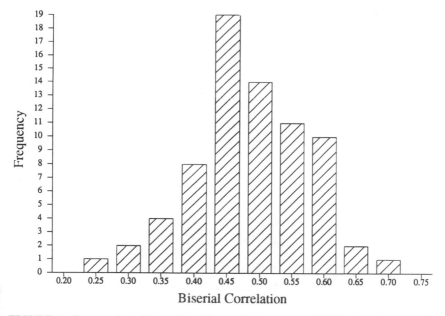

FIGURE 8. Frequencies of item biserial correlations in the SLAT calibration sample. (From S. E. Embretson [1992]. *Technical manual for the Spatial Learning Ability Test*)

biserial ($r = .25$) was not unacceptable. Thus, on the basis of classical test statistics, item attrition was virtually nil.

Further psychometric analysis was conducted with IRT models. The Rasch model, which contains only item difficulty as an item parameter, did not fit the data since the Andersen goodness of fit test was significant ($X^2{}_{162} = 252.65$, $p < .01$). A two-parameter logistic (2PL) IRT model (with both item difficulty and item discrimination) was also estimated, and fit increased significantly ($X^2{}_{76} = 132.20$, $p < .01$).

Although the Rasch model did not fit the whole set, the individual fit statistics indicated that only 4 of the 76 items failed to fit the Rasch model ($p < .05$). One item had a low difficulty level and slight graphic error. Estimating the 2PL model did improve fit for this item. The three other items were structurally equivalent variants, specified as 180 degrees of rotation, three surfaces carried with matched distractor orientations. These items had high difficulties. Estimating item discriminations in the 2PL model clearly improved fit for only one of these items. An inspection of the item characteristics curves for the items revealed substantial guessing at lower ability levels. Thus, these items could be fit by a 3PL model, which would include a parameter to represent guessing. Fitting an additional three items in the bank does not justify the additional complexity of the 3PL model compared to the Rasch model.

The results strongly indicate that the item specifications resulted in an internally consistent set of items that measure a single latent dimension. Classical item statistics indicated generally high biserial correlations, which is atypical for previously untried items. Further, applying a more stringent psychometric criterion, fit to the Rasch model, also yielded good results. The Rasch model does not fit the data exactly, but few departures from the model were observed. Only 4 of 76 items failed to fit. If the 4 nonfitting items were omitted from the item bank, attrition would be only .05. Since the observed item attrition rate is substantially less than is typical for most tryouts, the practical efficiency of the cognitive design approach is strongly supported.

Cognitive Properties

Mathematical modeling was used to determine the construct representation of the SLAT, using the calibration sample data. For response time, the item means are regressed on variables that reflect the stimulus specifications for each item. Thus, the independent variables are the degrees of rotation, number of surfaces carried, problem type, and distractor type as described above. Eight properties were scored for each item, which includes both a linear and quadratic trend variable for the degrees of rotation and the number of surfaces carried. Also, the degrees of rotation was scored separately for spatial and position problems. For item difficulty, the impact of the stimulus specifications was estimated with the linear logistic latent trait model (LLTM; Fischer, 1973). Estimating LLTM parameters is analogous to regressing the Rasch model item difficulties on independent variables for the stimulus complexity of the items. The independent variables in LLTM were identical to those in the regression analysis of response time. LLTM will be described more fully below because it is a psychometric model that has many advantages for item banking and score equating.

Table 3 shows the estimates of parameters obtained from a variant of the attached folding model for the SLAT items. The first two columns present results for response time while the second two columns present results for item difficulty.

It can be seen in Table 3 that overall prediction of item difficulty from LLTM was high, since the LLTM predictions correlated .88 with the Rasch model estimate of item difficulty. As anticipated, both the degrees of rotation and the number of surfaces carried were significant, which shows the impact of the spatial processes on task difficulty. Also as anticipated, the distractor type (matched vs. mixed) was not significant. Problem type (spatial vs. position) had a significant effect. It should be noted that the magnitude of the problem type effect on item difficulty is small (the mean for spatial items is .10 higher than the mean for position items) as compared to the large effect of the number of surfaces carried (.83 for each surface).

Table 3 also shows the results from modeling response time. As for item difficulty, overall prediction is high ($r = .87$). Furthermore, also similar to the item difficulty results, both the degrees of rotation and the number of surfaces carried have significant impact on response time, while

TABLE 3. Cognitive Models of Response Time
and Item Difficulty for the SLAT

Variable	Response Time ($R = .87$)		Item Difficulty ($R = .88$)	
	b	σ_b	η	σ_η
Problem type	−.16	.55	−.10**	.05
Distractor type	.78	.48	−.07+	.04
Spatial problems				
Degrees-linear	1.76**	.34	.16**	.03
Degrees-quadratic	.48*	.20	.10**	.02
Surfaces-linear	3.65**	.34	.83**	.03
Surfaces-quadratic	−1.09**	.20	−.18**	.02
Position problems				
Degrees-linear	−.07	.58	−.01	.05
Degrees-quadratic	.96**	.34	.19**	.03

distractor type did not have a significant impact. Unlike the item difficulty results, however, problem type was not significant in this analysis.

In summary, the impact of the degrees of rotation and the number of surfaces carried on both response time and item difficulty of the SLAT is strongly supported. These results support attaching and folding as defining the major aspect of construct representation. Problem type, spatial versus position, had no significant impact on response time and only a small effect on item difficulty. These results suggest that the same processes are applied to both problem types. Although the folding process is not required on the position problems, it may be applied anyway. Perhaps subjects fail to discriminate when folding is unnecessary.

Comparison to DAT Space Relations

The cognitive properties of the SLAT were compared to the DAT Space Relations Test by mathematically modeling item difficulty by LLTM (Embretson, in press). The mathematical models used above were not directly applicable for the comparisons for several reasons. First, the trend components for the degrees of rotation and the number of surfaces carried are highly correlated on the DAT Space Relations Test due to the overrepresentation of some combinations. Thus, only the linear component for both variables is included in the comparison. Second, although only two types of distractor sets are included on the SLAT, the distractor sets vary widely on the DAT Space Relations Test. Therefore, the qualities of the maximum distractor were scored by several variables, including the degrees of rotation, the number of surfaces carried, and the number of unanchorable (i.e., perceptually mismatched) distractors. Third, although the SLAT items have only directed markings, many DAT items have undirected markings. Thus, directed markings was included as a predictor for the DAT.

Table 4 shows the results of LLTM models of item difficulty for the SLAT and the DAT. Although the model for the DAT Space Relations items contained six independent variables, due to the greater variability in the item set, the correlation of LLTM estimates with the Rasch model item difficulties was only moderate ($r = .70$). Although the SLAT model contains only four independent variables, however, a much higher correlation was observed between the LLTM predictions and the Rasch model item difficulties ($r = .81$). Thus, the SLAT items are more predictable from the cognitive model than the DAT items.

Also important on Table 4 are the patterns of significance for the independent variables. For the DAT Space Relations Test, all the independent variables for the distractors are significant. Although two distractor variables operationalize spatial processes (degrees of rotation and surfaces carried), the other two variables represent the role of nonspatial

TABLE 4. Comparison of LLTM Parameter Estimates and Standard Errors
for Cognitive Models on Partial Tests

	DAT ($R = .70$)		SLAT ($R = .81$)	
	PE	SE	PE	SE
Stem to key variables				
Surfaces carried	−.01	.04	.81**	.07
Degrees rotation (/100)	−.09	.08	.17**	.03
Distractor variables				
Maximum degrees carried	.16**	.04	.01	.06
Maximum degrees rotation (/100)	.68**	.06	−.13**	.03
Unanchorable distractor	−.29**	.05	—	—
Directed markings	.33**	.10	—	—

processes (directed markings and unanchorable distractors). Table 4 shows that DAT items with unanchorable distractors and undirected markings are easier. The independent variables for the stem to key relationship had no significant unique contribution to item difficulty, however. Eliminating the distractor variables from the model, thus leaving only the two variables for the stem to key relationship, sharply reduced the predictability of DAT item difficulty ($r = .25$).

For the SLAT, in contrast, both the degrees of rotation and the number of surfaces carried were significant for the stem to key relationships, while only one distractor variable had a significant impact. Dropping the distractor variables from the model for the SLAT had virtually no impact on the prediction of item difficulty ($r = .81$).

These results indicate that the DAT Space Relations Test is less predictable than a model that is based on spatial processing involved in confirming the key. The DAT is more influenced by the processes involved in falsifying the item distractors, particularly the nonspatial processes, than by the stem to key relationships. The reverse pattern is true for the SLAT. The spatial processes involved in confirming the key account for nearly all the prediction of item difficulty.

The results are entirely consistent with the item specifications, as shown in Table 2 and in Figure 6. Thus, the implicit specifications of wide variability in the distractor set, coupled with relatively easy stem to key relationships in the DAT Space Relations Test, apparently results in the distractors exerting major influence on processing. The development of effective strategies for eliminating the distractors is seemingly more important than confirming the key. In comparison to the DAT Space Relations Test, accuracy on the SLAT items depends on spatial processes in confirming the key rather than on strategies for falsifying the distractors.

BANKING ITEMS BY COGNITIVE COMPLEXITY

The cognitive complexity of items is given by the LLTM estimates for the design features. Since LLTM is an item response theory (IRT) model, the LLTM cognitive complexity estimates have two major uses in test development. First, the items can be banked by estimates of the source of cognitive complexity (e.g., attaching or folding) rather than just by item difficulty. Parameter estimates of the specific source of item difficulty permits tests (even adaptive tests) to be counterbalanced for cognitive complexity. Second, the difficulty of new items can be predicted prior to tryout. Combined with the rather good results on SLAT item quality (i.e., biserial correlations and item fit), item attrition for inappropriate levels or poor fit should be virtually nil.

As for any IRT model, LLTM gives the probability for passing each item as a function of the item's difficulty and the examinee's ability. Unlike standard IRT models, however, item difficulty is determined by the source of cognitive complexity because the variables that operationalize the information processing model are entered as item complexity factor scores in LLTM. In LLTM, the probability that a person passes an item, $P(X_{ij} = 1)$, is given by the individual's ability, θ_j, and the item's information processing complexity as follows:

$$P(X_{ij} = 1) = \frac{\exp(\theta_j - \Sigma_m \eta_m q_{im} + d)}{1 + \exp(\theta_j - \Sigma_m \eta_m q_{im} + d)}. \tag{1}$$

where q_{im} is the score of item i on complexity factor m, η_m is the weight of factor m in item difficulty, and d is a normalization constant. Thus, in LLTM, the item parameters to be estimated describe the complexity of the item on the information processing factors.

Item difficulty is given by the sum of the complexity factor scores times their associated weights. That is, item difficulty, b_i^*, is the following in LLTM:

$$b_i^* = \Sigma_m \eta_m q_{im} + d \tag{2}$$

where all symbols are defined as for Equation 1.

The relative contribution of attaching, folding, and confirming to a specific item may be evaluated by examining the LLTM equation for the item. For the spatial folding data, the following equation for item difficulty was calibrated (Embretson, 1992c):

$$b_i^* = -.07q_1 - .10q_2 + .16q_3 + .10q_4 + .83q_5 - .18q_6$$

$$- .018_7 + .19q_8 \tag{3}$$

Where

q_1 = Distractor Type (0,1)
q_2 = Problem Type (0,1)
q_3 = Degrees Rotation-Linear (−1,0,1)
q_4 = Degrees Rotation-Quadratic (1,−2,1)
q_5 = Surfaces Carried-Linear (−1,0,1)
q_6 = Surfaces Carried-Quadratic (1,−2,1)
q_7 = Degrees Rotation Position-Linear (−1,0,1)
q_8 = Degrees Rotation Position-Quadratic (1,−2,1)

It should be noted that both the degrees of rotation and the number of surfaces carried are scored by orthogonal polynomials.

The contribution of each source of cognitive complexity to item difficulty is given by the product of the item score and the complexity factor weight, $\eta_m q_{im}$. Suppose that an item has distractors with mixed orientations (i.e., distractor type equals 1); thus the contribution of distractor type, q_1 to the complexity of the item is −.07 (−.07 × 1). Suppose that the item has three surfaces carried. The values for the orthogonal polynomial contrasts for three surfaces carried are 1 and 1, respectively, for q_5 and q_6. Thus, the contribution of the number of surfaces carried to item difficulty is given by the sum of the linear and quadratic components, which is .65 (i.e., ((.83 × 1) + (−.18 × 1))). Obviously, the number of surfaces carried has a far larger contribution to item difficulty than the distractor type.

Equation 3 also can be used to predict the difficulty of untried items on the basis of their stimulus characteristics. For example, suppose that a spatial item has two surfaces carried, a 90 degree rotation and matched orientation between the key and distractors. Then, item difficulty would be predicted as follows:

$$b_i^* = -.07(0) - .10(0) + .16(0) + .10(-2) + .83(0) - .18(-2) - \quad (3)$$

$$.01(0) + .19(0)$$

$$= .16.$$

VALIDATION: NOMOTHETIC SPAN

Both construct representation and nomothetic span are essential aspects of construct validity that can be influenced by the cognitive design system. Although the results on the cognitive model reported above are relevant to construct representation, nomothetic span data requires correlations of test scores with other variables.

The major goal for nomothetic span in designing the SLAT was to minimize the role of verbal abilities in the test. Embretson (in press) reports a study on the correlations of the SLAT pretest with some reference tests that were selected to represent verbal and spatial abilities. Verbal ability was represented by two tests, the Vocabulary and the Verbal Analogies subtests of the Cognitive Abilities Test (CAT). Spatial ability was represented by three tests, the Figure Analogy and Figure Synthesis subtests of the CAT and the Space Test of the Primary Mental Abilities Test (PMA).

Figure 9 presents the final model from a confirmatory factor analysis of the five reference tests and the SLAT in a sample of college undergraduates. It can be seen that the SLAT is the highest loading test on the Space factor but the SLAT does not load on the Verbal factor. A model that included a split loading for the SLAT on the Verbal factor did not significantly improve fit and, further, the nonsignificant loading of the SLAT on the Verbal factor was negative. Thus, these data support the relative independence of the SLAT from verbal abilities.

A second study (Embretson, 1992d) was undertaken to compare the nomothetic span of the SLAT to the DAT Space Relations Test. This study included eight reference tests to measure verbal reasoning and spatial ability in addition to the SLAT pretest and the DAT Space Relations Test. Verbal reasoning ability was measured by four tests: the Verbal Classification and the Verbal Analogy subtests from the CAT, and the Inference Test and the Deciphering Languages Test from the Kit of Cognitive Referenced Factors (KIT; Eckstrom, French, & Harman, 1987). Spatial ability was also measured by four tests: the Paper Folding Test, the Cube Comparison Test, the Form Board Test, and the Card Rotation Test from the KIT.

Figure 9 and Figure 10 show the final two-factor reference structures for the two groups. Both groups received both the SLAT and the DAT in different orders. Since a preliminary analysis indicated that the means of both the SLAT and the DAT depended on test position, however, only the first spatial folding test to be administered was included in the validation models. In the first group, shown on Figure 9, the SLAT was the first test administered. In the second group, shown on Figure 10, the DAT was the first test administered. The same pattern for the reference tests was specified in both groups, and the loadings for most tests were constrained across groups except where needed to achieve fit. In the final model, the SLAT loads only on the Space factor, while the DAT has a significant loading on the Verbal factor in addition to a correlated error with the Deciphering Languages Test. The latter test involves the translation of abstract symbols into language.

These results indicate that the role of verbal reasoning in the SLAT is less than in the DAT Space Relations Test. Unlike the DAT, the SLAT had no significant loading on Verbal ability and no significant correlated error with Deciphering Languages. The results are consistent with ex-

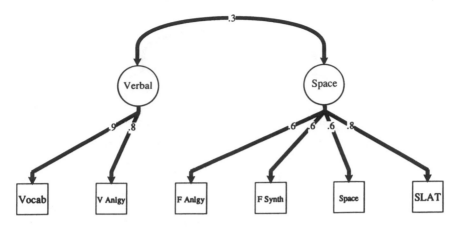

FIGURE 9. The reference factor structure of the SLAT (from Group 1). (From S. E. Embretson [under review]. *The nomothetic span of a spatial ability test: The impact of item design and test context.* Lawrence, KS: University of Kansas)

pectations from the construct representation findings, as well as with the item design specifications. The correlation of the DAT with the verbal tests, apparently results from the effectiveness of a verbal analytic strategy in solving items.

An interesting incidental result in the Embretson (1992) study concerned the loadings of the second spatial folding test. When the DAT Space Relations Test followed the SLAT, it had the same relationship to the verbal tests as the SLAT. When the SLAT followed the DAT, it had the same relationship to the verbal tests as the DAT.

These results indicate that one spatial folding test assumes the characteristics of the other, if it follows it. Such findings strongly suggest the role of strategies that develop during test taking. For the SLAT, spatial processing strategies are effective while verbal processing strategies are relatively ineffective. Thus, when the DAT Space Relations Test follows the SLAT, the spatial strategy may be sufficiently entrenched so as to be routinely applied. In contrast, verbal–analytic strategies are relatively effective on the DAT Space Relations Test. When the SLAT follows it, these same strategies may be applied, although not as effectively as the spatial strategy. The significantly lower mean of both the SLAT and the DAT when the SLAT follows the DATS adds further support to the strategy interpretation.

These results seem to suggest that the same nomothetic span can be obtained from the DAT Space Relations Test as from the SLAT. However, these results required a whole test's worth of training on the desired strategy. Since a 30-minute training period for a single test is not available in most testing situations, it appears that test design is the more practical method to achieve the desired pattern of nomothetic span.

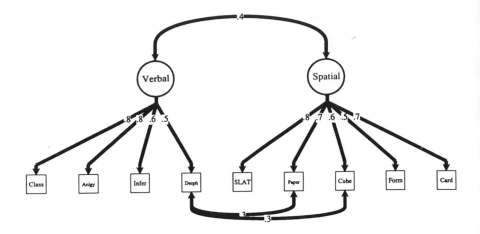

Group 1: SLAT Precedes DAT

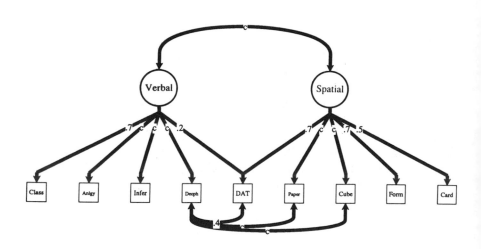

Group 2: DAT Precedes SLAT   c = constrained

FIGURE 10. The reference factor structure of the DAT (from Group 2). (From S. E. Embretson [under review]. *The nomothetic span of a spatial ability test: The impact of item design and test context.* Lawrence, KS: University of Kansas)

CONCLUSION

This chapter has shown how cognitive theory can be centralized in the development of an ability test. The chapter began by describing a conceptual and procedural framework that permits cognitive theory to be involved in all aspects of test development. The conceptual framework considered how a two-part conceptualization of construct validity (i.e., construct representation and nomothetic span) allowed cognitive design principles to have a clear role in test development. In contrast, the classic conceptualization does not define a role for test design, which may have contributed to the slow applications of cognitive theory in testing. The procedural framework is a series of stages for test development. Some stages, such as developing a cognitive model, are unfamiliar to test developers while other familiar stages are conducted in qualitatively different ways.

The cognitive design system was illustrated by the development of a test of spatial ability. The Spatial Learning Ability Test (SLAT) uses the spatial folding task to measure the mental manipulation of complex objects in space. A cognitive model for the task was postulated on the basis of related cognitive research on spatial processing. The model was supported by a series of studies that were conducted on potential items. The studies yielded several important results about the item stimulus features that would manipulate the difficulty of the spatial processes. Furthermore, other features were identified as contributing to the feasibility of using nonspatial processes in solving items. Item specifications were developed to maximize the role of spatial processing in the SLAT items. The item specifications yielded 24 item frames. Several items were developed for each item frame by varying features that were known not to influence processing difficulty.

Exceptionally good psychometric results were obtained on the first empirical tryout of the items. The biserial correlations were high and a wide range of item difficulties were observed. Furthermore, only 5 percent of the SLAT items did not fit the Rasch model. Since typical item attrition rates are much higher, these data show the efficiency of the cognitively based item specifications for test development. The further advantages of the cognitive parameters for item banking and equating were also described.

Good results were also obtained for construct validity. For construct representation, the SLAT item difficulties and response times were predictable from a cognitive model that included only spatial processes. These results are consistent with the item specifications that maximized spatial processing. Interestingly, the item difficulty for a rival test with spatial folding items, the DAT Space Relations Test, was less predictable from spatial processes. A comparison of the implicit item specifications of the DAT to the SLAT suggested that the DAT minimized spatial processing and maximized verbal analytic processing in item solving. For nomothetic span, the SLAT was found to load only on a spatial ability factor in two studies. Verbal reasoning was found to have little role in the SLAT. In contrast, the DAT Space Relations test was found to load on verbal reasoning and further also correlated with the ability to convert symbols into language.

In summary, the cognitive design principles in the SLAT were effective in influencing both construct representation and nomothetic span. Although centralizing cognitive principles in test design requires more effort in the early test development phase, construct validity is not clearly determined. Furthermore, once the design specifications are elaborated, creating new items with little attrition and carefully targeted difficulty levels become relatively easy. Thus, the initial cost of a cognitive design system in the early stages of test development, may be more than offset by subsequent advantages.

REFERENCES

Assessment Systems Corporation (1989). *User's manual for the MICROCAT Testing System*. Assessment Systems Corporation: St. Paul, Minnesota.

Bechtoldt, H. (1959). Construct validity: A critique. *American Psychologist, 14*, 619–629.

Bejar, I. (1990). A generative analysis of a three dimensional spatial task. *Applied Psychological Measurement, 14*, 237–245.

Bejar, I., Chaffin, R., & Embretson, S. E. (1990). *Cognitive and psychometric analysis of analogical problem solving*. New York: Springer-Verlag.

Carpenter, P., Just, M., & Shell, P. (1990). What one intelligence test measures: A theoretical account of processing in the Raven's Progressive Matrices Test. *Psychological Review, 97*, 404–431.

Carroll, J. B., & Maxwell, S. (1979). Individual differences in ability. *Annual Review of Psychology*, 603–640.

Cooper, L. A., & Shepard, R. N. (1973). Chronometric studies of the rotation of mental images. In W. G. Chase (Ed.), *Visual information processing*. New York: Academic Press.

Cronbach, L. J., & Meehl, P. E. (1955). Construct validity in psychological tests. *Psychological Bulletin, 52*, 281–302.

Eckstrom, R. B., French, J. W., Harman, H. H. (1987). *Manual for the Kit of Factor-Referenced Tests*. Research Report NR-150-329. Educational Testing Service: Princeton, NJ.

Embretson, S. E. (1983). Construct validity: Construct representation versus nomothetic span. *Psychological Bulletin, 93*, 179–197.

Embretson, S. (1984). A general latent trait model for response processes. *Psychometrika, 49*, 175–186.

Embretson, S. E. (1985). *Test design: Developments in psychology and psychometrics*. New York: Academic Press.

Embretson, S. E. (1992a). *A conceptual and procedural framework for designing tests by information-processing theory*. Unpublished manuscript, Department of Psychology, University of Kansas, Lawrence, Kansas.

Embretson, S. E. (1992b). Measuring and validity cognitive modifiability as an ability: A study in the spatial domain. *Journal of Educational Measurement, 29*, 25–50.

Embretson, S. E. (1992c). *Technical manual for the Spatial Learning Ability Test.* Technical Report 9201. Lawrence, KS: Department of Psychology, University of Kansas.

Embretson, S. E. (1992d). The construct validity of a spatial ability test: The impact of item design and test context. Paper under review. Department of Psychology, University of Kansas, Lawrence, Kansas.

Embretson, S. E. (in press). Development toward a cognitive design system for psychological tests. In R. Dawis and D. Lupinsky (Eds.), *Assessing individual differences in human behavior: New concepts and findings.* University of Minnesota Press: Minneapolis.

Embretson, S. E., & Waxman, M. (1989). Models for processing and individual differences in spatial folding. Unpublished manuscript. Lawrence, KS: University of Kansas.

Fischer, G. (1973). Linear logistic test model as an instrument in educational research. *Acta Psychologica, 37*, 359–374.

Hornke, L. F., & Habon, M. W. (1986). Rule-based item bank construction and evaluation within the linear logistic framework. *Applied Psychological Measurement, 10*, 364–380.

Just, M., & Carpenter, P. (1985). Cognitive coordinate systems: Accounts of mental rotation and individual differences in spatial ability. *Psychological Review, 92*, 137–172.

Mislevy, R., & Verhelst, N. (1990). Modeling item responses when different subjects employ different solution strategies. *Psychometrika, 55*, 195–215.

Pellegrino, J. W., & Lyon, D. W. (1979). The components of a cmponential analysis. *Intelligence, 3*, 169–186.

Pellegrino, J. W. (1985). Inductive reasoning ability. In R. J. Sternberg (Ed.), *Human abilities: An information processing approach* (pp. 195–225). New York: W. H. Freeman.

Shepard, R. N., & Feng, C. (1971). A chronometric study of mental paper folding. *Cognitive Psychology, 3*, 228–243.

Sternberg, R. J. (1985). *Beyond IQ: A triarchic theory of human intelligence.* New York: Cambridge University Press.

Whitely, S. E. (1980). Multicomponent latent trait models for ability tests. *Psychometrika, 45*, 479–494.

CHAPTER SEVEN

Evaluating Students' Errors on Cognitive Tasks: Applications of Polytomous Item Response Theory and Log-Linear Modeling

Jonna M. Kulikowich and Patricia A. Alexander

The adage, "We learn from our mistakes," is a familiar one. Most of us recognize that some of our most meaningful learning experiences have come about as a result of saying or doing the wrong thing. The value of mistakes, however, is dependent upon our ability to recognize them as such and to gather information from them that points us in a more positive direction. The errors that students make in classrooms can also be instructive if we acknowledge that mistakes typically arise from thoughtful, albeit misguided or incomplete, processing and if there is a systematic way to identify these mistakes and to unlock the diagnostic information they hold (Alexander, 1989; Alexander, Pate, Kulikowich, Farrell, & Wright, 1989).

In this chapter, we will consider how cognitive theory and psychometrics have been brought together to assist in unraveling the diagnostic data in students' incorrect responses. Specifically, we will discuss how cognitive researchers have analyzed errors to understand procedural "bugs" or "*mis*"-conceptions (Alexander, 1991; Brown & Burton, 1978) and how psychometricians have used information about wrong answers to improve the reliability of test scores (Bock, 1972; Smith, 1987; Thissen, 1976). Finally, we will summarize our recent efforts to merge cognitive

Jonna M. Kulikowich • Department of Educational Psychology, University of Connecticut, Storrs, Connecticut 06269   Patricia A. Alexander • Department of Educational Psychology, Texas A&M University, College Station, Texas 77843.
Cognitive Assessment: A Multidisciplinary Perspective, edited by Cecil R. Reynolds. Plenum Press, New York, 1994.

research in error analysis with that in psychometrics in an attempt to devise a more comprehensive system for assessing what students' know or do not know in a given content area. As have others (e.g., Judy, Alexander, Kulikowich, & Willson, 1988; Thissen & Steinberg, 1984), the psychometric procedures we turned to in these investigations were based on Item Response Theory (IRT), particularly polytomous IRT, and log-linear modeling.

PROCEDURAL "BUGS" AND "*MIS*"-CONCEPTIONS: A COGNITIVE VIEW OF ERRORS

As Payne and Squibb (1990) observed, "Theoreticians have long recognized that important insights into the nature of cognitive skill and its acquisition can be gained by examining errors" (p. 445). In general, the cognitive-based research on mistakes has fallen into one of two categories. First, there are procedural "bugs." "Bugs" are those errors, such as forgetting to carry digits during addition, that occur during the performance of a simple algorithmic routine (Brown & Burton, 1978). Second, there are nonrandom errors that are registered in more declarative-knowledge tasks (e.g., multiple-choice content tests) that signal incomplete or inaccurate conceptual or strategic knowledge (Alexander, 1991; Alexander et al., 1989; Kulikowich & Alexander, 1990).

For example, Clement (1982) found that undergraduates who failed to learn the relationship between mass, energy, and momentum consistently solved open-ended physics problems dealing with Newtonian mechanics incorrectly. Similarly, Geboyts and Claxton-Oldfield (1989) recognized that students failed to select correct multiple-choice answers on statistics questions designed to measure understanding of the central limit theorem and randomization because they did not have requisite amounts of knowledge in probability calculus. Thus, cognitive researchers have engaged in error analysis to assess deficits in procedural, strategic, conceptual, or domain-specific (i.e., subject-matter) knowledge. What has also been confirmed in these illustrative research programs is that errors contribute information about human information processing that may be over and above that contributed by correct responses.

Although cognitivists have come to realize the importance of inspecting errors (e.g., Alexander, 1991; Payne & Squibb, 1990), the means by which they engage in this inspection is often limited in scope. For one thing, most of the domains chosen for study have been well-structured fields such as physics and mathematics that rely heavily on rule-based procedures for solving problems (Alexander, 1991). Consequently, we know little about the kinds of procedural errors and potential misconceptions that might pervade problem solving in more ill-structured domains such as social studies or reading.

The tasks or tests created to assess students' knowledge in these more well-structured domains have typically been confined to well-defined mathematical isomorphs (Resnick, 1989) or traditional multiple-choice or short-answer items. These items have been developed without accounting for error patterns that might be exhibited in student performance (Guttman & Schlesinger, 1967; Smith, 1987). Only within the discipline of mathematics (e.g., algebra, simple arithmetic, fractional arithmetic) and the domain of spelling (e.g., consonant and vowel manipulation) have tasks been constructed so that potential error patterns were considered a priori and statistically predicted based on sophisticated computer programs that detect students' "bugs" or *mal*-rules (e.g., Brown & Van-Lehn, 1980; Matz, 1982; Payne & Squibb, 1990; Tatsuoka, 1983).

Many of the insights that cognitive researchers have gained regarding misconceptions have also been based on the analysis of verbal report data such as think-aloud protocols and interview data (e.g., Ericsson & Simon, 1980; Garner, 1987; White, 1985). For example, important understandings of how young children overcome misconceptions regarding the nature of living things (Carey, 1985); or how novices become frustrated with finding solutions to curvilinear motion problems due to their misconceptions (Chi, 1985), have been achieved through the analysis of verbal-report data. Verbal reports do not, however, permit as systematic an exploration of error patterns via psychometric analysis as would be the case for structured test formats such as multiple-choice items (White, 1985).

In summary, cognitive researchers have come to accept that errors arise from thoughtful, if incomplete or inaccurate, processing and are thus typically nonrandom (e.g., Alexander, Willson, White, & Fuqua, 1987). In addition, cognitive research has demonstrated that errors provide important clues for understanding human mental processing that cannot be garnered solely from the analysis of correct responses (Alexander, 1991). Yet, in few cases has the study of errors lead to the systematic detection, let alone the statistical or psychometric evaluation, of nonrandom mistakes (Kulikowich, 1990). The section that follows outlines how psychometrics has explored error analysis. Specifically, we discuss how item response theory (IRT) and log-linear modeling have used information from wrong answers as a means of improving the reliability of test scores and isolating item and test bias.

POLYTOMOUS IRT AND LOG-LINEAR MODELING: A PSYCHOMETRIC VIEW OF ERRORS

Cognitive researchers have not been the only group to engage in error analysis. Psychometricians have of late used subjects' incorrect responses as sources of information. Whereas cognitive researchers have seen errors as clues to human mental processing, psychometricians have viewed errors as indicators of test reliability (Guttman & Schlesinger, 1967; Thissen & Steinberg, 1984) or as a means of identifying components or tasks that result in item or test bias. In these latter programs of error-related research, the multiple-choice achievement or aptitude item remains the focus of study due mostly to its prevalence on large-scale testing examinations such as the Scholastic Aptitude Test or SAT (Linn, 1990).

For years, traditional test theories such as Classical True Score theory have recognized that incorrect alternatives within multiple-choice items need to be plausible (i.e., attractive) to students of moderate or below-average ability (Gronlund & Linn, 1989; Sax, 1989). Classical option weighting schemes, however, face limitations. First, weighting schemes that attempt to determine the degrees of correctness within a set of alternatives most often rest on the subjective rankings of experts. Typically, the alternatives are judged according to experts' frameworks for ranking rather than by some overriding option format (Hambleton, Roberts, & Traub, 1970).

Second, in some cases, when experts are not used to rank alternatives, respondents are asked to indicate what they perceive as the correctness of the alternatives (Hambleton et al., 1970). Neither the expert ranking method, however, nor the respondent ranking method provides psychometricians with knowledge about statistical properties related to the test items or the alternatives of which they consist, or with standard errors of estimate associated with varying ability levels.

Third, even when more sophisticated statistical procedures such as those associated with multiple regression are employed to weigh alternatives, there are limitations to consider. These limitations are mostly related to subject sampling. That is to say, item characteristics could not be estimated independently from the subject pool. As such, item parameters such as item difficulty and discrimination could change markedly as the sample changed (Hambleton & Cook, 1977).

Finally, when examining errors, traditional test theories are not sensitive to the dimensional nature of test data (i.e., how many different constructs underlie test performance). As far as weighting schemes for multiple-choice tests are concerned, many tests, particularly those designed to measure cognitive processes, are multidimensional in nature. Therefore, these tests measure several different aspects of ability, and the weights of the alternatives may change as the dimensions change. Consider, for example, a mathematics test designed to measure calculation ability as well as conceptual ability. Based on traditional weighting schemes, the degrees of correctness for the calculation alternatives would be ranked like the degrees of correctness for the conceptual alternatives.

Many of the remedies for these limitations (e.g., subjective rankings, subject-dependent sampling) came about as computer technologies advanced so that more sophisticated psychometric methods could be applied to test data. These psychometric methods modeled the relationship between test performance, or ability, and the selection of a multiple-choice response as generally nonlinear rather than as linear (Rasch, 1960). These psychometric tools were the basis for a family of latent trait techniques known as item response theory (IRT). Perhaps item response theory's greatest advantage over classical true score techniques is that item properties can be estimated independently from subject characteristics (Wright & Stone, 1979). For instance, subject abilities can be estimated independently from item attributes. This property of the psychometric model implies that item characteristics are sample independent, and once estimated, can be used across a large number of samples (Hambleton & Cook, 1977).

When considering multiple-choice items, polytomous IRT models (Bock, 1972; Samejima, 1969; Thissen & Steinberg, 1984) can be used to describe the performance of each alternative with respect to the cognitive proficiency or latent ability being measured. Therefore, subjective weighting schemes are not necessary because the actual responses to each of the alternatives are used to measure the attractiveness of each option to all levels of ability. As Thissen, Steinberg, and Fitzpatrick (1989) note:

> Thorough analysis of the behavior of alternatives is beyond the convenient reach of the traditional test theory, because the relationship between proficiency and most incorrect alternatives (distractors) is nonmonotonic; the traditional theory rests on correlations that summarize only monotonic relationships well. Here, we fit IRT models to the data from multiple-choice tests; each item is described numerically by a set of parameters and (equivalently) graphically by a set of curves that are trace lines relating the probability of each response to proficiency. (p. 162)

As mentioned, while there are many polytomous IRT models that may be used to examine multiple-choice alternatives (e.g., Bock's Nominal Model, 1972; Samejima's Graded Response Model, 1969), one model that has received considerable attention due to the availability of the computer software, MULTILOG, is the Multiple-Choice Model of Thissen and Steinberg (1984) that uses a multivariate logistic transformation to estimate the contribution of each alternative to test performance. Within each multiple-choice item, for m options, there are m response functions. Given the following equation:

$$Z_k = a_k \theta + c_k$$

$k = 1, 2, \ldots, m$ multiple-choice alternatives;
Z_k is a linear function of the latent ability, θ, measured by the test;

a_k is the slope related to the latent ability, θ; and,
c_k is an intercept parameter reflecting the overall attractiveness of option k.

In order to find the probability of choosing each alternative for any given ability level, the multivariate logistic transformation must be used to map the Z_k onto a categorical $[0,1]$ continuum. This permits the graphing of what is known as an option characteristic curve or trace line for every alternative. From this trace line, one can deduce the probability of any level of latent ability, θ, selecting that particular alternative. Mathematically, the probability of selecting a particular alternative within a set of options for a given level of ability using the Multiple-Choice Model (Thissen & Steinberg, 1984) is:

$$P(x_j = k|\theta;a,c,d) = \frac{\exp(Z_k) + d_k\exp(Z_o)}{\displaystyle\sum_{h=0}^{m_j} \exp(Z_h)}$$

where $x_j = k$ denotes the multiple-choice selection in which there are $k = 1, 2 \ldots , m$ alternatives for item j, a and c represent item parameter vectors that become subject to linear constraints,

$$\sum_{k=0}^{m_j} a_k = 0$$

and,

$$\sum_{k=0}^{m_j} c_k = 0$$

freeing $2(m_j - 1)$ parameters for the purpose of estimation. Finally, d_k is an adaptation of Samejima's (1969) Graded Response Model that incorporates an item characteristic for those who "do not know" or choose alternatives by guessing.

As mentioned, polytomous item response models are used for developing standardized achievement and aptitude items that will be administered to large samples (Thissen et al., 1989). Given the sophisticated mathematical estimation procedures required to evaluate item characteristics:

> It is important to note that the present state of technology of item parameter estimation permits such detailed item analysis only for small item sets, as each item is given individual attention in the calibration process. (Thissen et al., 1989, p. 168)

Thus, for large-scale test constructors, the Multiple-Choice Model assists item writers in the reduction or modification of distractors that do not distract or correct responses that do not attract higher ability levels because of ambiguous alternatives. As Thissen et al. (1989) have indicated, the model is much more difficult to apply when the estimation of the latent ability, θ, becomes the primary objective because of the reduction in the number of items that can be inspected at once.

From a cognitive view of error analysis, therefore, this truncation of the item pool may place constraints on the ability to detect the processing deficits triggering the selection of errors. That is, most widely used standardized tests (e.g., SAT, GRE) were not developed for the purpose of error analysis. Thus, these tests do not intend to show how errors arise from lack of domain knowledge or from procedural or strategic deficits within the test-taker (Alexander & Judy, 1988). As we will discuss later, the most successful attempts to merge cognitive and psychometric theories in error analysis have occurred when instruments have been specifically built around some a priori notions of how procedural or conceptual deficits would manifest themselves with regard to incorrect responses (Alexander et al., 1989; Ashlock, 1986; Brown & VanLehn, 1980; Tatsuoka, 1983).

Another polytomous IRT model that has been applied in the examination of distractors to multiple-choice items is the Partial Credit Model (Masters, 1982). This particular polytomous model may be better suited for estimating ability while considering the contributions made by individual multiple-choice alternatives. The Partial Credit Model is useful for providing information about the construct being measured by the items as well as the items themselves. This is a deviation from Thissen and Steinberg's Multiple-Choice Model (1984). The Multiple-Choice Model is better suited for detecting flaws in multiple-choice items and their alternatives than the Partial Credit Model, which is more effective at describing the construct that the test purports to measure (Thissen et al., 1989).

The Partial Credit Model has been used successfully to show increases in the reliability of vocabulary measures with multiple-choice alternatives designed to represent varying degrees of sophistication in understanding vocabulary terms (Smith, 1987). Specifically, the information garnered in ability and item estimation for those of low to moderate proficiency was greater than for a dichotomous model. Unlike the Multiple-Choice Model (Thissen & Steinberg, 1984), the Partial Credit Model is an extension of the Rasch model, and thus uses the statistic of total test score as the source of ability estimation (Masters, 1982).

Less mathematically cumbersome than the Multiple-Choice Model, the Partial Credit Model assumes equidistant thresholds between alternatives. This model seems well suited to tests designed on some a priori basis where options are constructed according to some cognitive hierarchical scheme denoting ordered performance levels that reflect option steps. Thus, a correct response to a four-option multiple-choice item, as in the following example, arguably requires three cognitive steps.

The capital city of Pennsylvania is:

a. Albany
b. Pittsburgh
c. Texas
d. Harrisburg

The first step is recognizing that Albany is more correct than Texas because Texas is a state. The second step is realizing that Pittsburgh is more correct than Albany because Albany is not a city in Pennsylvania. The final, third step involves selecting Harrisburg over Pittsburgh as the correct response because Harrisburg is, in fact, the capital of Pennsylvania. The probability of person n reaching performance level, or step, k on item i is:

$$P(y_{kni} = 1/\theta_{n}, \lambda_{ik}) = \frac{\exp(\theta_n - \lambda_{ik})}{1 + \exp(\theta_n - \lambda_{ik})}$$

where θ_n is the ability of person n; and λ_{ik} is the difficulty of reaching step k in item i.

Recently, another line of psychometric research incorporating log-linear modeling has evolved to inspect errors as sources of item bias (Green, Crone, & Folk, 1989). This body of research approaches error analysis as a means of finding out whether multiple-choice items and their distractors mean something different to different groups of people (e.g., cultural and ethnic groups), other than through the construct or ability measured by the test. Entitled "differential distractor functioning," log-linear modeling procedures are used to hold ability constant while subgroups (e.g., whites versus Hispanics) are compared based on their option choices.

Log-linear modeling is an extension of chi-square analyses for two-way contingency tables to higher-order tables (Bishop, Fienberg, & Holland, 1975). Therefore, rather than cross-tabulating two variables like ability level (high versus low) with item response (correct versus incorrect) as would be the case in a traditional chi-square analysis, one models the interactive effects of several variables simultaneously (e.g., ability level, racial background, and incorrect response selections). Specifically:

> Examinees are separated into several ability levels, and the frequency of each option choice is tabulated separately for each subgroup at each ability level, yielding a three-way contingency table. The ability

levels can be defined by an independent measure of ability, if one is available, but usually the total test score is used. (Green et al., 1989, p. 148)

The test for differential distractor functioning is based on comparing the fits of two specified models; one that includes the interaction between subgroup and option choices and one that does not. When the fit statistics are significantly different, it is assumed that distractors function differentially between subgroups, and that the errors denote a difference between groups not based on their cognitive ability.

Differential distractor functioning is much easier to apply to data than a polytomous item response model, since the former compares frequency counts while the latter uses frequency counts to estimate item characteristics. The differential distractor functioning method is not traditionally used to analyze errors for cognitive deficits. The section that follows describes how techniques from item response theory, particularly Masters Partial Credit Model (Masters, 1982), and log linear modeling can be incorporated to model the error patterns that students make on domain-specific tests.

COGNITIVE DIFFICULTY AND ERROR PATTERNS: MERGING THE COGNITIVE AND PSYCHOMETRIC VIEWS OF ERRORS

We have highlighted the ways in which cognitive researchers have looked at errors as indicators of knowledge deficits (Alexander, 1989; Alexander et al., 1989) and how psychometricians have used errors from incorrect responses on multiple-choice tests to improve the reliability of test scores (Thissen & Steinberg, 1984). In addition, an emerging camp of cognitive psychometricians (e.g., Embretson, 1984; Sheehan & Mislevy, 1990; Tatsuoka, 1983) has centered attention on how tasks can be built according to cognitive theory and how these tasks can subsequently be analyzed via psychometric techniques (e.g., IRT) to supply evidence of construct validity. The aim of these construct validity analyses is to define the difficulty of items or tasks as dependent on the cognitive processes (e.g., analogical reasoning) that the examinees do or do not employ. As Embretson (1984, 1985) has indicated, many of the cognitive constructs for which we need to build measures are complex problem-solving abilities that require careful task development if researchers are to gain insight into human mental performance (Baker & Herman, 1983).

Presently, IRT is being used to determine what is referred to as the cognitive difficulties of items (Sheehan & Mislevy, 1990). The focus in this analysis has primarily been on correct responses because many of the tasks constructed are novel in format reflecting departures from traditional multiple-choice items (Embretson, 1984). As such, one correct response may depend on several "components" that warrant consideration if the individual is to get the item right. For example, Whitely (1980) had subjects generate rules for solving analogy problems (e.g., A:B:C:___) in addition to choosing from among the alternatives provided.

Of the family of IRT models available for person and item parameter estimation of cognitive tasks, the Rasch model has been the method of choice. In part, this is because of the ability of the Rasch model to use total scores for people and item scores for components as sufficient statistics for estimation (Embretson, 1984; Masters, 1982). As mentioned, most of the efforts employing Rasch techniques on carefully constructed cognitive tasks have focused on correct responses. In the well-structured domain of mathematics, however, Tatsuoka (1983) and her associates (Birenbaum & Tatsuoka, 1983; Tatsuoka & Tatsuoka, 1983, 1987) have used the Rasch model to monitor the error patterns of students performing signed-number and fractional arithmetic problems where responses must be generated rather than selected.

Referred to as Rule Space (Tatsuoka, 1983), this extension of the Rasch model is used to: (1) predict the likelihood of each erroneous rule in a sample; and, (2) describe the rule according to some cognitive deficit. For example, Tatsuoka (1983) modeled signed-number addition and subtraction problems so that there were two additional ability estimates per person, one for the sign of the calculated value and one for its absolute value. Given the problem, $-2 - (-6) = +4$, if a respondent answered -9, then the vector to the response would be (0 0 0). In this case, the respondent not only gets the overall response incorrect, but also this response is incorrect in two respects: sign and absolute value.

In a study of 172 eighth graders administered simple arithmetic problems such as the above, Tatsuoka (1983) determined that 99% of the responses could be evaluated by one of the four pairs of calculations: (1) sign and absolute value incorrect (0,0); (2) sign incorrect and absolute value correct (0,1); (3) sign correct and absolute value incorrect (1,0); and, (4) sign and absolute value correct (1,1). In other words, "any erroneous rule in this study can be uniquely represented by the two component response patterns of signs and absolute value" (Tatsuoka, 1983, p. 347).

The Rule Space Model (Tatsuoka, 1983) permits an exhaustive account of the likelihood that an individual possesses a specific-error type in arithmetic. It is evident, however, that an account of the error pattern for more complex tasks in less rule-based algorithmic domains (e.g., human biology, social studies) would be much more difficult to model psychometrically. The answers to simple arithmetic models can be readily decomposed into two components (sign, absolute value). To extend this parameterization to multicomponent tasks or verbal-based measures (e.g., word problems or text comprehension) within a cognitive framework would seem an even more arduous task.

Before one could begin to predict possible error patterns, a researcher would most likely have to understand the mechanism by which a respondent could select or generate a correct response. Consider the number of components that could be modeled across a group of physics word problems, for instance. In addition to the vocabulary terms used, these components might include various mathematical functions plus reading comprehension strategies necessary to understand the text. As such, these tasks might not be as parsimonious as those used in the research of Tatsuoka (1983). To ascertain the number of components incorrectly processed that would contribute to a systematic or nonrandom error would clearly warrant an extensive amount of research.

In our research, we have not approached task development in a componential manner as would be the case with Embretson's research (1984). Since the instruments that we have developed are designed to measure domain-specific vocabulary, the number of facts, procedures, or conditions that could be modeled is virtually limitless. In our research, therefore, we have employed the Partial Credit Model of Masters (1982) to gather information from incorrect selections to our vocabulary multiple-choice items. Akin to a facet theory approach (Guttman & Schlesinger, 1967), we have constructed items in the domains of human biology (Alexander et al., 1989), physics (Garner, Alexander, Gillingham, Kulikowich, & Brown, 1991), and social studies (Pate, Alexander, & Kulikowich, 1989). These items consist of a stem (i.e., the term of interest) and four alternatives.

The alternatives for all items were developed according to a categorization scheme derived prior to the construction of each test. For example, a human biology item on a sixth grade test contained the following alternatives: (1) a correct human biology response; (2) an incorrect human biology response; (3) an incorrect science response; and, (4) an incorrect out-of-science response. Using Masters's (1982) notion of option steps, processing the item correctly would include the following: (1) recognizing the science distractor as more correct than the out-of-science distractor; (2) recognizing the human biology distractor as more correct than the science distractor; and (3) recognizing the correct response as more correct than the incorrect human biology response. For these alternatives to reflect the hierarchy psychometrically, the option steps should have difficulties that range from negative (i.e., easiest step) to positive (i.e., difficult step). These psychometric difficulties should match the hypothesized cognitive response hierarchy.

Table 1 presents two examples of multiple-choice items drawn from the domain of human biology along with their respective option-step difficulties and standard errors. For both items, we can see that the option step difficulties increased within items. That is, the option steps moved from least difficult (less than 0 logits) to most difficult (more than 0 logits) according to the hypothesized categorization scheme. These logit difficulties provide us information regarding the likelihood that a student with a specific level of ability will be able to bypass one option as less correct than another. Thus, when the logit difficulties are negative, we would expect that less able examinees would be able to pass that item step. When logit difficulties become positive, we would expect that less able examinees would not be able to pass that step.

The estimates from the Partial Credit Model permit us to explore how the level of difficulty per option step changed across items. For the "carpals" item shown in Table 1, we would expect that students with lower levels of ability (i.e., less than -1 logit) would be able to bypass the out-of-science and general science distractors. The .49 logit difficulty for option step 3 suggests that those of lower ability would have greater difficulty processing which of the two human biology alternatives was correct.

TABLE 1. Two Examples of Human Biology Multiple-Choice Items
with Option Step Difficulties and Option Step Standard Errors

| | Option Steps | | | | | |
| | Difficulties | | | Standard Errors | | |
Items	S1	S2	S3	S1	S2	S3
Carpals are	−.98	−.46	.49	.18	.15	.11
1. the small bones of the wrist (human biology, correct)						
2. muscles of the foot (human biology, incorrect)						
3. types of fish found in streams (science, incorrect)						
4. groups of people who travel to work together (out-of-science, incorrect)						
Amino acids are	−1.47	.11	1.08	.24	.14	.12
1. chemicals that make proteins (human biology, correct)						
2. liquids that help digest food (human biology, incorrect)						
3. substances found in batteries (science, incorrect)						
4. evil leaders found in fairy tales (out-of-science, incorrect)						

For the "amino acids" item, while the trend represented by the option step difficulties conforms to our expected hierarchical model, the difficulties per step indicate that lower ability students would have a much harder time bypassing some of the lower level distractors as incorrect. This is particularly evident with the change in difficulty between option step 1 (-1.47) and option step 2 ($.11$). Apparently, a student of low ability could discern that amino acids were not evil leaders found in fairy tales but would be far less sure that they were not substances found in batteries. Thus, for those of logit ability less than 0, determining which among the remaining three alternatives (science incorrect, human biology incorrect, and human biology correct) was the accurate response would be a more difficult task.

Once a test's scores are validated so that the alternatives function according to the cognitive model, response patterns can be examined across items as they are within each item. Using the ability estimates obtained from the polytomous scoring of items, groups can be formed based on the normal distribution of logit abilities (thetas), and the frequency of errors per alternative category tallied. The dependence between ability and option choices can be examined by a traditional chi-square procedure (Green et al., 1989).

This model can be altered or extended to include other variables such as level of instruction or gender. Responses are then analyzed in more of a log-linear fashion. We performed such an analysis with sixth-grade students in the domain of social studies. First, a vocabulary measure was constructed that contained a cognitive hierarchy of alternatives per item. Within this more ill-structured domain of social studies, we focused on the subject area of ancient Roman civilization (Pate et al., 1989). As with the human biology measure, each item possessed a stem and four options: (1) ancient Roman civilization, correct; (2) ancient civilizations, incorrect; (3) general social studies, incorrect; and (4) out-of-social studies, incorrect.

Once an inspection of options steps reflected the predicted cognitive trends in difficulty patterns per item (i.e., negative to position option steps) we examined the frequency counts per alternative category across items with respect to instruction and gender for a specific level of ability. Table 2 displays these alternative selections (frequencies and percentages) with respect to whether students did or did not receive instruction on ancient Rome while Table 3 presents option selection differences by gender.

An analysis of Table 2 reveals that students who received instruction related to ancient Rome improved substantially over those who did not receive such instruction when it came to correctly bypassing the out-of-social studies and social studies distractors. Thus, in addition to the fact that the test items were constructed according to a cognitive perspective

TABLE 2. Frequencies and Percentages for Social Studies Response Options for Sixth-Grade Students With and Without Training on Ancient Roman Civilization

| | Response Options | | | | | | | |
| | A | | B | | C | | D | |
Instruction	f	%	f	%	f	%	f	%
Training	330	39.00	186	21.90	181	21.30	149	17.62
(n = 40)								
No training	361	34.41	238	22.69	197	18.78	253	24.12
(n = 40)								

X^2 (3) = 400.14, $p < .0001$
Note: A = Roman Civilization, correct; B = ancient civilizations, incorrect; C = social studies, incorrect;
      D = out-of-social studies, incorrect.

of learning substantiated via polytomous modeling, log-linear analysis permitted us to inspect how external variables to the test responses affected the manner in which error patterns changed. Theoretically, those who receive instruction about a subject area should improve in their ability to bypass more irrelevant distractors. Such was the case in the present analysis.

Further, log-linear modeling can be used to inspect the relationship between response options and other variables that are not necessarily tied to instruction. Table 3 shows that females who took the Roman Civilization test were more adept in selecting domain-related responses than males. In addition to choosing a greater percentage of correct responses than males, when incorrect, females were less inclined to select distractors that were not domain related.

TABLE 3. Frequencies and Percentages for Social Studies Response Options for Males and Females

| | Response Options | | | | | | | |
| | A | | B | | C | | D | |
Gender	f	%	f	%	f	%	f	%
Males	579	66.48	105	12.06	105	12.06	82	9.41
(n = 46)								
Females	751	77.03	81	8.31	76	7.79	67	6.87
(n = 61)								

X^2 (3) = 25.72, $p < .0001$
Note: A = Roman Civilization, correct; B = ancient civilizations, incorrect; C = social studies, incorrect;
      D = out-of-social studies, incorrect.

Together polytomous IRT and log-linear modeling can assist both in the construction of tests (e.g., multiple-choice measures) and the analysis of these instruments with respect to a cognitive perspective of learning. As we can see in these examples, these psychometric techniques can help us build tasks where errors not only contribute to more reliable observations but also offer us information about knowledge deficits. Still, the cognitive and psychometric research agenda before us promises to challenge us with greater complexity. In the section that follows, we offer some concluding thoughts about the nature of the complexity that confronts us as cognitive researchers and psychometricians. We provide what we think are some useful considerations for how we might continue merging cognitive psychology and psychometrics.

CONCLUDING THOUGHTS

Those concerned with assessment and information processing should be encouraged by the growing body of research that has begun to bridge the wide expanse between cognitive psychology and psychometrics. Embretson's work on spatial reasoning tasks (this volume), Sheehan and Mislevy's (1990) analysis of document literacy, and Wilson's (1989) survey of children's problem-solving development using Siegler's balance beam tasks are a few examples of successful mergers of cognition and psychometrics.

Further, the body of research of Tatsuoka and her associates (Birenbaum & Tatsuoka, 1983; Tatsuoka & Tatsuoka, 1987) on arithmetic bug distributions, as well as our own research on incorrect responses to domain knowledge tasks (Alexander et al., 1989) show signs of the increasing sensitivity to the information provided by errors. Many researchers are no longer settling for an independent cognitive account of errors that provides them with only qualitative perceptions of human processing deficits. Likewise, these researchers are no longer content with an independent psychometric study of errors that merely contributes to better test score reliability without regard for the underlying cognitive processing. Instead, this new breed of researcher is beginning to build tasks that integrate both cognitive theory and psychometric modeling; tasks that reveal not only what students do not know but also give more detailed and systematic information about the source or extent of those deficits. Increasing awareness about what students know as well as what they do not know may well be the best source of information for effective classroom instruction (Snow & Mandinach, 1991).

Still, those seeking to combine cognitive theory and psychometrics have many obstacles to face in their attempts to build tasks that are not only informative but also reliable and valid. First, little is known about knowledge domains, particularly those such as social studies or reading that can be described as ill-structured (Alexander, 1991). Consequently, the complexity involved in developing appropriate tasks for ill-structured content areas remains great. When one considers what range of errors might occur from ill-defined tasks and how these errors might be modeled systematically, the obstacles to research appear even more formidable. Of course, researchers can continue to focus on simple, well-defined tasks in well-structured domains and can continue to treat content areas as completely separate entities as if subject-matter knowledge was all tightly organized and noninteractive (Mislevy, Yamamoto, & Anacker, 1991). This research perspective, however, appears too limited if the goal is a more complete understanding of human mental processing.

While we could continue to document the difficulties that lie ahead for those engaged in integrating cognition and psychometrics in assessment, we need to point out that the knowledge gained from exploring simpler, algorithmic tasks in domains like mathematics and physics is indeed encouraging. The understanding garnered from these tasks form the building blocks of more extensive research. Further, such activity improves the knowledge base for the subsequent efforts that are necessary to study cognitive processing in varying domains and with a variety of tasks (Sheehan & Mislevy, 1990). Only through this continued maturation can we begin to map the topography of individual differences with the sophistication and resolution that is warranted.

REFERENCES

Alexander, P. A. (1989). Categorizing learner responses on domain-specific analogy tests: A case for error analysis. Paper presented at the annual meeting of the American Educational Research Association, San Francisco.

Alexander, P. A. (1992). Domain knowledge: Evolving themes and emerging concerns. *Educational Psychologist, 27*, 33–51.

Alexander, P. A., & Judy, J. E. (1988). The interaction of domain-specific and strategic knowledge in academic performance. *Review of Educational Research, 58*, 375–404.

Alexander, P. A., Pate, P. E., Kulikowich, J. M., Farrell, D. M., & Wright, N. L. (1989). Domain-specific and strategic knowledge: Effects of training on students of differing ages or competence levels. *Learning and Individual Differences, 1*, 283–325.

Alexander, P. A., Willson, V. L., White, C. S., & Fuqua, J. D. (1987). Analogical reasoning in young children. *Journal of Educational Psychology, 26*, 401–408.

Ashlock, R. B. (1986). *Error patterns in computation: A semi-programmed approach.* Columbus, OH: Merrill.

Baker, E. L., & Herman, J. L. (1983). Task structure design: Beyond linkage. *Journal of Educational Measurement, 20*, 149–164.

Bishop, Y. M. M., Fienberg, S. E., & Holland, P. W. (1975). *Discrete multivariate analysis: Theory and practice.* Cambridge, MA: MIT Press.

Birenbaum, M., & Tatsuoka, K. K. (1983). The effect of a scoring system based on the algorithm underlying the students' response patterns on the dimensionality of achievement test data of the problem solving type. *Journal of Educational Measurement, 20*, 17–26.

Bock, R. D. (1972). Estimating item parameters and latent proficiency when the responses are scored in two or more nominal categories. *Psychometrika, 37*, 29–51.

Brown, J. S., & Burton, R. (1978). Diagnostic models for procedural bugs in basic mathematical skills. *Cognitive Science, 2*, 155–192.

Brown, J. S., & VanLehn, K. (1980). Repair theory: A generative theory of bugs in procedural skills. *Cognitive Science, 4*, 379–426.

Carey, S. (1985). Are children fundamentally different kinds of thinkers and learners than adults? In S. F. Chipman, J. W. Segal, & R. Glaser (Eds.), *Thinking and learning skills* (Vol. 2: pp. 485–517). Hillsdale, NJ: Lawrence Erlbaum.

Chi, M. T. H. (1985). Interactive roles of knowledge and strategies in the development of organized sorting and recall. In S. F. Chipman, J. W. Segal, & R. Glaser (Eds.), *Thinking and learning skills* (Vol. 2: pp. 457–484). Hillsdale, NJ: Lawrence Erlbaum.

Clement, J. (1982). Students' preconceptions in introductory mechanics. *American Journal of Physics, 50*, 66–71.

Embretson, S. E. (1984). A general latent trait model for response processes. *Psychometrika, 49*, 175–186.

Embretson, S. E. (1985). Multicomponent latent trait models for test design. In S. E. Embretson (Ed.), *Test design: Developments in psychology and psychometrics* (pp. 195–218). Orlando, FL: Academic Press.

Ericsson, K. A., & Simon, H. A. (1980). Verbal reports as data. *Psychological Review, 87*, 215–251.

Garner, R. (1987). *Metacognition and reading comprehension.* Norwood, NJ: Ablex.

Garner, R., Alexander, P. A., Gillingham, M. G., Kulikowich, J. M., & Brown, R. (1991). Interest and learning from text. *American Educational Research Journal, 28*, 643–659.

Geboyts, R. J., & Claxton-Oldfield, S. P. (1989). Errors in the quantification of uncertainty: A product of heuristics or minimal probability knowledge base? *Applied Cognitive Psychology, 3*, 157–170.

Green, B. F., Crone, C. R., & Folk, V. G. (1989). A method of studying differential distractor functioning. *Journal of Educational Measurement, 26*, 147–160.

Gronlund, N. E., & Linn, R. L. (1990). *Measurement and evaluation in teaching.* New York: Macmillan.

Guttman, L., & Schlesinger, I. M. (1967). Systematic construction of distractors for ability and achievement test items. *Educational and Psychological Measurement, 27*, 569–580.

Hambleton, R. K., & Cook, L. L. (1977). Latent trait models and their use in the analysis of educational test data. *Journal of Educational Measurement, 14*, 75–96.

Hambleton, R. K., Roberts, D., & Traub, R. E. (1970). A comparison of the reliability and validity of two methods for assessing partial knowledge on a multiple-choice test. *Journal of Educational Measurement, 7*, 75–82.

Judy, J. E., Alexander, P. A., Kulikowich, J. M., & Willson, V. L. (1988). Effects of two instructional approaches and peer tutoring on gifted and nongifted sixth graders' analogy performance. *Reading Research Quarterly, 23*, 236–256.

Kulikowich, J. M. (1990). *Application of latent trait and multidimensional scaling models to cognitive domain-specific tests.* Unpublished doctoral dissertation, Texas A&M University, College Station, TX.

Kulikowich, J. M., & Alexander, P. A. (1990). Application of a General Euclidean Model to analyze hierarchically-constructed achievement tests. Paper presented at the annual meeting of the American Educational Research Association, Boston.

Linn, R. L. (1990). Has item response theory increased the validity of achievement test scores? *Applied Measurement in Education, 3*, 115–141.

Masters, G. N. (1982). A Rasch model for partial credit scoring. *Psychometrika, 47*, 149–174.

Matz, M. (1982). A process model for high school algebra errors. In D. Sleeman & J. S. Brown (Eds.), *Intelligent tutoring systems.* London: Academic.

Mislevy, R. J., Yamamoto, K., & Anacker, S. (1991). *Toward a test theory for assessing student understanding.* (Tech. Rep. No. RR-91-32-ONR). Princeton, NJ: Educational Testing Service.

Pate, P. E., Alexander, P. A., & Kulikowich, J. M. (1989). Assessing the effects of training social studies content and analogical reasoning processes on sixth-graders' domain-specific and strategic knowledge. In D. B. Strahan (Ed.), *Middle school research: Selected studies 1989* (pp. 19–29). Columbus, OH: Research Committee of the National Middle School Association.

Payne, S. J., & Squibb, H. R. (1990). Algebra mal-rules and cognitive accounts of error. *Cognitive Science, 14*, 445–481.

Rasch, G. (1960). *Probabilistic models for some intelligence and attainment tests.* Copenhagen: Danmarks Paedagogiske Institut.

Resnick, L. B. (1989). Treating mathematics as an ill-structured discipline. In R. I. Charles & E. A. Silver (Eds.), *The teaching and assessing of mathematical problem solving* (pp. 32–60). Reston, VA: National Council of Teachers of Mathematics.

Samejima, F. (1969). Estimation of latent ability using a response pattern of graded scores. *Psychometrika Monograph Supplement No. 17.*

Sax, G. (1989). *Principles of educational and psychological measurement and evaluation.* Belmont, CA: Wadsworth.

Sheehan, K., & Mislevy, R. J. (1990). Integrating cognitive & psychometric models to measure document literary. *Journal of Educational Measurement, 27*, 255–272.

Smith, R. (1987). Assessing partial knowledge in vocabulary. *Journal of Educational Measurement, 13*, 130–141.

Snow, R. E., & Mandinach, E. B. (1991). *Integrating assessment and instruction: A research and development agenda.* (Tech. Rep. No. RR-91-8). Princeton, NJ: Educational Testing Service.

Tatsuoka, K. K. (1983). Rule space: An approach for dealing with misconceptions based on Item Response Theory. *Journal of Educational Measurement, 20*, 345–354.

Tatsuoka, K. K., & Tatsuoka, M. M. (1983). Spotting erroneous rules of operation by the individual consistency index. *Journal of Educational Measurement, 3*, 221–230.

Tatsuoka, K. K., & Tatsuoka, M. M. (1987). Bug distributions and statistical pattern classification. *Psychometrika, 52*, 193–206.

Thissen, D. (1976). Information in wrong responses to the Ravens Progressive Matrices. *Journal of Educational Measurement, 13*, 201–214.

Thissen, D., & Steinberg, L. (1984). A response model for multiple choice items. *Psychometrika, 49*, 501–519.

Thissen, D., Steinberg, L., & Fitzpatrick, A. R. (1989). Multiple-choice models: The distractors are also part of the item. *Journal of Educational Measurement, 26*, 161–176.

White, R. T. (1985). Interview protocols and dimensions of cognitive structure. In L. H. T. West & A. L. Pines (Eds.), *Cognitive structure and conceptual change* (pp. 51–59). New York: Academic Press.

Whitely, S. E. (1980). Multicomponent latent trait models for ability tests. *Psychometrika, 45*, 479–494.

Wilson, M. R. (1989). Saltus: A psychometric model of discontinuity in cognitive development. *Psychological Bulletin, 105*, 276–289.

Wright, B. D., & Stone, M. H. (1979). *Best test design.* Chicago: MESA.

CHAPTER EIGHT

Cognitive Modeling of Individual Responses in Test Design

VICTOR L. WILLSON

This chapter proposes a model for test design that breaks with classical psychometric traditions, although it is consistent with the general orientation of the general linear model paradigm of representation in social science. The model is based on cognitive theory principles and includes the assumption that any test must be designed formally to consider task structure and information processes. Another assumption is that cognitive theory is fundamentally always representative of each individual, and that there is always the potential for separate, unique individual responses to the test that should be modeled. The following sections of the chapter develop the theses and present both theory and example of such test development.

INTRODUCTION

Intelligence and achievement test design has for over 50 years followed a model based on true score theory that has systematically excluded substantive psychological theory (Willson, 1989). The reliance on psychometric principles for the selection of items, maximization of coefficient alpha, and establishment of various validities is understandable, given the orientation of learning theory toward behaviorism. The unspoken assumption was that all information is resident in the subjects'

VICTOR L. WILLSON • Department of Educational Psychology, Texas A&M University, College Station, Texas 77843-4243.
Cognitive Assessment: A Multidisciplinary Perspective, edited by Cecil R. Reynolds. Plenum Press, New York, 1994.

responses and recovery of latent variables was a function of parsing the response variance. While strong true score theory provided new models for examination of responses, it remained within the same tradition as the classical formulation. Only within the last two decades have alternative conceptualizations within psychology permitted consideration of alternatives to the classical paradigm.

Cognitive theory fundamentally changed the constructs of learning theory, seeking mechanisms to explain responses that were more complex than S-R circuits. Memory mechanisms, neural networks, and processors are all permissible constructs within cognitive psychology, and researchers investigating them have developed intellectual tasks that are intended to be sensitive to the theoretical processes they invoke. Fischer (1973, 1983) and Embretson (1984, 1985, chapter 6) have sought to formalize the theoretical formulations mathematically through models that extend strong true score theory to accommodate task features. This seemingly straightforward concept has revolutionary implications for test design (Willson, 1989; Embretson, chapter 6).

Although Cronbach and his colleagues (Cronbach, Gleser, Nanda, & Rajaratnam, 1972) indicated the need to expand the list of sources of variation in the true score model through generalizability theory, their work did not affect test development. Generalizability was examined after test development as evidence for limits to the populations and places in which the test could reasonably be used. In some decision modes the theory might provide evidence for test length but had almost nothing to say about the structure of the test. Achievement test development has most commonly followed a weak theoretical structure due to Bloom, (1956), or an even weaker theory of content structure or behavioral objectives. Intelligence test development has followed a somewhat more complex model (Wagner & Sternberg, 1984) that included child development as well as factor analysis. Nevertheless, psychometric principles have driven the selection of items and construction of subtests in both areas.

The first nod toward cognitive theory came with Kaufman and Kaufman's (1983) *Kaufman Assessment Battery for Children* (K-ABC), which was intended to reflect Luria's and others' theories of information processing. The theory in the K-ABC dictated the general nature of the subtests. The items were developed and selected from classical psychometric procedures (point biserials, p-values, factor loadings, item discriminations). Other test development agencies also still develop their tests using classical procedures and then examine them from cognitive perspectives (Mislevy & Sheehan, 1989; Schmidt & Dorans, 1990). Cognitive researchers have thus been forced to develop their own tests to measure the variables they hypothesize to affect cognitive responses. One branch has eschewed such measurement in favor of reaction time or simple decisions (yes-no) (Willson, 1989), while others (Alexander, Willson, White, & Fuqua, 1987; Embretson, 1985, chapter 6), have systematically developed tests whose items assessed the cognitive processes hypothesized to function in the subjects under study.

The important distinction between an item developed psychometrically and one developed theoretically is that the information contained in the latter is always informative, while in the former it is often ignored. For example, Alexander et al. (1987) discussed numerous multiple-choice items in a geometric analogies test that had difficulties near chance level, which in a psychometric framework would have been discarded since their contribution to coefficient alpha is nil. The items were intended to discriminate among children who employed different reasoning strategies. A portion of the population, sometimes small, was expected to be able to solve the problems, while others were expected to select specific and theoretically predictable incorrect responses, depending on the level or stage of analogical reasoning they had attained. Item difficulty in the cognitive paradigm is never the explanation of anything; it is the outcome of the interplay among task, process, prior knowledge, metacognition, instruction, and affect. While not all of those variables are explicitly represented in a given model, a salient feature of cognitive test development is the formal inclusion of two or more in representations of subjects' responses.

MODEL REPRESENTATIONS

GENERAL LINEAR MODEL

The classical true score model, as formulated in comprehensive fashion by Lord and Novick (1968), parses an observed score for each individual into true and error components. All other assumptions follow from that. It is in principle no different from the general linear model used throughout social science research:

$$Y_{ijk} = \tau_{ijk} + e_{ijk} \tag{1}$$

where i = subject, j = item, and k = occasion. As Lord and Novick note, we usually condition on some subscripts, such as k, and make assumptions about the expectations, variances, and covariances of the parts τ and e. This leads to virtually all classical true score outcomes with which we are familiar. The true score term τ is assumed to be nonrandom in the general linear model (Hocking, 1985), and all of the terms that τ is partitioned into are also nonrandom. Estimation of τ has, under the classical model, been based on the expected value of a sample mean of replicates (the items of a test or subtest), but there is no requirement that τ be

estimated internally. Of course additional concerns arise if external variates are the basis for estimation, such as their own errors. A model in
these terms is given by:

$$y_{ijk} = \sum_{1} \beta_{ijl} x_{jl} + \beta_{0ijk} + e_{ijk}. \tag{2}$$

In this model error is an occasion-dependent random variate while the x
variates are known without error, although their values vary with item j
and component l. The weights β_{ijl} in this model are both item and subject
dependent. This is more general than might be assumed; for example, the
weights might be instead β_{il}, β_{jl}, or β_l. Each represents a different theoretical model for item functioning by the subject. Adding time depen-
dence k to each weight may also be a reasonable extension of the model. If
variates are unrelated for an individual, the model reduces to Equation 1.

The distribution of e in the model is assumed to be normal, both for
the joint subscript condition ijk and for all conditional distributions across
one or more subscripts. Cross-occasion, or even cross-item errors may in
reality have autoregressive structure. For binary items the normality
assumption is clearly violated, except that it is common to assume the
binary quality of the item is merely an approximation or information-loss
estimate of the random variate score y. The effect of this violation on
estimation in the general linear model (GLM) depends on the underlying
distribution of y.

Subject-Component Interaction Models (β_{il} Terms)

If the model assumes weights β_{il}, a different weight on component l
for subject i, then l parameters are needed for each subject. Mathematically, of course, the number of items must be at least one more than
the number of parameters if all parameters and error are to be independently estimated, and the usual linear rank restrictions apply to the
design matrix.

Item-Component Interaction Models (β_{jl} Terms)

This model is not particularly attractive since it assumes that there is
a peculiarity to an item that cannot be captured by the x variates and
cannot be included in the random error term. While in practice such items
are quite likely, they are theoretically unpalatable. There is nothing resident in the item itself that is in theory indescribable, so that what occurs
under this model is the invocation of a different component than is intended (and included in the model) or there exist significant component
interactions that have not been included.

Population-Independent Component Model (β_1)

Components that are independent of item or subject are quite desirable, even though there is always likely to be a qualifier such as "independent within ages 8–10." Under such conditions populations of items can be specified for use in building tailored tests or sampling the universe of the task.

MULTICOMPONENT LATENT TRAIT MODEL

Embretson (1984, 1985) developed her general multicomponent latent trait model as a generalization of item response theory (IRT) to include both task features and processing components as parameters. Her model is, for the composite task T, made up of k components,

$$P(x_{ijT} = 1|\theta_i,\mu_m,d) = (a - g)\prod_k \frac{\exp[\theta_{jk} - (\Sigma_m c_{imk}\mu_{mk} + d_k)]}{1 + \exp[\theta_{jk} - (\Sigma_m c_{imk}\mu_{mk} + d_k)]} + g \quad (3)$$

where i = item, j = person, m = factor, k = component, θ = ability, μ = difficulty, c = complexity, d = normalization constant, a = probability of solution when requisite component information is available, g = probability of solution when requisite component information is not available, and x = score of 0 or 1. The complexity coefficients are estimated independently from the responses of the subjects, using a previous sample or other criteria. The components are specified theoretically. Embretson showed that the various response patterns are functions of the joint probabilities of solution under presence or absence of the requisite components in the item. Estimation is based on the joint maximum likelihood solution for I equations on each component.

The particular formulation of Embretson's model is based on the product of the probabilities of solution to components and requires both a finite and complete space of complexities by components. One limitation of this approach is that many theoretical formulations make this space virtually infinite, or at least so large that any practical solution is problematic. In effect the model require a complete representation of the independent variable space without any restrictions. It is in the specification of restrictions that other models become attractive, particularly those of the general linear model presented above. While these models are simplifications of Embretson's Equation 3 model, the term does not capture the gains in conceptualization and practicalities of design attendant to the simplification.

Logistic Regression Models

Logistic regression is a GLM approach that requires underlying multivariate normality for the independent variables while retaining the binary distribution of the dependent (Bishop, Fienberg, & Holland, 1975). This model is given by

$$P(x_{ijT} = 1 \mid \theta_i, \mu_m, d) = 1/[1 + \exp\{\sum_k b_k \theta_{jk} + \sum_m c_m \mu_{im} + d_i\}], \quad (4)$$

with the terms consistent with Embretson's model, with one major exception: abilities are not estimated from within the model, they may be represented as specific values from independent test scores or as dummy coded effects in an ANOVA-type design. In the latter case the intercept d_i carries the meaning of an average ability performance measure for the item. Model 4 is consistent with the general linear model formulation in Equation 2. Zwinderman (1992) has similarly represented the model in a recent paper, but has retained an item difficulty parameter in Embretson's formulation. He acknowledges that without further assumptions the item parameter and the intercept cannot simultaneously be estimated.

Equation 4 was represented with two discrete parameter sets to note formally that the sets are related to different theoretical constructs. Mathematically one summation term is sufficient to represent all parameters. Equation 4 need not be restricted to two cognitive variable sets, ability/processing variables, and task variables. Additional sets of variables, such as instruction condition, metacognition, and affect, may be added as theoretically required. In any case, the model is clearly a rejection of classical and IRT models that attempt to estimate independent subject variables from within the information of the item covariance structure. The contention made here is that independent information is necessary to further theory; covariance structure decomposition, the fundamental model for individual differences psychology, is not the central methodological tenet of cognitive psychology (Wagner & Sternberg, 1984). The appeal is, instead, to independent measures of processing based on stimuli strength or salience. This is fundamentally an association model translated into cognitive framework. Stimulus variation is required for estimation, a within-subjects model. While this orientation is restrictive and requires more measurement, at the same time it makes much more likely estimation at the level of the individual, which under the classical or IRT models has usually been fruitless.

Estimation of logistic regression for Equation 4 can take two paths: maximum likelihood (ML) or generalized least squares (GLS). Maximum likelihood estimation is well known to users of IRT and covariance structure methods, and GLS to experimental design methodologists. Zwinderman (1992) has summarized the estimation requirements, which under his restrictions, yield a model identical to Equation 4. One consequence of a manifest (no latent variables) model is that in many applications discriminant analysis is the preferred method. In many situations logistic regression and discriminant analysis via standard regression can be expected to yield almost identical results, although empirically, convergence is more likely to be a problem in logistic regression. It must also pointed out that in principle all estimation may be carried out *separately* for each subject when independent variables are the basis for the regression. Under the classical model a single subject analysis is only possible under specific assumptions, such as stationarity in a time series design (Willson, 1980), since an assumption of randomly parallel items provides no other information. As with time series models, when a structure is imposed internally or due to independent variables, reliability can be defined as an information measure, discussed below.

RELIABILITY

Following general linear model concepts, reliability for the logistic regression model extends the generalizability model to continuous variable predictors. While variance components in the general linear model are estimable, the expectations are cumbersome. An alternative is to consider the population covariance matrix and represent the information in interrelationships in standardized form. For samples this becomes the multiple and partial R^2 values relating item score to independent predictors. Separate reliabilities can be computed for each subject, and reliability is an attribute to be studied both within and between subjects. Since the space of independent variable values may be exhausted or only sampled, variances associated with the independent variables may be considered fixed or random in design terms. This leads to a generalizability conceptualization in which variance components may be estimated, whether within each subject or between subjects, and a more general framework, g-theory, employed.

While the general theory is straightforward, what is perhaps of greater benefit is to consider how to conceptualize the independent variables and generate the real values used in equation 4.

TEST DEVELOPMENT

INDEPENDENT VARIABLE ANALYSIS

Since the emphasis in this paper is on theoretical formulation, every behavior to be assessed is assumed to be the result of cognitive operations on a specified task. If affect is ignored for a particular assessment it is assumed to vary independently and randomly across subjects, and within each subject will be expected to be constant for the assessment being examined. Similarly, instruction is assumed to be constant unless it occurs between sets of items, say in a Vygotskian approach, for which it is then coded as a binary or otherwise fixed variable (see Glass, Willson, & Gottman, 1975, for time-series designs that might be modeled).

Cognitive Operations

There has not yet occurred any consensus regarding either the number or quality of cognitive processes, although general areas such as spatial ability, reasoning, and memory have general currency. Thus, theory is intimately linked to test development, for the items developed must conform to the theory invoked, and the item performance, good or bad, becomes an indicator of theoretical validity without regard to external measures. To amplify, let us look at a process widely investigated, analogical reasoning, and specifically, two-dimensional geometric figure analogies.

Willson, Goetz, Hall, and Applegate (1986) evaluated items from the Matrix Analogies subtest of the Kaufman Assessment Battery for Children (K-ABC), an intelligence test developed for children by Kaufman and Kaufman (1983). Each item of the subtest consists of a 2 × 2 arrangement of figure drawings on an easel with the bottom right term blank and a selection of possible answers available to the child to be physically manipulated and placed in the blank area. While the items were selected from a larger pool based on psychometric and developmental principles (high correlations with total score, increasing ease with age, increasing difficulty within age), it is possible to assign to each item three variable scores based on a fairly well developed theory (Mulholland, Pellegrino, and Glaser, 1980; Sternberg, 1977) based on the number of elements, visually perceptible units that are perceived to change, in the top left figure, and the number and kind of transformation represented in the top right (termed an A-B transformation) and bottom left (termed A-C transformation) figures. For example, in Figure 1 the number of elements is 2, the number of A-B transformations is 1, and the number of A-C transformations is 1. Transformations can be additive, subtractive, and substitutional (one figure feature for another), and others can be found in other sets such as Raven's (1962) work. These are theoretically linked to processes termed encoding (number of elements encoded), inferring (deciding on the number and character of A-B transformation), mapping (A-C transformations), and applying (selecting or producing a solution based on the three processes). Thus, it is assumed that the task invokes the process. The components of the task are varied in complexity from item to item, permitting examination of the independent effects of each component on performance, and by inference, the relation of each process to

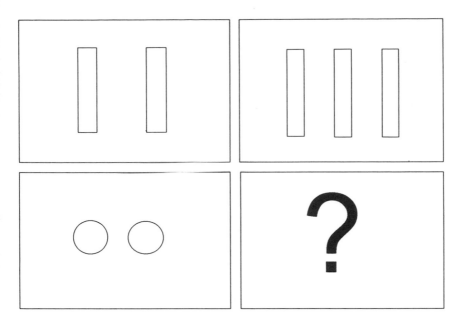

FIGURE 1. Matrix analogy example with two elements, one A-B transformation, and one A-C transformation.

others in solution of the problem. A population of items can be constructed from a set of specifications for a limited number of elements, say 5, A-B transformations, perhaps up to 5, and A-C transformations, again 5. This yields 125 items for a given set of geometric shapes or forms, and multiple sets can be constructed to parallel a given set. This was the basis for the items in Alexander, Willson, White, and Fuqua (1987). They worked with only color, shape, and size, since children aged 3 to 6 were the target population.

Visual/Spatial Features

While in theory every aspect of an item's presentation, the entire experience, should be linked to a cognitive process, in practice we are simply not at that level of specificity with respect to cognitive modeling. Nevertheless, it has been long known that various features of an item can affect performance. For example, with elementary children the percentage able to add together two two-digit numbers varies with horizontal or vertical presentations of the numbers. This has to do with familiarity of the format and the particular routines that are invoked to perform the processes needed. Clearly, the unfamiliar format of horizontal addition terms invokes different processes that typically reduce correct solution.

Such formats can be included as independent variables in the theoretical model when the format is known or suspected to change processing mechanisms, but the mechanisms are not fully linked theoretically to the primary processes being examined.

In Willson and Olivarez (1987) visually presented arithmetic items were examined for the number and kind of mental transformations required for their solutions. In these items the pictures presented to the children contained all information required to solve the problem, although in many items a transformation was required (such as recognizing that ice cream cones were 5 cents, and six people buying ice cream cones, the problem, would require 30 cents payment). The pictures under investigation all were represented as taking place at a zoo, and there were interesting, and potentially distracting, features in each picture. Several variables were coded as theoretically affecting a child's mental transformation processing: amount of information presented (coded as number of chunks available to the child, the more gross visual organization of the picture; and total number of visually identifiable units or elements in the picture), and spatial orientation of the information (primarily horizontal, vertical, or two-dimensionally complex).

Instructional Variables

Vygotsky's (1978) theory of the zone of proximal development in intelligence incorporates in it a critical testing component, the degree to which a learner's performance changes after instruction. This represents at present the most formal theory that incorporates instruction (or instructability) into testing, and testing into intellectual development. Most cognitive researchers now incorporate instruction as a salient variable in their theories. The functional form of an item may thus incorporate one or more instructional variables; these variables may be simply binary (instruction has or has not occurred), or they may include more elaborated components, such as amount of instructional time, salience of instruction, or form of instruction.

Metacognition and Learning Strategies

While no consistent theory has emerged regarding the role of metacognition, and its related learning strategy use, there is now consensus that it is an important part of intellectual activity. The extent to which such factors are modeled directly in item performance will be dictated by the nature of the cognitive task proposed, the instruction an individual has already been given in strategy use, and the specifics of the theory being invoked. For example, if field dependence and attribution are selected as components to be modeled, they may have little bearing on specific item processing; if, however, an item can be linked to specific strategy use, such as using analogical reasoning, the respondent's knowledge and ability to use analogy may be important to code.

Prior Knowledge

The role of prior knowledge is now universally acknowledged as important to item performance. What is meant by prior knowledge, however, is less clear (Alexander & Judy, 1988). There are several theories of information storage and access, including level-of-processing, schema, neural network, and distributed processing models. Also, there is a connection to instruction, although it is not necessary. Instruction of a fact may have produced assimilation (using a Piagetian concept) or augmented a particular schema. Whether an item is successfully answered may hinge on the student's correct selection of schema, network, or whatever, assuming that the correct action or fact was ever learned. Item failure may be due to incorrect selection of process or prior knowledge condition rather than lack of knowledge. Correct response is generally due (guessing on multiple choice aside) to correct cognitive process selection and appropriate prior knowledge linkage, although incautiously generated items may allow correct response from incorrect process.

ITEM POPULATION SPECIFICATION

Given the independent variable set described above, item populations must be defined for each variable as fixed or random, and whether to be randomly sampled, systematically sampled, or allowed to vary randomly. The most common model assumes a given minimal constellation of prior knowledge, some specific instruction, and positive affect. Content and task structure vary independently, and task structure is often selected based on individual idiosyncracies or economic constraints rather than analysis of the processes to be invoked. Alternatives exist that can systematize the definition of item populations.

DETAILED EXAMPLE

An example of linking theory to item development can be found in Willson & Rupley (1991). Words were drawn from the population commonly found in elementary school populations' vocabularies. They represented both irregular and regular English orthographies. Each word in an oral decoding (also called word identification) task of 28 words was decomposed into eight orthographic and phonological structural components based on linguistic theory. The words and the decomposition are given in Table 1. Since the word list is proprietary, they are not identified.

TABLE 1. Components of Words in a Word Identification Task

Word	Number of								
	Gra	Phon	Mor	ConBl	ConDi	SiMkr	RConV	VoDig	Syll
1	6	5	1	0	0	0	1	0	2
2	5	4	1	1	0	0	0	0	2
3	6	4	1	0	1	0	1	0	2
4	6	5	1	1	0	0	0	0	2
5	7	4	1	0	0	0	1	0	2
6	6	6	1	0	0	0	0	0	3
7	4	3	1	0	0	1	0	0	1
8	4	2	1	0	1	0	0	0	1
9	9	7	2	0	1	0	0	0	3
10	7	5	1	0	0	2	0	0	2
11	9	6	1	0	0	2	0	0	3
12	10	8	1	0	0	0	1	1	5
13	11	8	1	1	1	0	0	0	4
14	5	4	1	0	0	0	0	0	1
15	11	10	2	0	0	0	1	0	5
16	5	4	1	0	1	0	0	0	2

A coherent theory of reading, due to Adams (1990) and others, predicted both importance of certain components and shifts in importance with age. For this example children of age 12½ years are presented for detailed study. Each of the 100 students at this age received 16 words visually and was requested to pronounce the word. Raters were trained to near 1.0 reliability to score the pronunciation as correct or incorrect (Kaufman & Kaufman, 1983).

Two analyses were conducted at the single subject level: logistic regression and direct regression on the binary scores, mathematically equivalent for two scores to discriminant analysis (Tatsuoka, 1988, p. 228). Each will be discussed below. An initial evaluation of the predictor intercorrelations indicated that phonemes, syllables, and graphemes intercorrelated about .9, so that only phonemes was retained. This is due to the high degree of similarity of the orthographic properties of these variables. From Willson & Rupley (1991) five predictors exhibited major influence at this age level from either a logistic or linear model perspective: phonemes, consonant blends, consonant digraphs, silent markers, and r-controlled vowels.

Logistic Regression

Of the 100 analyses, 8 were rejected for zero variance. With all seven predictors, not a single analysis converged in the iterated maximum likelihood procedure (SAS, 1989) employed after 25 iterations. Consequently, the five predictors from Willson and Rupley (1991) were entered to investigate convergence for fewer predictors. Of the 92 cases, 24 converged to provide parameter estimates. The limited number of observations per subject is a major factor preventing convergence. Of those cases that converged, all were in the middle of the total score distribution (5–10 correct, frequencies 1, 2, 2, 6, 4, 7), while the observed distribution of 100 scores ranged from 1 to 16 correct (frequencies 1, 5, 2, 2, 3, 7, 9, 7, 5, 13, 11, 7, 7, 7, 6, 8). Two measures of the association between predicted and observed binary scores of interest were the simple concordance (SAS Institute, Inc., 1989) and the Goodman-Kruskal gamma. The concordances ranged from .52 to .97, with twenty values above .80, and mean of .84. The gamma statistics correlated .99 with the concordance, with values between .03 to .95, and all but four values above .60, mean of .69.

An inspection of the individual analyses revealed potentially interesting outliers among the subjects. The case with very low association measures (gamma of .03, concordance of .52) also exhibited nearly zero logistic regression coefficients for all predictors, the only such case. Coefficients were seemingly quite interpretable from subject to subject; standardized coefficients indicated relative importance of a particular predictor. For all 24 cases the sign of the phoneme weight was positive, while 23 consonant blend weights were negative, and 21 were positive for consonant digraphs and r-controlled vowels. Weight signs were quite mixed for silent markers. The signs may be interpreted as follows: positive weights are associated with decreased performance, so that increasing the number of phonemes in a word decreased the probability of children's correct pronunciation, while increasing the number of consonant blends and consonant digraphs consistently assists children's correct pronunciation.

While such analysis may prove to be quite useful for instruction on an individual basis, that only 24 cases could be analyzed leaves the question whether increasing the number of items will assist convergence, as theoretically it should, or whether decreasing the number of predictors might help. In this case it seems dysfunctional to eliminate predictors that, while not seemingly important for most students, are important for certain individuals.

Regression Analysis

Using a discriminant analysis approach yielded estimates from all 94 cases. The distributions of within-subject regression R^2 values are given in Table 2. These correlated over .9 with both gamma and concordance for the 24 cases in the logistic regression, indicating high consistency between the measures.

The regression coefficients associated with phonemes were negative

TABLE 2. Stem-and-Leaf Plots for R^2
for Within-Subject Regressions

	Entire Sample	Logistic Regression Sample
10		
9		
8	00	
7	224568999	
6	333599	33
5	001112367777788888	11777
4	0111123333488	0111
3	0011111123666666667789	011267
2	111112334444788	4444
1	1479999	47
0	1	1

for all 92 cases (excluding the perfect scores), and 91 were positive for consonant blends; 85 weights were positive for r-controlled vowels, while signs were mixed for consonant digraphs and silent markers. The signs in these analyses have reversed meaning from the logistic regressions: negative signs are associated with decreased probability of correct pronunciation. Stem-and-leaf plots for the predictors are given in Table 3. Normality was rejected for none at the .01 level.

A correlation analysis was performed on the 24 cases identified by the logistic regression to compare regression and logistic coefficient order. For phonemes the weights from the two analyses correlated .62; for consonant blends, .91; for consonant digraphs, .65; for silent markers, .92; and for r-controlled vowels, .88.

Among the 24 cases the same outliers appeared as with the logistic regression. The coefficients were also all nearly zero for the extreme case.

The prediction models for both the logistic and regression analyses were used to generate predicted scores for items 11 and 13. The predictions were correlated for the 24 cases. The mean for item 11 under logistic modeling was .257 (SD = .22) and under regression was .442 (SD = .45). For item 11 the two correlated .97. For item 13, the logistic mean was .236 (SD = .15) and the regression mean was .455 (SD = .33). The two predicted scores correlated .90. These data clearly illustrate one of the problems of regression methods, extensive range for probability of success beyond [0–1]. The minimum score for item 11 under regression was −.20, and for item 13, −.10, with maxima of 1.06 and 1.16, respectively. The regression estimate more closely predicted the mean subject performance on item 11 (.50), while for item 13 (.34), logistic modeling underpredicted and regression modeling overpredicted.

TABLE 3. Stem-and-Leaf Plots of Regression Weights for Five Components of Word Identification

Phonemes		Consonant Blends		Consonant Digraphs	
1	5	10	9	2	11
0	778	9		1	777
−0		8	23	0	12234
−1	8	7	112244459	−0	23455555777777778889999
−2	147	6	1134456	−1	0000111222355666666799
−3	248	5	0013	−2	0000113355688
−4	33467	4	03344466777	−3	02346
−5	111999	3	0135555677888	−4	2229
−6	000677888	2	0012222344468		Multiply by .01
−7	38	1	0145566666677999999		
−8	99	0	013334679		
−9	344	−0	4		
−10	01114	−1	06		
−11	12333	−2	2		
−12	44455558899		Multiply by .01 (eg., −2 2 becomes −.22)		
−13	23779				
−14	000011678				
−15	15559				
−16	78				
−17	1499				
−18	22667				
−21	33				

Silent Markers		*R-controlled vowels*	
3	7	8	13789
2	0034444679	7	45567
1	00001234446799	6	0388
0	000111222333345555667777777899	5	0024557899
−0	00002334555566788	4	022333467
−1	02444477	3	0013666778889
−2	01112344477	2	011222566
−3		1	022344555555666999999
−4	32	0	033357777
	Multiply by .01	−0	34679
		−1	2
		−2	3
			Multiply by .01

MODELING POOLED SUBJECT REGRESSION WEIGHTS

While the evidence presented in the tables suggests individual models may be quite beneficial instructionally, a model in which all subjects' weights are assumed to be equal may in some cases be appropriate. Since subject average differences must be modeled, one approach is to use a general linear model with subject a random factor. In practice, with a

TABLE 4. Prediction of Word Identification Residual Item Scores
by Five-Word Identification Components

Source	Parameter Estimate	Type I SS	F	Type II SS
Intercept	.41	0	–	24.23
Phonemes	−.104	33.90	221.96	56.92
Consonant blends	.335	8.34	54.61	18.04
Consonant digraphs	−.0938	5.94	38.89	2.22
Silent markers	.0089	5.22	34.18	.04
R-controlled vowels	.323	19.34	126.63	19.34
Error		210.01		
$df_{error} = 1372$				
$R^2 = .257$				

large subject pool and large item bank the design size can become enormous, exhausting even the resources of large mainframes. Removing subject mean performance from each item score (within subject) is a space-saving approach. This leaves each subject with two possible scores and the distribution of possible item scores with $i − 1 \times 2$ possible values. In the case of the word identification task, there were 30 different possible item scores. This rapidly approaches a continuous variable distribution as the item pool increases.

Running an analysis on the 92 subjects with a pooled regression weight model, the weights associated with the components are given in Table 4.

Under this model, phonemes, consonant blends, and r-controlled vowels are the most salient variables, consistent with the individual regression model. The R^2 predicted was about .26. Note that this is prediction of residuals subsequent to the removal of between-subject variance, which is an order of magnitude larger in sum of squares.

CONSTRUCT VALIDATION WITH READING COMPREHENSION

The argument advanced in this paper has been that basic theoretical constructs should be the basis for both item and test construction, and that the constructs should be linked directly to the individual's performance. Further, theoretical relationships to other constructs should be demonstrable. Ideally, this will occur multivariately, or at least in structural models in which each construct is tied to all others as theory dictates. There is nothing new about this, except that when construct regression weights replace omnibus true scores, as shown in the example above, then the regression weights must be related to other constructs.

Word identification, in its theoretical construct, is hardly of importance except as it promotes greater automaticity and fluency in decoding, a theoretical prerequisite to reading comprehension (Adams, 1990). Reading comprehension itself has many competing theoretical models, although there has been some coherence in recent years (Adams, 1990). For the example presented here, reading comprehension was measured in a manner that minimizes any other verbal demands: each student read a card containing instructions for them to perform a physical action such as touch their nose with a finger of their right hand. A total score for each child represented the reading comprehension variable. No attempt was made to deconstruct any components for this study, although such an analysis should be performed.

The regression weights for the 92 subjects in the earlier analysis were entered into a multiple regression analysis. The summary table is given in Table 5.

At this particular age the individual weights predicted almost 28% of the variance. Rupley and Willson (1991) reported that the predictable variance in reading comprehension due to word identification dropped from about 80% at age 6 to about 60% at age 12. For this group the proportion of variance predictable from total word identification score was .591. Thus, using individual components instead to the total score reduced variance accountable by about half. Clearly, other factors are important at this age rather than just decoding fluency. In an unpublished paper, Willson and Rupley (1992) showed that for older children increasing variance is accounted for by other constructs, particularly listening comprehension, replacing word identification. Thus, the results reported here must be integrated into a more comprehensive model of reading comprehension to be properly interpreted.

TABLE 5. Prediction of Reading Comprehension by Individual Regression Weights from Five Word Identification Components

Source	Parameter Estimate	Type I SS	F	Type II SS
Phonemes	−2.58	73.36	7.59	1.42
Consonant blends	−3.96	231.32	23.93	29.94
Consonant digraphs	−.10	1.01	.10	.02
R-controlled vowels	−3.64	42.42	4.39	30.95
Vowel digraphs	.48	3.64	.38	3.64
Error		908.76		
n = 92				
R^2 = .279				

SUMMARY

Modeling individual responses has been ignored because there did not seem to be an appropriate theoretical or methodological venue. It is argued here that both are now available, although application will require a willingness to break with now long-standing psychometric tradition, particularly in the development of items and their integration into tests. It is impossible to make any claim that major problems have been solved in item and test development, but the promise of individual modeling of response from structural features of the task must surely promote its investigation. Test items need no longer be generated from either vague specifications or theoretically bankrupt behavioral algorithms, and individual responses to the items need no longer be only indicators of a theoretically sterile true score. Cognitive approaches to learning have allowed new conceptualizations of brain function; there is now promise of linking the physiological with the mental, and this is fundamentally a process conducted at the level of the individual. Our measurement of mental activity should reflect this new emphasis.

REFERENCES

Adams, M. J. (1990). *Beginning to read*. Cambridge, MA: MIT Press.

Alexander, P. A. and Judy, J. E. The interaction of domain-specific and strategic knowledge in academic performance. *Review of Educational Research, 58*, 375–404.

Alexander, P. A., Willson, V. L., White, C. S., & Fuqua, J. D. (1987). Analogical reasoning in young children. *Journal of Educational Psychology, 79*, 401–408.

Bishop, Y. M. M., Fienberg, S. E., & Holland, P. W. (1975). *Discrete multivariate analysis*. Cambridge: MIT Press.

Bloom, B., (1956). *Taxonomy of educational objectives: Handbook I, Cognitive domain*. New York: David McKay.

Cronbach, L. J., Gleser, G. C., Nanda, H., & Rajaratnam, N. (1972). *The Dependability of behavioral measurements: Theory of generalizability for scores and profiles*. New York: Wiley.

Embretson, S. E. (1984). A general latent trait model for response process. *Psychometrika, 49*, 175–186.

Embretson, S. E. (1985). Multicomponent latent trait models for test design. In S. E. Embretson (Ed.), *Test design: Developments in psychology and psychometrics* (pp. 195–218). New York: Academic Press.

Fischer, G. (1973). Linear logistic test model as an instrument in educational research. *Acta Psychologica, 37*, 359–374.

Fischer, G. (1983). Logistic linear trait models with linear constraints. *Psychometrika, 48*, 3–26.

Glass, G. V., Willson, V. L., & Gottman, J. (1975). *Design and analysis of time-series experiments*. Boulder: University of Colorado Press.

Hocking, R. (1985). *The analysis of linear models*. Monterey, CA: Brooks/Cole Pub.

Kaufman, A. S., & Kaufman, N. L. (1983). *Kaufman Assessment Battery for Children Interpretive Manuel*. Circle Pines, MN: American Guidance Services.

Lord, F., & Novick, M. (1968). *Statistical theories of mental test scores*. Reading, MA: Addison-Wesley.

Mislevy, R. J., & Sheehan, K. M. (1989). The role of collateral information about examinees in item parameter estimation. *Psychometrika, 54*, 661–679.

Mulholland, T. M., Pellegrino, J. W., & Glaser, R. (1980). Components of geometric analogy solution. *Cognitive Psychology, 12*, 252–284.

Raven, J. C. (1962). *Advanced progressive matrices, sets I and II*. London, England: H. K. Lewis & Co., Ltd.

SAS Institute, Inc. (1989). SAS/STAT® User's Guide, Version 6, Fourth Edition, Volume 1. Cary, NC: SAS Institute, Inc.

Schmidt, A., & Dorans, N. (1990). Differential item functioning for minority examinees on the SAT. *Journal of Educational Measurement, 27*, 67–81.

Sternberg, R. J. (1977). *Intelligence, information processing, and analogical reasoning: The componential analysis of human abilities*. Hillsdale, NJ: Lawrence Erlbaum.

Tatsuoka, M. (1988). *Multivariate analysis: Techniques for educational and psychological research*. New York: Macmillan.

Vygotsky, L. S. (1978). *Mind in Society*. Cambridge, MA: Harvard University Press.

Wagner, R. K., & Sternberg, R. J. (1984). Alternative conceptions of intelligence and their implications for education. *Review of Educational Research, 54*, 179–223.

Willson, V. L. (1980). Stationary time-series models of true score theory. Paper presented at the annual meeting of the Psychometric Society, Iowa City, May.

Willson, V. L. (1989). Cognitive and developmental effects on item performance in intelligence and achievement tests for young children. *Journal of Educational Measurement, 26*, 103–119.

Willson, V. L., Goetz, E. T., Hall, R. J., & Applegate III, E. B. (1986). Effects of varying the number of elements and transformations of matrix analogies on children ages 5–12. Paper presented at the annual meeting of the American Educational Research Association, San Francisco, April.

Willson, V. L., & Olivarez Jr., A. O. (1987). Information processing of pictorial arithmetic problems. Unpublished manuscript, Texas A & M University, College Station.

Willson, V. L., & Rupley, W. H. (1991). Relationship of reading comprehension to components of word decoding: Support for developmental shifts. Paper presented at the annual meeting of the National Reading Conference, Palm Springs, CA, December.

Zwinderman, A. (1992). A generalized Rasch model for manifest predictors. *Psychometrika, 56*, 589–600.

CHAPTER NINE

Variance Components in Generalizability Theory

ROBERT L. BRENNAN

Generalizability theory is described most extensively in a book by Cronbach, Gleser, Nanda, and Rajaratnam (1972) entitled *The Dependability of Behavioral Measurements*. Brennan (1983) has provided a monograph on generalizability theory that is less comprehensive than Cronbach et al. (1972) but still detailed enough to convey many of the conceptual and statistical issues inherent in generalizability theory. Also, Shavelson and Webb (1991) have provided a primer on generalizability theory. Recent overviews of generalizability theory are provided by Feldt and Brennan (1989) and Shavelson, Webb, and Rowley (1989).

Generalizability theory can be viewed as liberalizing classical test theory through the application of certain analysis of variance procedures to measurement situations. In this sense, classical theory and analysis of variance can be viewed as precursors of generalizability theory, but the theory itself is both less and more than a conjunction of classical theory and analysis of variance. For example, generalizability theory has virtually no role for F-tests. Also, generalizability theory is a weak theory in the sense that the theory per se requires no assumptions about distributional form (e.g., normality). Most importantly, generalizability theory constitutes a broadly defined psychometric model with a rich conceptual framework for simultaneously examining multiple sources of error in tests and other types of measurement procedures. Indeed, the conceptual

ROBERT L. BRENNAN • Research Division, American College Testing, Iowa City, Iowa 52243.
Cognitive Assessment: A Multidisciplinary Perspective, edited by Cecil R. Reynolds. Plenum Press, New York, 1994.

framework of generalizability theory may well outlive the statistical procedures currently employed in applying the theory.

Although this paper concentrates on certain statistical issues in generalizability theory, the statistical issues should not be viewed as driving the theory. On the contrary, the statistical issues should be driven by the conceptual framework. Indeed, one point this paper attempts to make is that some analysis of variance procedures in the statistical literature are inappropriate in generalizability theory because they are inconsistent with the conceptual framework of the theory.

The most important parameters considered in generalizability theory are universe score variance and error variances of various types. Universe score variance is the variance for the objects of measurement (usually, but not necessarily, persons) of their expected scores over all conditions of all facets in the universe of generalization (i.e., the universe to which an investigator wants to generalize). Error variances are dependent on both the universe of generalization and the data collection design actually employed to make decisions about objects of measurement.

In the framework of (univariate) generalizability theory, both universe score variance and error variances can be expressed in terms of components of score variance; that is, variance components. Indeed, the *Standards for Educational and Psychological Testing* (APA, 1985) state that:

> [T]he estimation of clearly labeled components of observed and error score variance is a particularly useful outcome of a reliability study, both for the test developer who wishes to improve the reliability of an instrument and for the user who wants to interpret test scores in particular circumstances with maximum understanding. Reporting standard errors, confidence intervals, or other measures of imprecision of estimates is also helpful. (p. 19)

In the sense considered in the previous paragraph, variance components can be viewed as the building blocks of generalizability theory. Consequently, issues concerning the definition and estimation of variance components are crucial in generalizability theory. Although these issues are the central focus of this paper, the reader is cautioned not to equate generalizability theory with *variance components analysis*, as that term is often used in statistical literature. There are two reasons for this caveat: First, variance components can be viewed as the building blocks of the theory, but they are not the edifice itself. Second, the statistical literature on variance components is uneven with respect to its applicability in generalizability theory. Indeed, one purpose of this paper is to consider the relevance of some of the statistical literature on variance components from the perspective of generalizability theory. Another purpose is to aid users of generalizability theory in understanding how some conceptual issues in the theory influence how variance components are defined and, hence, estimated.

DEFINITIONS OF VARIANCE COMPONENTS

Because variance components are central to generalizability theory, it is important that definitions of variance components be considered carefully. Unfortunately, a substantial amount of the literature on generalizability theory treats definitional issues only vaguely, with emphasis placed too quickly on estimation issues. Of course, it is not possible to evaluate the characteristics of estimates without a clear understanding of the parameters.

VARIANCE COMPONENTS FOR UNIVERSES WITH INFINITE FACETS

The usual statistical treatment of a random model begins with the linear model for the decomposition of observed scores into a grand mean and certain score effects. For example, consider the $p \times (i{:}h)$ balanced design in which n persons are crossed with items; an equal number of items, k, are nested within each of the r levels of some other facet, h; and the symbols "x" and ":" denote crossing and nesting, respectively. For this design, the linear model can be represented as:

$$X_{\text{pih}} = \mu + \upsilon_p + \upsilon_h + \upsilon_{i{:}h} + \upsilon_{ph} + \upsilon_{pi{:}h,e} \tag{1}$$

where μ is the grand mean, υ designates a score effect, and $\upsilon_{pi{:}h,e}$ represents the interaction effect which is confounded with residual error. It is typically assumed that the expectation of each of the score effects is zero, and the score effects are uncorrelated or, more strongly, independent. Often, it is even assumed a priori that all score effects, or at least the residuals, are normally distributed.

The variance components are defined as the expectation (E) of the square of the score effects. The second column in Table 1 provides the definitions of each of these random effects variance components, and Table 2 provides the expected mean square (EMS) equations in terms of the variance components.

Although the above description of the random model is typical of the statistical literature, it is a bit misleading from the perspective of generalizability theory. In particular, generalizability theory does *not* begin with the linear model for a data collection design such as Equation 1. Rather, generalizability theory begins with an explicit consideration of the structure of a population and universe and the number of levels for all facets in the population and universe. (For example, even though a data

TABLE 1. Cornfield and Tukey (1956)
Definitions of Variance Components
for the $p \times (i{:}h)$ Design

Effect α	$\sigma^2(\alpha)$: $N \to \infty$, $K \to \infty$, $R \to \infty$	$\sigma^2(\alpha\|H)$: $N \to \infty$, $K \to \infty$, $R < \infty$
p	$E\, \nu_p{}^2$	$E\, \nu_p{}^2$
h	$E\, \nu_h{}^2$	$\displaystyle\sum_h \nu_h{}^2/(R-1)$
$i{:}h$	$E\, \nu_{i{:}h}{}^2$	$\displaystyle\sum_h (E\, \nu_{i{:}h}{}^2)/R$
ph	$E\, \nu_{ph}{}^2$	$\displaystyle\sum_h (E\, \nu_{ph}{}^2)/(R-1)$
$pi{:}h,e$	$E\, \nu_{pi{:}h,e}{}^2$	$\displaystyle\sum_h (E\, \nu_{pi{:}h,e}{}^2)/R$

Note. The population/universe sizes for p, i, and h are
N, K, and R, respectively.

TABLE 2. EMS Equations for the $p \times (i{:}h)$ Design
in Terms of $\sigma^2(\alpha)$
$(N \to \infty,\ K \to \infty,\ R \to \infty)$

$$
\begin{aligned}
\text{EMS}(p) &= \sigma^2(pi{:}h,e) + k\sigma^2(ph) + kr\sigma^2(p) \\
\text{EMS}(h) &= \sigma^2(pi{:}h,e) + k\sigma^2(ph) + n\sigma^2(i{:}h) + nk\sigma^2(h) \\
\text{EMS}(i{:}h) &= \sigma^2(pi{:}h,e) + n\sigma^2(i{:}h) \\
\text{EMS}(ph) &= \sigma^2(pi{:}h,e) + k\sigma^2(ph) \\
\text{EMS}(pi{:}h,e) &= \sigma^2(pi{:}h,e)
\end{aligned}
$$

Note. The (sample, population/universe sizes) for p, i, and h are
(n,N), (k,K), and (r,R), respectively.

collection design may have levels of i nested within levels of h, the structure of the universe may have levels of i crossed with levels of h.) Furthermore, mean scores are defined for the population and universe *before* a data collection design and its linear model are specified.

Suppose the structure of a population and universe is $p \times (i{:}h)$ with $p = 1, \ldots, N \to \infty$, $i = 1, \ldots, K \to \infty$, and $h = 1, \ldots, R \to \infty$ (for the facets p, i, and h, respectively). This type of structure occurs, for example, when items are associated with reading passages. For such a population and universe the following mean scores are defined *prior* to specifying a data collection design and its linear model:

$$
\mu_h \equiv \mathop{E}_{p}\mathop{E}_{i} X_{pih}, \quad \mu_{ph} \equiv \mathop{E}_{i} X_{pih}, \quad \mu_i\mu_{i{:}h} \equiv \mathop{E}_{p} X_{pih}, \tag{2}
$$

$$\mu \equiv \underset{p \ \ i \ \ h}{E \ E \ E} \ X_{pih}, \text{ and} \tag{3}$$

$$\mu_p \equiv \underset{i \ \ h}{E \ E} \ X_{pih}. \tag{4}$$

Now, suppose the data collection design is also $p \times (i{:}h)$, and we take independent random samples of sizes n, k, and r (for the facets p, i, and h respectively). Equation 1 is still the linear model for this design, but in generalizability theory the score effects in Equation 1 for this model ($n < N \rightarrow \infty$, $k < K \rightarrow \infty$, and $r < R \rightarrow \infty$) and *defined* as:

$$\nu_p \equiv \mu_p - \mu, \ \nu_h \equiv \mu_h - \mu, \ \nu_{i{:}h} \equiv \mu_{i{:}h} - \mu_h,$$

$$\nu_{ph} \equiv \mu_{ph} - \mu_p - \mu_h + \mu, \text{ and} \tag{5}$$

$$\nu_{pi{:}h,e} \equiv X_{pih} - \mu_{ph} - \mu_{i{:}h} + \mu_h,$$

which makes the linear model a tautology.

Clearly, given these definitions it *necessarily* follows that the expectation of all score effects is zero; i.e., an assumption of zero expectations is not required. It is also true, although less obvious, that the above development implies that all score effects for the random model are necessarily uncorrelated—again, no such assumption is required. For example $E(\nu_p)(\nu_{p'}) = 0$ (for $p \neq p'$) because of independent sampling, and $E(\nu_p)(\nu_{ph}) = 0$ because score effects are defined as deviation effects. Finally, nothing in the above development requires normality assumptions. In this sense, as stated previously, generalizability is a weak model.

The above development of the random model in generalizability theory emphasizes the distinction between a design for data collection and a population/universe. This distinction is often crucial in generalizability theory, although it is frequently overlooked or irrelevant in other treatments of linear models. Also, the above development specifically defines score effects in terms of mean scores for the population and universe. Doing so may make little practical difference for random models and infinite universes, but, as discussed below, it has important implications for other models and universes with one or more finite facets.

VARIANCE COMPONENTS FOR UNIVERSES
WITH ONE OR MORE FINITE FACETS

Suppose that the structure of a population and universe is $p \times (i{:}h)$ with $N \rightarrow \infty$, $K \rightarrow \infty$, and $R < \infty$, which means that the universe has a finite facet, h. In this case, the mean scores for the population and universe are given by Equation Set 2, with Equations 3 and 4 replaced by

$$\mu \equiv \sum_{h=1}^{R} (E_p E_i X_{\text{pih}})/R, \text{ and} \tag{6}$$

$$\mu_p \equiv \sum_{h=1}^{R} (E_i X_{\text{pih}})/R. \tag{7}$$

Model Restrictions

Now, if the data collection design is also $p \times (i{:}h)$, then the linear model is given by Equation 1, with the score effects defined by Equation Set 5 using the mean scores in Equations 2, 6, and 7. Given this development it *necessarily* follows that

$$E_p v_p = E_i v_{i{:}h} = E_p v_{pi{:}h,e} = E_i v_{pi{:}h,e} = 0 \quad \text{and}$$

$$\sum_{h=1}^{R} v_h = \sum_{h=1}^{R} v_{ph} = 0. \tag{8}$$

In particular, from the perspective of generalizability theory, the zero sums in Equation 8 are not *constraints* that are *sometimes* imposed on the score effects a posteriori for estimation purposes. Rather, both zero sums are *restrictions* on the score effects that are derivable from the manner in which one *defines* mean scores a priori in the population and universe.

If this issue of model restrictions were simply a terminological quibble, it would be unimportant. In many treatments of variance components, however, no such restrictions are employed (see, for example, Searle, 1971, chapter 9). Consequently, some of the statistical literature concerning variance components is not applicable in generalizability theory.

Also, it can be shown that since all sampling is assumed to be independent, and since score effects are defined as deviation scores, it necessarily follows that all effects are uncorrelated except for pairs of the form (v_p, v_{ph}) and $v_{ph}, v_{ph'})$, $h \neq h'$.

Cornfield and Tukey Definitions

Cronbach et al. (1972), Brennan (1983), and most of the literature on generalizability theory implicitly or explicitly employ the Cornfield and Tukey (1956) definitions of variance components. Table 1 provides two examples of these definitions for the $p \times (i{:}h)$ design. The first example provides definitions of the random effects variance components, which will be denoted generically as $\sigma^2(\alpha)$. The second example provides definitions of the variance components when $N \to \infty$, $K \to \infty$, and $R < \infty$. These variance components will be denoted $\sigma^2(\alpha|H)$ to emphasize that the h facet is finite ($R < \infty$). It is particularly important to note that, for sampling from a finite population and/or universe (e.g., mixed models), the Cornfield and Tukey (1956) definitions are consistent with the restrictions discussed above. From the perspective of generalizability theory, these restrictions are crucial. Other characteristics of these definitions that are less important theoretically are considered below.

Consider the definitions of the $\sigma^2(\alpha|H)$ and note that a divisor of R is used whenever h appears after a colon, and otherwise $(R-1)$ is used. This convention is consistent with the degrees of freedom for the effects. For example, the degrees of freedom for the ph effect are $(n-1)(r-1)$, and the degrees of freedom for the $(pi{:}h,e)$ effect are $r(n-1)(k-1)$.

Given *these* definitions of variance components, Tables 2 and 3 provide the EMS equations in terms of the $\sigma^2(\alpha)$ and $\sigma^2(\alpha|H)$, respectively. If $r = R$, then the term with $(1 - r/R)$ in Table 3 disappears and the resulting EMS equations are for the so-called mixed model with the h facet fixed.

A principal motivation behind the Cornfield and Tukey (1956) manner of defining variance components when the population and/or universe are finite is that doing so leads to simpler expressions for the EMS equations (and, hence, simpler expressions for unbiased estimators of the variance components) than the obvious alternative of replacing all occurrences of $N-1$ with N, $K-1$ with K, and $R-1$ with R. If, for example one uses R rather than $R-1$ in the denominators of the definitions of $\sigma^2(h|H)$ and $\sigma^2(ph|H)$ then, for the EMS equations in Table 3, terms involving $\sigma^2(h|H)$ and $\sigma^2(ph|H)$ need to be multiplied by $R/(R-1)$. To make this distinction explicit, I will use σ^2 to designate the Cornfield and Tukey (1956) definitions of variance components and θ^2 to designate the definitions that use N, K, or R whenever a finite facet size is required in the denominator of the definition of a variance component.

TABLE 3. EMS Equations for the $p \times (i{:}h)$ Design in Terms of $\sigma^2(\alpha|H)$
$(N \to \infty, K \to \infty, R < \infty)$

EMS(p)	$= \sigma^2(pi{:}h,e|H) + (1 - r/R)k\sigma^2(ph|H) + kr\sigma^2(p|H)$
EMS(h)	$= \sigma^2(pi{:}h,e|H) + k\sigma^2(ph|H) + n\sigma^2(i{:}h|H) + nk\sigma^2(h|H)$
EMS($i{:}h$)	$= \sigma^2(pi{:}h,e|H) + n\sigma^2(i{:}h|H)$
EMS(ph)	$= \sigma^2(pi{:}h,e|H) + k\sigma^2(ph|H)$
EMS($pi{:}h,e$)	$= \sigma^2(pi{:}h,e|H)$

Note. The (sample, population/universe sizes) for p, i, and h are $(n,N)k$, (k,K), and (r,R), respectively.

There is some precedent for using the θ^2 rather than the σ^2 definitions in variance components analyses. For example, in multiple matrix sampling and incidence sampling (Sirotnik & Wellington, 1977) the θ^2 definitions are sometimes used rather than the σ^2 definitions. In examining such literature, however, one needs to be careful about a potential notational confusion; namely, some of the literature on multiple matrix sampling and incidence sampling uses θ^2 to reference the Cornfield and Tukey (1956) definitions and σ^2 to designate the other definitions (see, for example, Sirotnik & Wellington, 1977, p. 354–355).

Also, Cardinet, Tourneur, and Allal (1981) and Cardinet and Allal (1983) have taken steps in the direction of always using θ^2 definitions of variance components in generalizability theory. (They refer to these definitions as "expectancies of variance" and denote them E^2.) Since there is nothing inherently right or wrong in using these definitions, it is reasonable to consider the consequences of employing θ^2 rather than σ^2 definitions. The most obvious consequence is, of course, the one mentioned above; that is, somewhat more complex expressions for EMS equations. Consequently, if one employs the θ^2 definitions, then certain modifications are *sometimes* required in the expressions (and estimates) for universe score variance and error variances. Note, however, that no modifications are required when $N \to \infty$ for the objects of measurement (see Brennan, 1984, for a consideration of this and various other cases).

As stated previously, there is no compelling theoretical basis for preferring σ^2 to θ^2 definitions of variance components. Usually, however, in generalizability theory I would argue in favor of the Cornfield and Tukey (1956) σ^2 definitions for the following pragmatic reasons. First the EMS equations are simpler when they are expressed in terms of the σ^2 definitions. Second, the σ^2 definitions are often employed in statistical literature and almost always employed in literature on generalizability theory. Third, virtually all readily available computer programs that provide EMS equations and/or estimates of variance components use the σ^2 definitions (e.g., BMDP8V, Dixon, 1985; GENOVA, Crick & Brennan, 1983).

Comment

Suppose the model is mixed in the sense that, for every facet, the sample and universe size are identical or the universe size is infinite. In this case, it is possible to avoid arguments about definitions of variance components through using multivariate generalizability theory in which a random model is associated with each level of a fixed facet (see Cronbach et al., 1972, chapter 9; Brennan, 1983, section 6.5). Doing so is often preferable theoretically, but it is usually more complicated in at least some respects.

ESTIMATORS OF VARIANCE COMPONENTS

This section considers estimators of variance components for both balanced and unbalanced designs. A great deal of statistical literature has been devoted to this topic. The intent here is to summarize aspects of this literature in order to make judgments about the applicability of various estimation procedures for generalizability analyses.

ESTIMATORS FOR BALANCED DESIGNS

The most common procedure currently employed in generalizability theory for estimating variance components with balanced designs is called the ANOVA procedure and involves equating mean squares to their expected values, where the expected values are expressed in terms of σ^2 definitions of variance components. This set of simultaneous linear EMS equations can be solved to obtain unbiased estimates of the σ^2 variance components.

Given the definitions and model restrictions discussed in the previous section, these EMS equations are identical to those obtained using the Cornfield and Tukey (1956) procedures; or the so-called "EMS algorithm" described by Kirk (1982), Millman and Glass (1967), and Winer (1971). (For the types of designs typically encountered in generalizability theory, Brennan, 1983, p. 50 provides a general formula for these EMS equations.) It is especially important to note that the ANOVA procedure makes no normality assumptions. Also, contrary to some statements in current literature on generalizability theory, the ANOVA procedure does not assume that observed scores are from a continuous distribution.

Three approaches to implementing the ANOVA procedure have been discussed in the literature on generalizability theory. First, Cronbach et al. (1972) suggest solving the EMS equations by starting at the bottom, given the order in which the equations are usually expressed (as in Tables 2 and 3, for example), and working upwards. Using this approach with the equations in Table 2 we replace parameters with their estimators and obtain, for example,

$$
\begin{aligned}
MS(pi{:}h,e) &= \hat{\sigma}^2(pi{:}h,e) \text{ and} \\
MS(ph) &= \hat{\sigma}^2(pi{:}h,e) + k\hat{\sigma}^2(ph) \\
&= MS(pi{:}h,e) + k\hat{\sigma}^2(ph) ,
\end{aligned}
$$

which means that $\hat{\sigma}^2(ph) = [MS(ph) - MS(pi{:}h,e)]/k$. This approach is straightforward provided none of the estimates is negative. If any estimate is negative, Cronbach et al. (1972) suggest setting it to zero *everywhere* it occurs in the set of equations.

Second, Brennan (1983, p. 41) provides an algorithm that can be used to obtain estimated *random* effects variance components directly from mean squares without having to explicitly write out the EMS equations. Brennan (1983, p. 51) also provides a simple equation for using estimated random effects variance components to obtain estimated variance components for any model—again without explicitly writing out the EMS equations.

Third, one can obtain the estimates using the following matrix formulation (see Searle, 1971, pp. 405–406). Let m designate the total number of effects in the linear model (both main and interaction effects) for a design, let $\mathbf{P}$ be the $m \times m$ upper triangular matrix of coefficients of the variance components in the EMS equations, and let $\mathbf{a}$ be the $m \times 1$ vector of mean squares. Then $\hat{\boldsymbol{\sigma}}^2 = \mathbf{P}^{-1}\mathbf{a}$ is an $m \times 1$ vector whose elements are unbiased estimates of the variance components.

Brennan's (1983) algorithmic approach and the matrix approach provide identical results even if one or more of the estimates is negative, and all three approaches given identical results provided none of the estimates is negative. If one or more estimates is negative, however, then the Cronbach et al. (1972) approach will usually give *slightly* different results for one or more of the nonnegative estimates of variance components, and any altered estimates are no longer unbiased. For this reason, with negative estimates, strictly speaking the Cronbach et al. (1972) approach is not equivalent to the ANOVA procedure.

Since variance components are non-negative by definition, and since the general procedure of equating mean squares to their expected values can lead to negative estimates, the ANOVA procedure for estimating variance components is sometimes intensely criticized. In partial defense of this procedure, I would offer the following two comments.

First, the occurrence of one or more negative estimates usually indicates rather large sampling variability in the estimate(s). In such a case, it is reasonable to be circumspect about the interpretation and use of not only the negative estimate(s) but also (perhaps) other estimated variance components. From a rather pragmatic viewpoint, therefore, I find that the occurrence of one or more negative estimates can be a useful indicator of potential problems with a generalizability analysis.

Second, one can preclude the possibility of obtaining negative estimates by using maximum likelihood procedures (discussed later) or Bayesian procedures such as those discussed by Box and Tiao (1973). To do so, however, one must make a distributional form assumption (almost always normality) for the score effects. (No such assumption is required when one uses the ANOVA procedure.) Also, for the most part, the literature on Bayesian procedures for estimating variance components assumes a noninformative prior because it is difficult to incorporate an informative one. Finally, Bayesian results are currently available for only a limited number of designs. On balance, I am not convinced that it is generally worthwhile precluding the possibility of negative estimates at the expense of making additional assumptions about distributional form and a noninformative prior.

Next, consideration is given to procedures for estimating variance components for unbalanced designs. In principal, of course, procedures that are appropriate for unbalanced designs in generalizability theory could also be used with balanced designs. The ANOVA procedure has many advantages, however, including simplicity, widespread use, and computational ease. In addition, the ANOVA procedure gives locally best quadratic unbiased estimators of the variance components for balanced designs (see Searle, 1971, p. 470).

ESTIMATORS FOR UNBALANCED SITUATIONS[1]

Frequently, the term *unbalanced design* is something of a misnomer in that an unbalanced situation does not necessarily arise by design, especially when the unbalancing occurs because of missing observations, as opposed to nesting. Also, even when unbalancing occurs with respect to nesting, only, such lack of balance is frequently unintended. Consider, for example, the unbalanced $p \times (i{:}h)$ design with the i facet representing items and the h facet representing raters or judges. It is not uncommon that, for reasons beyond the investigator's control, judges rate unequal numbers of items and, therefore, the situation is unbalanced with respect to nesting as a result of less than ideal experimental control. By contrast, when tests are developed according to a table of specifications, it frequently occurs *by design* that unequal numbers of items are nested within content categories.

This distinction between an unbalanced "design" and an unbalanced "situation" seems to be conceptually useful in generalizability theory, because the theory itself places considerable emphasis on a priori considerations of a population, universe, and design. Unfortunately, however, the rather extensive statistical literature on unbalanced "designs" seldom makes this distinction.

Also, it should be noted that statistical discussions of both balanced and unbalanced situations with mixed models do not always clearly indicate the definitions of the variance components or the restrictions (or constraints), if any, that are employed. In particular, it is not always recognized that the general unbalanced mixed model typically presented in the literature (e.g., Searle, 1971, chapters 9 and 10) does *not* make restrictions similar to those in Equation 8. Consequently, the general unbalanced mixed model does *not* give results that are consistent with

---

[1]Parts of this section are edited versions of one major section in Brennan, Jarjoura, and Deaton (1980).

the assumptions of generalizability theory. In short, as pointed out by Hartley and Searle (1969), there exists a "discontinuity" between some treatments of the balanced mixed model (those using restrictions similar to Equation 8) and the general unbalanced mixed model. (From a slightly different perspective, consequences of using or not using restrictions have received recent attention by Samuels, Casella, & McCabe, 1991.)

Even with these caveats, however, Searle (1971, 1979) and Harville (1977) provide excellent reviews of procedures discussed in the statistical literature for estimating variance components in unbalanced situations (see also, Marcoulides, 1987; Rao & Kleffe, 1988). A brief overview of many of these procedures is provided below, followed by a discussion of some procedures for special consideration in generalizability theory.

ANOVA-Like Procedures

For unbalanced situations there are a number of procedures reported in the literature for estimating variance components that are similar to the basic ANOVA procedure for balanced designs—similar in that each involves the following steps: (1) calculate specified quadratic forms of the observations; (2) determine the expected values of the quadratic forms in terms of the variance components in the model; and (3) solve the set of simultaneous linear equations that result from equating the quadratic forms to their expected values.

It should be noted, however, that the choice of a procedure implies the choice of a set of quadratic forms, and different procedures sometimes produce quite disparate estimates. Even so, these procedures have certain desirable characteristics. For example, none requires assumptions about distributional form, and all produce the same estimates when used with balanced designs (i.e., they reduce to the basic ANOVA procedure). The ANOVA-like procedures briefly considered below are Henderson's (1953) methods, the analysis of means, and the use of symmetric sums.

For Henderson's method 1, the quadratic forms are very similar in appearance to the sum of squares for balanced designs. The quadratic forms are not always true sums of squares, however, as evidenced by the fact that they can be negative. Consequently, they are often referred to as "analogous" sums of squares. One difficulty with method 1 is that determining expected values can be an extensive algebraic exercise, although the process is considerably facilitated by using Hartley's (1967) method of "synthesis." It is important to note that Henderson's method 1 usually produces biased estimates of variance components with models involving fixed effects.

Henderson's method 2 was developed for use with mixed models. The observations are first adjusted by estimating the fixed effects in the model, and then method 1 is usually applied to these adjusted observations. The principal limitation of this approach is that it does not permit the possibility of including interactions between fixed and random effects in the model, and this limitation makes Henderson's method 2 virtually inapplicable in generalizability theory.

Henderson's method 3 provides unbiased estimates for any mixed model. It is often referred to as the fitting constants method because it employs reductions in sums of squares due to fitting specified submodels. The investigator must specify the order of fitting the submodels, however, and a change in the order usually results in a change in the variance component estimates. (The type I sums of squares in SAS, 1989, GLM and VARCOMP are those employed in Henderson's method 3.)

In the analysis of means procedure, the lack of balance in a design is "removed" by using subclass means in the calculation of quadratic forms. In this sense, a subclass mean is treated as a single observation. Either a weighted or an unweighted means analysis can be employed. Because of computational ease and conceptual simplicity, the analysis of means procedure appears attractive. In the context of generalizability theory, however, the procedure is often not defensible. Consider, for example, the $p \times (i{:}h)$ design with unequal numbers of items nested within subtests. If an investigator performs an analysis using the subtest means, then the analysis will confound variability due to subtests with variability due to items within subtests, and it will confound variability due to the person–subtest interaction with variability due to the interaction of persons and items within subtests. This type of confounding is problematic, at best, from the perspective of generalizability theory.

Koch (1968) developed a procedure based on certain "symmetric sums" of products of the observations. This procedure makes use of the fact that expected values of products of observations are linear functions of the variance components. The symmetric sums procedure can be viewed as a competitor to Henderson's Method 1 for completely random models. In particular, for the symmetric sums procedure the basis for the computing formulas is simple, expectations of symmetric sums are determinable beforehand, and tedious algebra is usually not required. Incidence sampling procedures (Sirotnik & Wellington, 1977) have similarities with the symmetric sums procedure, but incidence sampling procedures frequently necessitate a considerable amount of tedious algebra.

Maximum Likelihood Procedures

The maximum likelihood (ML) procedures suggested in the literature are based on the assumption of normality. They can be categorized into two basic approaches: general ML and restricted maximum likelihood (REML). With the general ML approach, fixed effects and variance components are estimated simultaneously, while they are obtained separately in REML. For both procedures the variance component estimates are nonnegative and invariant with respect to values of the fixed effects. REML is usually more convenient, and with balanced designs REML produces the same estimates as the ANOVA procedure except when negative variance component estimates are obtained. Even when negative estimates do occur, at least some research suggests that the ANOVA and REML sets of estimates tend to be quite similar in generalizability analyses (see, for example, Marcoulides, 1987, pp. 91ff).

A principal advantage of maximum likelihood procedures is that the estimates have certain desirable properties, that is, they are functions of sufficient statistics, asymptotically normal and efficient, and provide asymptotic variances and covariances of the estimates. However, these properties depend on the normality assumptions.

MINQUE

Minimum norm quadratic unbiased estimation (MINQUE) is a general theoretical framework developed by Rao (1971). No assumptions about distributional form are required, and the variance component estimates are designed to be invariant with respect to fixed effects. The estimates are quadratic functions of the observations, which are determined through the minimization of a suitable norm. Minimization involves the calculation of certain matrix products and generalized inverses associated with the design matrix. Weights are used in the estimation process and are chosen a priori to correspond to the relative sizes of the variance components.

A special case of MINQUE, sometimes referred to as MIVQUE0, was developed by Hartley, Rao, and LaMotte (1978) and uses a priori weights of zero except for the residual variance components.[2] MIVQUE0 is also a special case of the first iterate solution of the REML equations of Corbeil and Searle (1976). The development of the MIVQUE0 algorithm was motivated by a need for a computationally efficient method for estimating variance components when the number of observations is large. MIVQUE0 estimates have a number of "optimality properties," including being asymptotically consistent and locally best quadratic unbiased estimators (see Hartley et al., 1978, p. 238).

Many of the procedures outlined above for estimating variance components in unbalanced situations are conceptually complex, and some

---

[2]Marcoulides (1987) argues that MIVQUE0 is not appropriate in generalizability theory because in generalizability theory, he says, it is desirable that the residual variance be small relative to universe score variance. While it is desirable that this occur, almost always the residual variance component is relatively large. Indeed, a principal reason for using average (or total) scores over conditions of measurement, rather than single scores, is to reduce the effect of the residual error on generalizability.

involve normality assumptions. Also, for generalizability analyses involving mixed models, an investigator should be aware of the way in which variance components are defined and make sure that the restrictions discussed previously are taken into account. Furthermore, for generalizability analyses, many of these procedures are computationally burdensome, if not impractical, in part because the usual designs employed in generalizability analyses have (at most) one observation per cell, which means that design matrices are often prohibitively large. Given these considerations, it can be argued that, when a procedure is computationally straightforward and conceptually clear, for a given unbalanced situation, that procedure may be preferred in a practical sense.

Procedures for Special Consideration in Generalizability Theory

For unbalanced completely nested situations, straightforward and unambiguous ANOVA solutions exist for the random effects model (see, for examples, Edelman, 1974; Gates & Shiue, 1962; Gower, 1962; and Searle, 1971, pp. 473–479).

Also, for the $p \times (i{:}h)$ design, when unbalancing exists with respect to nesting only (not with respect to missing data), Henderson's method 3 yields only one decomposition of the total sums of squares, no matter what logical ordering is used to obtain reductions in sums of squares. Furthermore, this decomposition yields the sums of squares for Henderson's method 1 (the ANOVA procedure). It follows that, by expressing expected mean squares in a very general form, unbiased estimates of variance components can be obtained for random models (see Jarjoura & Brennan, 1981). These sums of squares can also be used to obtain estimates of variance components for a mixed model with h fixed, but a better approach is to employ multivariate generalizability theory.

In multivariate generalizability theory (see Cronbach et al., 1972, chapter 9; Brennan, 1983, section 6.5), each object of measurement (e.g., a person) has multiple universe scores, with each such universe score associated with a level of a fixed facet, or a combination of levels of two or more fixed facets. Consider, for example, the $p \times (i{:}h)$ design with unequal numbers of items nested within $r = R$ fixed levels of h. In this case, estimation can proceed as follows: (1) estimate the variance components for the r balanced $p \times i$ designs using the ANOVA procedure, and (2) estimate the universe score covariances by computing the observed covariances between person mean scores for the pairs of levels of h.

Cronbach et al. (1972), Shavelson and Webb (1981), and Webb, Shavelson, and Maddahian (1983) provide examples of estimating variance and covariance components using multivariate generalizability theory with more complicated designs. One of the distinct advantages of multivariate generalizability theory is that estimation for unbalanced, mixed models is only slightly more complicated than for balanced, mixed models as long as the unbalancing is with respect to nesting, only. Furthermore, multivariate generalizability approaches to estimation with mixed models (balanced or unbalanced) produce a richer set of results that are, in some ways, easier to interpret than the results obtained using other procedures that average results over the levels of a fixed facet (or facets).

Other Procedures

Another procedure recommended by Cronbach et al. (1972) for unbalanced situations involves categorizing conditions into sets of conditions such as half-tests, and performing analyses in terms of these sets of conditions. This procedure has similarities with an unweighted means analysis, but it does not involve the type of confounding described in the discussion of the analysis of means procedures. However, estimates obtained using this procedure can be influenced by which conditions happen to be assigned to which half-test.

Finally, no discussion of approaches to estimation in unbalanced situations would be complete without referencing the frequently employed procedure of randomly discarding data to make an inherently unbalanced situation into an apparently balanced one. The advisability of employing this procedure is usually inversely related to the amount of data discarded. Unfortunately, too frequently in generalizability analyses this procedure necessitates discarding so much data that one wonders about the credibility of the procedure and the stability of resulting estimates.

COMPUTER PROGRAMS

Brennan (1983) provides a discussion of computer programs for use in generalizability analyses. Although his discussion is somewhat dated, parts of it are still applicable. As he points out, in evaluating computer programs for use in generalizability theory it is necessary to be sensitive to underlying assumptions in the estimation procedure. It is especially important for mixed models that the estimation procedure take into account the restrictions previously discussed. Also, since the designs usually employed in generalizability theory have one observation per cell, often design matrices are *very* large, especially when the number of persons is large. (This author often encounters designs with over 100,000 cells.) With virtual memory, large design matrices are less problematic, but computational efficiency is still a relevant concern.

BMDP8V (Dixon, 1985), GENOVA (Crick & Brennan, 1983), and SAS VARCOMP (SAS, 1989) are the principal, general purpose programs that directly provide estimated variance components. These programs are widely available and relatively well known to the measurement community. (For completely nested, random effects designs SAS NESTED can be employed with both balanced and unbalanced data.)

Both BMDP8V and GENOVA are appropriate for generalizability analyses with balanced designs. For mixed models they both employ model restrictions. Also, they are both very fast, easy to use, and pretty much unrestricted with respect to the size of the design matrix. The principal advantage of GENOVA is that it was written specifically for generalizability analyses and, therefore, it provides many types of output that are tailored to generalizability theory.

The SAS VARCOMP procedure provides estimates of variance components using four procedures: Type I (which is essentially Henderson's method 3), MIVQUEO, ML, and REML, with the default procedure being MIVQUEO (BMDP3V also provides REML estimates). For balanced random effects designs with no negative estimates, the type I, MIVQUEO and REML estimated variance components are identical, and they are the same as those provided by BMDP8V and GENOVA. For balanced random effects designs with negative estimates the type I and MIVQUEO results are the same as those provided by BMDP8V and GENOVA. For unbalanced designs, however, the four procedures in SAS VARCOMP give different estimates.

Most importantly, however, as implemented in SAS *none* of the four procedures employ the restrictions discussed previously for mixed models in generalizability theory. Therefore, with mixed models SAS VARCOMP is *not* appropriate for use in generalizability theory, except perhaps to get the type I (Henderson's Method 3) sums of squares and compute appropriate variance component estimates using these sums of squares.[3]

In a review of MIVQUEO in SAS, Bell (1985) suggests that, all things considered, MIVQUEO is currently the best general-purpose alternative for unbalanced designs in generalizability theory. Bell's suggestion seems sensible, *provided* the model is random. Even though MIVQUEO was designed to be computationally efficient, however, it still makes very heavy use of computer resources with designs of the type employed in many generalizability analyses (see Chastain & Willson, 1986).

VARIABILITY OF ESTIMATED VARIANCE COMPONENTS[4]

Estimated variance components are subject to sampling variability and, in general, the smaller the sample sizes the larger the variability.

---

[3]When SAS ANOVA is employed with an unbalanced design, it appears to provide the so-called "analogous" ANOVA sums of squares used in Henderson's Method 1 procedure.

[4]This section is largely a summary of Brennan et al., 1987.

Procedures for examining the variability of estimated variance components have been surveyed by Cronbach et al. (1972, pp. 49–57) and more recently Smith (1978, 1982), Brennan (1983, 1984), and Brennan, Harris, and Hanson (1987) have addressed this issue in the context of generalizability theory.

The variability of estimated variance components can be addressed through reporting estimated standard errors and/or confidence intervals. Unfortunately, however, one of the most serious limitations of the vast majority of published generalizability studies is that they report neither estimated standard errors nor approximate confidence intervals for estimated variance components. This is especially problematic for studies (and there are many of them) that employ small sample sizes. Disclaimers such as "of course, estimated variance components are subject to sampling variability" are seldom, if ever, sufficient for meaningful interpretation of the magnitudes of estimated variance components.

In principal, standard errors of estimated variance components can be estimated by replicating a study several times and directly computing the standard deviations of the resulting sets of estimated variance components. Indeed, in theory, this procedure may be preferred over others because it is conceptually straightforward, it is empirically based without assumptions about distributional form, and it is directly related to a basic notion in generalizability theory, namely, generalizing over randomly parallel sets of conditions from a universe. In the context of generalizability theory, however, this procedure has been applied only rarely (e.g., Colton, 1983; Jarjoura & Brennan, 1982, 1983) for the obvious reason that multiple, randomly parallel data sets are difficult to obtain.

Because replicated studies are seldom feasible, the procedures discussed below involve data from a single study only. The price paid for employing only one study is either strong statistical assumptions or extensive computation.

TRADITIONAL PROCEDURE

The traditional (i.e., usual) approach to examining the variability of estimated variance components makes normal distribution assumptions. In particular, Searle (1971, pp. 415–417) shows that, under the assumptions that score effects have a multivariate normal distribution, and estimated variance components are linear combinations of independent mean squares, an estimator of the standard error of an estimated variance components is:

$$\hat{\sigma}[\hat{\sigma}^2(\alpha|M)] = \sqrt{\sum_j \frac{2(f_j MS_j)^2}{df_j + 2}} \, , \tag{9}$$

where M designates the specific model under consideration, j indexes the mean squares (MS) that enter $\hat{\sigma}^2(\alpha|M)$, and f_j is the coefficient of MS_j in the linear combination of the MS_j that gives $\hat{\sigma}^2(\alpha|M)$. Technically, $\hat{\sigma}[\hat{\sigma}^2(\alpha|M)]$ in Equation 9 is not unbiased although its square is an unbiased estimator of the variance of $\hat{\sigma}^2(\alpha|M)$.

The form of Equation 9 suggests that the standard error of $\hat{\sigma}^2(\alpha|M)$ will usually decrease as the degrees of freedom for the means squares that enter α increase. Also, Equation 9 suggests that, for estimated variance components that involve several mean squares, the estimated standard errors are likely (although not necessarily) larger than for estimated variance components that involve fewer mean squares.

Even though, under normality assumptions, it is relatively simple to obtain an unbiased estimate of the variance of estimates of a variance component, the exact distribution of estimates of a variance component is usually very complex. Consequently, with few exceptions (see Searle, 1971, p. 414), formulas for exact confidence intervals for variance components are unavailable, even under the assumption that the score effects have a multivariate normal distribution.

When the multivariate normality assumption is met and degrees of freedom are very large, a simple normal approximation to a $100(P)\%$ confidence interval for $\sigma^2(\alpha|M)$ is $\hat{\sigma}^2(\alpha|M) \pm (z)\hat{\sigma}[\hat{\sigma}^2(\alpha|M)]$, where z is the normal deviate corresponding to the $(1 + P)/2$ upper percentage point (see Welch, 1956, p. 136). With even moderately large degrees of freedom, however, the normal approximation may be quite inaccurate. In particular, the computed upper limit is frequently too small, which gives an interval that is too short.

The literature suggests that, under the assumption of multivariate normality, a usually better procedure of obtaining approximate confidence intervals is one attributed to Satterthwaite (1941, 1946) and summarized by Graybill (1976, pp. 642–643). Brennan (1983, p. 137) demonstrates that Satterthwaite's procedure can be employed very easily using the ratio of an estimated variance component to its estimated standard error.

JACKKNIFE PROCEDURE

Quenouille (1949) invented a nonparametric estimator of bias, subsequently called the jackknife, although the term *jackknife* is usually associated with Tukey, probably because of his extension of Quenouille's idea to a nonparametric estimator of the standard error of a statistic (Tukey, 1958). An often referenced overview of the jackknife is given by Mosteller and Tukey (1968) who also discuss how to use the jackknife in obtaining confidence intervals.

Suppose θ is some parameter of interest and one obtains a set of s

data points to estimate θ. In general terms, the steps involved in using the jackknife are as follows: (1) obtain $\hat{\theta}$ for all s data points; (2) obtain the s estimates of θ that result from eliminating each one of the data points, and let each such estimate be designated $\hat{\theta}_{-j}$; (3) obtain the s "pseudo-values" $\hat{\theta}_{*j} = \hat{\theta} + (s-1)(\hat{\theta} - \hat{\theta}_{-j})$; (4) obtain the jackknife estimator of θ, $\hat{\theta}_J$, which is the mean of the pseudovalues; (5) obtain the estimate of the standard error of the jackknife estimate of θ:

$$\hat{\sigma}(\hat{\theta}_J) = \left\{ \sum_{j=1}^{s} (\hat{\theta}_{*j} - \hat{\theta}_J)^2 / [s(s-1)] \right\}^{1/2},$$

which is simply the sample standard deviation of the pseudovalues divided by $\sqrt{s}$; and (vi), if desired, obtain the jackknife 100(P)% percent confidence interval for θ:

$$\hat{\theta}_J - t\hat{\sigma}(\hat{\theta}_J) \leq \theta \leq \hat{\theta}_J + t\hat{\sigma}(\hat{\theta}_J),$$

where t is the $(1+P)/2$ upper percentage point of Student's t distribution with $s - 1$ degrees of freedom. The extension of the steps 1 to 5 to estimated variance components resulting from data for a random effects $p \times i$ design is provided in appendix A. The basic steps are those outlined above, but several of the steps are quite a bit more complicated conceptually and computationally.

Bootstrap Procedure

The bootstrap is a general methodology for assessing how accurate a particular $\hat{\theta}$ is as an estimate of θ (see Efron, 1982, for a comprehensive theoretical treatment and Efron & Tibshirani, 1986, for a simpler and more applied treatment). The bootstrap substitutes considerable amounts of computation for traditional, theoretical analysis. Furthermore, the bootstrap need not (and usually does not) involve any assumptions about distributional form. In this sense, it is (usually) a completely nonparametric procedure.

The bootstrap algorithm is based on the results of multiple bootstrap samples, where each bootstrap sample consists of a random sample of size t drawn *with replacement* from the actual sample of size t. The three steps in the algorithm are: (1) using a random number generator, independently draw a large number of bootstrap samples, say B of them; (2) for each sample evaluate the statistic of interest, say $\hat{\theta}_b(b = 1, 2, \ldots, B)$; and (3) calculate the sample standard deviation of the $\hat{\theta}_b$, which is the bootstrap standard error:

$$\hat{\sigma}(\hat{\theta}_b) = \left\{ \frac{1}{B-1} \sum_{b=1}^{B} (\hat{\theta}_b - \hat{\theta}_\cdot)^2 \right\}^{1/2}$$

where

$$\hat{\theta}_\cdot = \sum_{b=1}^{B} \hat{\theta}_b / B$$

will be called here the "bootstrap estimate" of θ. For estimating standard errors, B in the range of 50 to 200 is quite adequate according to Efron and Tibshirani (1986, p. 56).

The bootstrap can also be used to produce approximate confidence intervals. For example, an 80% approximate confidence interval for θ can be defined as the 10th and 90th percentile points of the distribution of the $\hat{\theta}_b$. For confidence intervals, however, the computational requirements are more substantial. Usually, one wants $B \geq 1000$ bootstrap samples (see Efron & Tibshirani, 1986, p. 67).

Although the bootstrap is conceptually simple in univariate situations, it is unclear how to extend it to estimates of variance components for designs typically used in generalizability theory. Consider, for example, the random effects $p \times i$ design with each of n sampled persons taking each of k sampled items. The crux of the matter is to specify how to draw a bootstrap sample from the $n \times k$ matrix of observed scores. It might seem that the obvious way to do so is: (1) draw a random sample of n persons with replacement from the sampled persons; (2) draw an independent random sample of k items with replacement from the sampled items; and (3) let the bootstrap sample consist of the responses of the sampled persons to the sampled items. This double sampling procedure will be denoted "boot-p,i."

The boot-p,i procedure seems obvious in that it is similar to the random sampling process that generates the observed $n \times k$ data matrix. It is important to note, however, that the boot-p,i procedure involves sampling *with replacement* from the observed data. This means that, except when the bootstrap sample is identical to the observed sample, the bootstrap sample matrix will contain some repeated persons and/or some repeated items. For the ANOVA estimators of $\sigma^2(p)$ and $\sigma^2(i)$ with the $p \times i$ design, this replication of some persons and items seems likely to occasionally lead to inflated estimates of $\sigma^2(p)$ and $\sigma^2(i)$ for bootstrap samples. This seems obvious when one recognizes, for example, that the ANOVA estimator of $\sigma^2(p)$ is a function of the average of the unbiased estimates of the $k(k-1)$ item covariances. Clearly, if there are repeated items, then some of these covariances will be artificially inflated (relative to the expected value of the covariance), and this problem should be exacerbated by small values of k. A similar line of reasoning suggests that the bootstrap estimate of $\sigma^2(i)$ is likely to be inflated, especially for small values of n. Now, since the "inflation factor" will not be the same for all bootstrap samples, it seems sensible to have some doubts about the accuracy of the bootstrap estimates of the standard errors under this double sampling procedure.

The reasoning in the above paragraph is admittedly ad hoc, but it does suggest that the double sampling in the boot-p,i procedure *may* produce suspect results. Consequently, one might want to consider obtaining bootstrap samples by sampling only one dimension. Two such procedures are possible. The "boot-p" procedure involves sampling n persons with replacement, but not items. The "boot-i" procedure involves sampling k items with replacement, but not persons. The boot-p and boot-i procedures keep items and persons fixed, respectively, in obtaining bootstrap sample. Since results are wanted for the situation in which both persons and items are random, one might expect that neither of these procedures would be completely satisfactory for all variance components.

Efron (1982) considers in some detail similarities and dissimilarities between the bootstrap and the jackknife. Both are based on resampling models and are primarily nonparametric procedures. As such, they are quite flexible and seem to have considerable appeal in complicated contexts. For the context here, however, an important difference is that the bootstrap involves sampling with replacement while the jackknife does not.

SOME SIMULATION RESULTS

To examine the traditional, jackknife, and bootstrap procedures, Brennan et al. (1987) employed a small simulation study using normally distributed data and more extensive simulations using binary data. For purposes of simplicity, without too much loss of generality, they employed the $p \times i$ design, only.

For the normal data, the traditional approach worked very well, which is to be expected since this approach assumes the score effects are normally distributed. The jackknife procedure also provided very accurate estimates of standard errors and confidence intervals for estimates of variance components. For the bootstrap procedure, however, the results were mixed.

With normal data there seems to be no compelling reason to use any procedure more complicated than the traditional one. In the vast majority of generalizability analyses, however, it is unreasonable to assume that the score effects are normally distributed. This assumption is particularly unreasonable with binary data.

To examine the three approaches with binary data, Brennan et al. (1987) used a subset of a real data set consisting of a finite population of $N = 2000$ persons and a finite universe of $K = 200$ items. Let the population, universe, and grand means be μ_p, μ_i, and μ respectively. Then the linear model can be represented as

$$X_{pi} = \mu + (\mu_p - \mu) + (\mu_i - \mu) + (X_{pi} - \mu_p - \mu_i + \mu)$$
$$= \mu + v_p + v_i + v_{pi,e} ,$$

where $v_{pi,e}$ represents the confounded effect of the (p,i) interaction and other sources of error. For this model, based on the Cornfield & Tukey (1956) definitions, the variance components are

$$\sigma^2(p) = \sum_{p=1}^{N} v_p^2/(N - 1),$$

$$\sigma^2(i) = \sum_{i=1}^{K} v_i^2/(K - 1), \quad \text{and}$$

$$\sigma^2(pi,e) = \sum_{p=1}^{N} \sum_{i=1}^{K} v_{pi,e}^2/[(N - 1)(K - 1)].$$

[Since the context here is a finite population and universe, each of the variance components could be designated more explicitly $\sigma^2(\alpha|P,I)$ to be consistent with previous notation. Here $\sigma^2(\alpha)$ is used for simplicity.] For these variance components, the ANOVA estimators for a sample of n persons and k items are

$$\hat{\sigma}^2(p) \quad = [MS(p) - (1-k/K)MS(pi,e)]/k,$$
$$\hat{\sigma}^2(i) \quad = [MS(i) - (1-n/N)MS(pi,e)]/n, \text{ and}$$
$$\hat{\sigma}^2(pi,e) = MS(pi,e).$$

For the finite population of 2000 persons and the finite universe of 200 items, $\sigma^2(p)$, $\sigma^2(i)$, and $\sigma^2(pi,e)$ are reported in the last row of Table 4 (labeled "Parameters"), along with standard errors of estimated variance components for $n = 200$ and $k = 20$. These standard errors are the standard deviations of the distributions of $\hat{\sigma}^2(p)$, $\hat{\sigma}^2(i)$, and $\hat{\sigma}^2(pi,e)$ resulting from 200 random samples of size $n = 200$ and $k = 20$ from the finite population and universe. Technically, these standard errors are approximations, but they were judged to be sufficiently accurate to be viewed as parameters.

TABLE 4. Traditional, Bootstrap, and Jackknife Estimates of Variance
Components and Their Standard Errors for Binary Data Based on Random
Samples (Trials) of Size $n = 200$ and $k = 20$ From a Finite Population and
Universe of Sizes $N = 2000$ and $K = 200$, Respectively

	Persons		Items		Interaction	
Procedure	$\hat{\sigma}^2(p)$	$\hat{\sigma}[\hat{\sigma}^2(p)]$	$\hat{\sigma}^2(i)$	$\hat{\sigma}[\hat{\sigma}^2(i)]$	$\hat{\sigma}^2(pi,e)$	$\hat{\sigma}[\hat{\sigma}^2(pi,e)]$
Traditional	.0067	.0015	.0350	.0116	.1903	.0044
Boot-p	.0069[a]	.0016[a]	.0360	.0025	.1898[a]	.0033[a]
Boot-i	.0164	.0043	.0334[b]	.0098[b]	.1901[b]	.0121[b]
Boot-p,i	.0161	.0047	.0039	.0103	.1911[c]	.0123[c]
Jackknife	.0068	.0021	.0344	.0101	.1905	.0116
Parameters	.0068	.0021	.0346	.0101	.1902	.0118

[a]Computed estimates multipled by the bias correction factor $n/(n - 1) = 1.00503$.
[b]Computed estimates multipled by the bias correction factor $k/(k - 1) = 1.05263$.
[c]Computed estimates multipled by the bias correction factor $[n/(n = 1)][k/(k - 1)] = 1.05792$.
Note. An individual trial involves sampling without replacement from the population and universe,
whereas a bootstrap sample involves sampling with replacement from the person and/or item vectors
constituting a given trial.

Standard Errors

The results in Table 4 for the traditional procedure are means over
1000 trials, with each trial consisting of a random sample (without replacement) of size $n = 200$ and $k = 20$. The most noticeable result about
the traditional procedure is that the standard error of $\hat{\sigma}^2(pi,e)$ is *dramatically* underestimated. Also, the estimated standard error for $\hat{\sigma}^2(p)$ is too
small.

The bootstrap results in Table 4 involved taking 100 random samples
(trials) of size $n = 200$ and $k = 20$ with $B = 100$ bootstrap samples per
trial. (Note that each trial involved independent random sampling *without* replacement.) Consider, for example, the boot-p results for persons.
Since there were 100 trials, there were 100 values of $\hat{\sigma}^2(p)$, with each
value being the average $\hat{\sigma}_b^2(p)$ for 100 bootstrap samples. The mean, over
the 100 trials, of the $\hat{\sigma}^2(p)$ was .0069. Similarly, there were 100 values of
$\hat{\sigma}[\hat{\sigma}_b^2(p)]$ with each value being the standard deviation of the $\hat{\sigma}_b^2(p)$ for 100
bootstrap samples. The mean, over 100 trials, of the $\hat{\sigma}[\hat{\sigma}_b^2(p)]$ was .0016.

Note that the boot-p,i results for $\hat{\sigma}^2(p)$ and its estimated standard
error are poor. The bootstrap estimate of $\sigma^2(p)$ is much too high, and the
bootstrap estimate of the standard error of $\hat{\sigma}^2(p)$ is much too low. This is
consistent with the concern expressed previously about using boot-p,i for
$\hat{\sigma}^2(p)$ and its estimated standard error, especially when k is small. (Recall
that here $k = 20$.) On the other hand, the boot-p,i results for $\sigma^2(i)$ and its
estimated standard error are quite close to the parameter values. This

difference in performance of boot-p,i for persons and items is probably attributable to the fact that there are 10 times mores persons than items in the data matrix ($n = 200$).

All things considered, the bootstrap results in Table 4 suggest that boot-p is preferable for the estimated variance component and standard error for persons, boot-i is preferable for the estimated variance component and standard error for items, and boot-p,i and boot-i provide quite accurate results for the residuals. Note, however, that even though boot-p is preferable to boot-i and boot-p,i for estimating the standard error of $\hat{\sigma}^2(p)$, this standard error is still not very well estimated. The parameter value is .0021, and the boot-p estimate is .0016 with a standard deviation of .003 (not reported in Table 4).

In Table 4 the jackknife estimates of variance components and standard errors are based on 1000 trials, with each trial consisting of a random sample (without replacement) of size $n = 200$ and $k = 20$. All variance components and standard errors appear to be very well estimated by the jackknife. (Cronbach et al. [1972] suggest jackknifing the logarithm of the estimated variance components, but doing so for this simulation provided less accurate results. Therefore, in Table 4 and elsewhere the jackknife results are *not* based on logarithms.)

Confidence Intervals

Brennan et al. (1987) also report results for computing 1000 Satterthwaite and jackknife confidence intervals for each variance component using nominal coverage coefficients of 50, 80, and 90%. The percents of intervals that actually covered the parameters are reported in Table 5. Comparable bootstrap results were not obtained because doing so would have required $B \geq 1000$ bootstrap samples for boot-p, boot-i, and boot-p,i for each of the 1000 trials. This was judged to be excessively expensive.

For the Satterthwaite intervals, the actual coverages for $\sigma^2(p)$ are somewhat low, and the actual coverages for $\sigma^2(i)$ are somewhat high.

TABLE 5. Confidence Interval Coverage Results for Satterthwaite and Jackknife Procedures for Binary Data and 1000 Trials

| Normal Coverage (%) | Actual Coverage (%) | | | | | |
| | Satterthwaite | | | Jackknife | | |
	$\sigma^2(p)$	$\sigma^2(i)$	$\sigma^2(pi,e)$	$\sigma^2(p)$	$\sigma^2(i)$	$\sigma^2(pi,e)$
50	49.5	54.0	19.2	51.3	49.7	48.1
80	72.4	83.9	36.8	78.9	76.4	77.2
90	85.3	93.2	46.0	87.4	84.2	86.9

Most importantly, however, the actual coverages for $\sigma^2(pi,e)$ are dramatically too low, which means that the confidence intervals for $\sigma^2(pi,e)$ using Satterthwaite's procedure are *much* too narrow with binary data. This result is consistent with the excessively low value for $\hat{\sigma}[\hat{\sigma}^2(pi,e)]$ using the traditional approach (see Table 4). Clearly, the fact that binary data violate the normality assumptions in Satterthwaite's procedure causes this procedure to work poorly for the residual variance component.

Almost without exception, the actual coverages for the jackknife intervals are somewhat too low, implying that the intervals are a little bit too narrow. However, the results in Table 5 for the jackknife suggest that, all things considered, the jackknife provides confidence intervals that are quite accurate.

Summary

In the judgment of this author, these simulation results suggest that, for binary data: (1) the traditional procedure is suspect, especially for estimating the standard error of $\hat{\sigma}^2(pi,e)$; (2) the jackknife procedure works very well; and (3) the bootstrap procedure can be "made to work" reasonably well by using boot-p for persons, boot-i for items, and boot-p,i for residuals, but generally the bootstrap gives less accurate results than the jackknife, and the bootstrap confidence intervals are relatively expensive to obtain. For normal data, the traditional approach works quite well.

RECOMMENDATIONS AND CONCLUSIONS

As discussed in this chapter, procedures in the statistical literature for estimating variance components are not always appropriate in generalizability theory for any one of four reasons.

First, some procedures for mixed models do not employ restrictions (or constraints) of the type in Equation 8. These restrictions are crucial in generalizability theory because they are a consequence of certain aspects of the conceptual framework of the theory—in particular, the manner in which population and universe mean scores and score effects are defined. Second, some procedures make normality assumptions which may be inappropriate for some generalizability analyses, especially those with binary data. Third, some procedures directly or indirectly assume that certain interactions are zero, which is highly questionable in most generalizability analyses. Fourth, many procedures are so computationally intensive that they are impractical for many generalizability analyses. This is largely a consequence of the fact that most generalizability designs have one observation per cell, which leads to very large design matrices whenever there are a large number of persons and/or conditions of measurement (e.g., items)—a rather common occurrence.

For all of these reasons, care needs to be exercised when employing general-purpose statistical packages in generalizability analyses. For balanced designs, all things considered, BMDP8V and GENOVA are likely to be the best alternatives in most cases.

For unbalanced designs, SAS VARCOMP's MIVQUEO may be the best alternative in many cases *provided* the model is random. If the model is mixed, it may be reasonable to use the random effects estimated variance components to estimate mixed model results using a formula provided by Brennan (1983, p. 51). For example, letting $\hat{\sigma}^2(p)$ and $\hat{\sigma}^2(ph)$ be random effects estimated variance components, then for the mixed model with h fixed ($r = R$), the estimated variance component for persons is $\hat{\sigma}^2(p|H) = \hat{\sigma}^2(p) + \hat{\sigma}^2(ph)/r$. With unbalanced data, however, the properties of the resulting estimates for the mixed model are unknown, and if the design is purposely unbalanced this approach may be unacceptable a priori.

Alternatively, for designs that are unbalanced with respect to nesting, only, in principle a multivariate generalizability analysis can be performed in which there is a random effects design for each level of the conditions of one or more fixed facets. (See, for example, Brennan, 1983, p. 113.) Indeed, this approach corresponds well with Scheffé's (1959) treatment of mixed models. Also, from the perspective of generalizability theory, a multivariate analysis is preferable, in principal, because generalizability theory is primarily a random effects theory (see Shavelson & Webb, 1981).

No matter how variance components are estimated, they are always subject to sampling variability. The traditional approach to estimating the standard errors of estimated variance components, as well as confidence intervals, is relatively simple to employ, but it makes normality assumptions that are likely violated in many generalizability analyses, especially those with binary data. In principle, jackknife and bootstrap procedures are alternatives to the traditional approach. A limited number of simulations suggest that the jackknife procedure work quite well, and the bootstrap can be "made to work" reasonably well.

Both the jackknife and bootstrap procedures are computationally very intensive, even for relatively simple designs and moderate sample sizes, and especially for establishing confidence intervals. Also, no computer programs are generally available that employ the jackknife or bootstrap procedures. (GENOVA provides estimated standard errors using the traditional approach.) Therefore, in the near future, the traditional approach is probably the only viable alternative for most users of generalizability theory. What this paper suggests, however, is that the results of the traditional approach (especially for residual variance components) should be interpreted with caution when the score effects are not normally distributed.

Probably no discussion of variance components in generalizability theory would be complete without some consideration of random sampling issues. Generalizability theory is, after all, a sampling theory. This was emphasized early in this paper when population and universe issues were introduced. One of the most frequently voiced criticisms of generalizability theory is the assumption of random sampling. In some contexts such criticisms seem moot. For example, given a well-defined item pool, or rules for generating items from item forms, it is possible to closely approximate the assumption of random sampling (Bock, 1972). In other contexts, random sampling assumptions can be viewed as useful idealizations.

This latter point has been made by Lord and Novick (1968) who argue that:

> A possible objection to the item-sampling model (for example, see Loevinger, 1965) is that one does not ordinarily build tests by drawing items at random from a pool. There is, however, a similar and equally strong objection to classical test theory: Classical theory requires test forms that are parallel, and yet no one has ever produced two strictly parallel forms for any ordinary paper-and-pencil test. Classical test theory is to be considered a useful idealization of situations encountered with actual mental tests. The assumption of random sampling of items may be considered in the same way. Further, even if the items of a particular test have not actually been drawn at random, we can still make certain interesting projections: We can conceive an item population from which the items of the test might have been randomly drawn and then consider the score the examinee would be expected to achieve over this population. The abundant information available on such expected scores enhances their natural interest to the examiner. (p. 235)

In a similar vein, but in the broader context of inferential statistics, Cornfield and Tukey (1956, pp. 912–913) justify random sampling assumptions using their classic bridge analogy.

Also, any inferential theory involves certain assumptions about random sampling, independence, or uncorrelated effects that are likely to be idealized to some extent. Some investigators seem to view independence assumptions and/or assumptions about uncorrelated effects more positively than random sampling assumptions. When one asks how such assumptions might be fulfilled, however, one usually reverts, in part, to random sampling explanations.

Finally, generalizability theory does not dictate that, say, all items in a test be considered a random sample from the same undifferentiated universe. (Recall, for example, previous discussion of the $p \times [i{:}h]$ design with items nested within cells of a table of specifications.) Almost always, one can structure a universe in such a way that random sampling assumptions are a more realistic idealization. Doing so may lead to more complex, multifaceted universes, but serious consideration of universes usually reveals that they are in fact complex, without even considering sampling assumptions.

On balance, then, this author is usually persuaded that the random sampling assumptions in generalizability theory are defensible as useful idealizations. However, each application of generalizability theory (or any measurement theory, for that matter) is a special case that needs to be evaluated on its own merits with respect to the match between assumptions and data/design issues.

ACKNOWLEDGMENTS: The author gratefully acknowledges that various parts of this paper summarize work performed by Bradley A. Hanson, Deborah J. Harris, and David Jarjoura in collaboration with the author.

APPENDIX: JACKKNIFE ESTIMATES AND THEIR STANDARD ERRORS FOR THE $P \times I$ RANDOM EFFECTS DESIGN

Based on advice from John Tukey, Cronbach et al. (1972, pp. 54–57, 66, 70–72) outline a jackknife procedure for estimating the standard errors of estimated variance components. Collins (1970) also discusses jackknifing estimated variance components. Provided below is an outline of how to employ the jackknife with the $p \times i$ design.

Consider the following notational conventions:

$\hat{\theta}$ = any estimated variance component for the $p \times i$ design based on analyzing the full $n \times k$ matrix—i.e., $\hat{\theta}$ could be

$$\hat{\sigma}^2(p) = [MS(p) - (1-k/K)MS(pi,e)]/k, \qquad (A1)$$

$$\hat{\sigma}^2(i) = [MS(i) - (1-n/N)MS(pi,e)]/n, \text{ or} \qquad (A2)$$

$$\hat{\sigma}^2(pi,e) = MS(pi,e); \qquad (A3)$$

$\hat{\theta}_{-pi}$ = value of $\hat{\theta}$ for the $(n-1) \times (k-1)$ matrix that results from eliminating person p and item i;

$\hat{\theta}_{-po}$ = value of $\hat{\theta}$ for $(n-1) \times k$ matrix that results from eliminating person p;

$\hat{\theta}_{-oi}$ = value of $\hat{\theta}$ for the $n \times (k-1)$ matrix that results from eliminating item i;

$\hat{\theta}_{-oo}$ = value of $\hat{\theta}$ for original $n \times k$ matrix (i.e., $\hat{\theta} = \hat{\theta}_{-oo}$). Now, the pseudovalue for person p and item i is:

$$\hat{\theta}_{*pi} = nk\hat{\theta}_{-oo} - (n-1)k\hat{\theta}_{-po} - n(k-1)\hat{\theta}_{-oi}$$
$$+ (n-1)(k-1)\hat{\theta}_{-pi}. \tag{A4}$$

The mean of all nk pseudovalues is the jackknife estimator of θ:

$$\hat{\theta}_J = \sum_{p=1}^{n} \sum_{i=1}^{k} \hat{\theta}_{*pi}/nk. \tag{A5}$$

For the estimators in Equations A1–A3, $\hat{\theta}_J = \hat{\theta}$ which is an unbiased estimator of θ.

To estimate the standard error of $\hat{\theta}_J = \hat{\theta}$ using the jackknife procedure, we employ the matrix of pseudovalues, which has n rows and k columns. For this matrix let $\hat{\sigma}^2(\text{rows})$, $\hat{\sigma}^2(\text{cols})$, and $\hat{\sigma}^2(\text{res})$ be the estimated variance components taking into account sampling from a finite population and/or universe if $N < \infty$ and/or $K < \infty$, respectively. (Use Equations A1, A2, and A3 with "rows," "cols," and "res" replacing p, i, and pi,e, respectively.) Then the estimated standard error of $\hat{\theta}_J$ is:

$$\hat{\sigma}(\hat{\theta}_J) = [c_n\hat{\sigma}^2(\text{rows})/n + c_k\hat{\sigma}^2(\text{cols})/k + c_nc_k\hat{\sigma}^2(\text{res})/nk]^{1/2}, \tag{A6}$$

where $c_n = 1 - n/N$ and $c_k = 1 - k/K$ are the finite population and universe correction factors, respectively. (Note that, in their discussion of the jackknife, Cronbach et al. (1972, pp. 56, 71) incorrectly suggest that the result in Equation A6 be divided by the square root of nk.)

REFERENCES

American Psychological Association. (1985). *Standards for educational and psychological testing*. Washington, DC: Author.

Bell, J. F. (1985). Generalizability theory: The software problem. *Journal of Educational Statistics, 10*, 19–29.

Bock, R. D. (1972). [Review of *The dependability of behavioral measurements*]. *Science, 178*, 1275–1276.

Box, G. E. P., & Tiao, G. C. (1973). *Bayesian inference in statistical analysis*. Reading, MA: Addison-Wesley.

Brennan, R. L. (1983). *Elements of generalizability theory*. Iowa City, IA: American College Testing.

Brennan, R. L. (1984). *Some statistical issues in generalizability theory*. (ACT Technical Bulletin No. 46). Iowa City: American College Testing.

Brennan, R. L., Harris, D. J., & Hanson, B. A. (1987). *The bootstrap and other procedures for examining the variability of estimated variance components in testing contexts*. (ACT Research Report No. 87-7). Iowa City, IA: American College Testing.

Brennan, R. L., Jarjoura, D., & Deaton, E. L. (1980). *Some issues concerning the estimation and interpretation of variance components in generalizability theory.* (ACT Technical Bulletin No. 36.) Iowa City, IA: American College Testing.

Cardinet, J., & Allal, L. (1983). Estimation of generalizability parameters. In L. J. Fyans (Ed.), *Generalizability theory: Inferences and practical applications* (pp. 17–48). San Francisco: Jossey-Bass.

Cardinet, J., Tourneur, Y., & Allal, L. (1981). Extension of generalizability theory and its applications in educational measurement. *Journal of Educational Measurement, 18,* 183–204. Errata, *Journal of Educational Measurement,* 1982, *19,* 331–332.

Chastain, R. L., & Willson, V. L. (1986). *Effect on generalizability coefficients when estimating variance components using computer packages.* Paper presented at the Annual Meeting of the American Educational Research Association, San Francisco, CA, April.

Collins, J. D. (1970). *Jackknifing generalizability.* Unpublished doctoral dissertation, University of Colorado, Boulder.

Colton, D. A. (1983). *A multivariate generalizability analysis of a test developed according to a table of specifications.* Unpublished master's thesis. The University of Iowa, Iowa City.

Corbeil, R. R., & Searle, S. (1976). Restricted maximum likelihood (REML) estimation of variance components in the mixed model. *Technometrics, 15,* 819–826.

Cornfield, J., & Tukey, J. W. (1956). Average values of mean squares in factorials. *Annals of Mathematical Statistics, 27,* 907–949.

Crick, J. E., & Brennan, R. L. (1983). *Manual for GENOVA: A GENeralized analysis Of VAriance system* (ACT Technical Bulletin No. 43). Iowa City, IA: American College Testing.

Cronbach, L. J., Gleser, G. C., Nanda, H., & Rajaratnam, N. (1972). *The dependability of behavioral measurements: Theory of generalizability for scores and profiles.* New York: Wiley.

Dixon, W. J. (Ed.) (1985). *BMDP statistical software.* Los Angeles: University of California Press.

Edelman, D. A. (1974). Three-stage nested designs with composite samples. *Technometrics, 16,* 409–417.

Efron, B. (1982). The jackknife, the bootstrap, and other resampling plans. *Society for Industrial and Applied Mathematics, CBMS-NSF Monograph 38,* Philadelphia.

Efron, B., & Tibshirani, R. (1986). Bootstrap methods for standard errors, confidence intervals, and other measures of statistical accuracy. *Statistical Science, 1,* 54–77.

Feldt, L. S., & Brennan, R. L. (1989). Reliability. In R. L. Linn (Ed.), *Educational measurement* (3rd ed., pp. 105–146). New York: Macmillan.

Gates, C. E., & Shiue, C. (1962). The analysis of variance of the S-stage hierarchical classification. *Biometrics, 18,* 529–536.

Gower, J. C. (1962). Variance component estimation for unbalanced hierarchical classifications. *Biometrics, 18,* 537–542.

Graybill, F. A. (1976). *Theory and application of the linear model.* North Scituate, MA: Duxbury Press.

Hartley, H. O. (1967). Expectation, variances, and covariances of ANOVA mean squares by 'synthesis.' *Biometrics, 23,* 105–114, and Corrigenda, 853.

Hartley, H. O., Rao, J. N. K., & LaMotte, L. R. (1978). A simple 'synthesis'-based method of variance component estimation. *Biometrics, 34,* 233–242.

Hartley, H. O., & Searle, S. R. (1969). A discontinuity in mixed model analyses. *Biometrics, 25,* 573–576.

Harville, D. A. (1977). Maximum likelihood approaches to variance component estimation and to related problems. *Journal of the American Statistical Association, 72,* 320–338.

Henderson, C. R. (1953). Estimation of variance and covariance components. *Biometrics, 9,* 226–252.

Jarjoura, D., & Brennan, R. L. (1981). *Three variance components models for some measurement procedures in which unequal numbers of items fall into discrete categories* (ACT Technical Bulletin No. 37). Iowa City, IA: American College Testing.

Jarjoura, D., & Brennan, R. L. (1982). A variance components model for measurement procedures associated with a table of specifications. *Applied Psychological Measurement, 6,* 161–171.

Jarjoura, D., & Brennan, R. L. (1983). Multivariate generalizability models for tests developed from tables of specifications. In L. J. Fyans (Ed.), *Generalizability theory: Inferences and practical applications* (pp. 83–101). San Francisco: Jossey-Bass.

Kirk, R. E. (1982). *Experimental design* (2nd ed.). Belmont, CA: Wadsworth.

Koch, G. G. (1968). Some further remarks concerning "A general approach to the estimation of variance components." *Technometrics, 10,* 551–558.

Loevinger, J. (1965). Person and population as psychometric concepts. *Psychological Review, 72,* 143–155.

Lord, F. M., & Novick, M. R. (1968). *Statistical theories of mental test scores.* Reading, MA: Addison-Wesley.

Marcoulides, G. A. (1987). *An alternative method for variance component estimation: Applications to generalizability theory.* Unpublished doctoral dissertation, University of California, Los Angeles.

Millman, J., & Glass, G. C. (1967). Rules of thumb for writing the ANOVA table. *Journal of Educational Measurement, 4,* 41–51.

Mosteller, F., & Tukey, J. W. (1968). Data analysis, including statistics. In G. Lindzey & E. Aronson (Eds.). *The handbook of social psychology, Vol. 2. Research methods* (2nd ed., pp. 80–203). Reading, MA: Addison-Wesley.

Quenouille, M. (1949). Approximate tests of correlation in time series. *Journal of the Royal Statistical Society—Series B, 11,* 18–84.

Rao, C. R. (1971). Estimation of variance and covariance components—MINQUE theory. *Journal of Multivariate Analysis, 1,* 257–275.

Rao, C. R., & Kleffe, J. (1988). *Estimation of variance components and applications.* New York: Elsevier Science Publishing.

Samuels, M. L., Casella, G., & McCabe, G. P. (1991). Interpreting blocks and random factors. *Journal of the American Statistical Association, 86,* 798–808.

SAS Institute. (1989). *SAS/STAT User's Guide* (version 6, 4th ed.). Cary, NC: SAS Institute Inc.

Satterthwaite, F. E. (1941). Synthesis of variance. *Psychometrika, 6,* 309–316.

Satterthwaite, F. E. (1946). An approximate distribution of estimates of variance components. *Biometrics Bulletin, 2,* 110–114.

Scheffé, H. (1959). *The analysis of variance.* New York: Wiley.

Searle, S. R. (1971). *Linear models.* New York: Wiley.

Searle, S. R. (1979). *Notes on variance component estimation—A detailed account of maximum likelihood and kindred methodologies.* Unpublished manuscript, Cornell University, Biometrics Unit, Ithica, NY.

Shavelson, R. J., & Webb, N. M. (1981). Generalizability theory: 1973–1980. *British Journal of Mathematical and Statistical Psychology, 34,* 133–166.

Shavelson, R. J., & Webb, N. M. (1991). *Generalizability theory: A primer.* Newbury Park, CA: Sage.

Shavelson, R. J., Webb, N. M., & Rowley, G. L. (1989). Generalizability theory. *American Psychologist, 44,* 922–932.

Sirotnik, K., & Wellington, R. (1977). Incidence sampling: An integrated theory for "matrix sampling." *Journal of Educational Measurement, 14,* 343–399.

Smith, P. L. (1978). Sampling errors of variance components in small sample generalizability studies. *Journal of Educational Statistics, 3,* 319–346.

Smith, P. L. (1982). A confidence interval approach for variance component estimates in the context of generalizability theory. *Educational and Psychological Measurement*, *42*, 459–466.

Tukey, J. (1958). Bias and confidence in not quite large samples. Abstract in *Annals of Mathematical Statistics*, *29*, 614.

Webb, N. M., Shavelson, R. J., & Maddahian, E. (1983). Multivariate generalizability theory. In L. J. Fyans (Ed.), *Generalizability theory: Inferences and practical applications* (pp. 67–81). San Francisco: Jossey-Bass.

Welch, B. L. (1956). On linear combinations of several variances. *American Statistical Association Journal*, *51*, 132–148.

Winer, B. J. (1971). *Statistical principles in experimental design* (2nd ed.). New York: McGraw-Hill.

CHAPTER TEN

Kant, Wittgenstein, Objectivity, and Structural Equations Modeling

STANLEY A. MULAIK

Since 1980 I have written a number of papers on how philosophy of science themes relate to statistical practices. My earliest and latest efforts in this regard have exposed and criticized the pervasive influence of classical empiricism on multivariate statistical practice (Mulaik 1985, 1987a, 1988, 1991a, in press). Classical multivariate statistics, I argue, are but mathematical emulations of the associative processes that empiricism postulated were the basis by which we acquire knowledge. But empiricism is no longer the received view of the philosophy of science and should no longer be the philosophical foundation on which multivariate statistical practice rests.

In a related vein I have also been deeply interested in the philosophy of causality because causality as a concept is central to a proper use of structural equation modeling, which I regard, as Susan Embretson once expressed it, as a "paradigm shift" in multivariate statistics. My work on causality (Mulaik 1986, 1987a) has led me in the mean time to see that causality is only part of a larger schema or framework for understanding nature: *objectivity*. I touched on this theme in a paper (Mulaik, 1991) in the *British Journal for the Philosophy of Science* in which I argued that objectivity is a regulative concept used by scientific communities as a norm for evaluating theoretical and instrumentational practices. In a yet-to-be published chapter (Mulaik, in press), titled, "The Critique of Pure

STANLEY A. MULAIK • School of Psychology, Georgia Institute of Technology, Atlanta, Georgia 30332.

Cognitive Assessment: A Multidisciplinary Perspective, edited by Cecil R. Reynolds. Plenum Press, New York, 1994.

Statistics," I explore why classical multivariate statistics is so frequently vulnerable to the accusation that it is replete with artifacts of method. My answer is that by way of Karl Pearson (1892/1911) multivariate statistics absorbed from the empiricist philosophy, for example, David Hume's, a distorted meaning of "object" and the derivative concept of objectivity, which declared ordinary objects to be illusions or fictions of the mind and sense impressions to be the only true objects of consciousness.

It was the philosopher Immanuel Kant who arose after Hume to attempt a defense of the notion of object and objectivity in his famous *Critique of Pure Reason*. What preoccupied Kant in that work were ideas like causality, object, number, unity, substance, ideas that empiricists like Hume regarded with skepticism because they had no referents as objects of experience, being nothing more they said than names linked to collages and sequences of sensory impressions joined together by the associative processes. In the light of the empiricist critique of such concepts, Kant's question was "How are such concepts to be justified?"

To understand Kant's answer to this question has preoccupied much of my time over the past 6 years and led me deeply into the murky world of Kantian scholarship and exegesis. My reason as a psychological statistician for making this major excursion into philosophy is because I believe that just as the empiricist philosophy of Locke, Berkeley, Hume, and Mill underlies classical multivariate statistics, Kant's philosophy of objectivity may be seen as the forerunner of a philosophical base for structural equation modeling.

Kant's works concerned with the topic of objects, causality, and objectivity and related matters are *Critique of Pure Reason, The Prolegomena*, and *Logic*. These are not works easy to understand. But because I think structural modelers can benefit from studying Kant, particularly in terms of his concepts of an object and causality, I am going to present a view of Kant that makes him both plausible and relevant for structural modeling today. What has eventually helped me to get a better understanding of Kant is to master another equally difficult and obscure philosopher, Ludwig Wittgenstein (1953). I first had to understand the more contemporary Wittgenstein before I could understand what Kant was trying to do in his often quaint, obscure, and convoluted way. In saying I see similarities between Wittgenstein and Kant I must indicate that I use principles and concepts of Wittgenstein to help me interpret Kant. My doing this is not to be confused with the way some relate Wittgenstein to traditional interpretations of Kant, which I think are often misinterpretations. Seeing Kant in Wittgensteinian terms brings out aspects of Kant's thought not recognized in traditional accounts of Kant that were strongly influenced by rationalist and empiricist points of view. The view of Kant I am going to present is somewhat new, being based on some very recent insights and discoveries by contemporary Kantian scholars.

Both Kant and Wittgenstein, I now believe, have much that is essential in common. Both of them are concerned with the a priori. For Kant in his early middle years the a priori concerned acquired (not innate) concepts abstracted from attending to the actions of the mind on the occasion of an experience (Kant 1770/1968, p. 59) and codifying these actions to serve as rules governing the application of thought to experience. But in *Critique of Pure Reason (CPR)* the a priori becomes concerned with the *transcendental*, which is "the mode of our knowledge of objects in so far as this mode of knowledge is to be possible *a priori*" (Kant, *CPR*, p. 59). For Wittgenstein (1953) the a priori was to be found in *grammar*, the rules for use of language in the contexts in which it is applied. Language, broadly understood, was for Wittgenstein the medium by which we organize, express, and communicate our experiences. To understand Wittgenstein's emphasis on language and the grammar of its use I think it is essential to realize that there are numerous forms by which in language we may organize, express, and communicate our experiences. To reduce the indeterminacies in such activities so that we may act and communicate consistently, we as members of language communities have developed rules that stipulate a priori the forms of language use. Language is thus a normative practice governed by rules. Grammar concerns the codification of these rules and the criteria for their correct application. Much of Wittgenstein's efforts concerned not simply the grammar of language use but the grammar of grammar, that is, what it means to follow a rule (cf. Canfield (1971/1985)).

Both Kant and Wittgenstein had a sense of the normative, social aspect of our use of concepts. Both of them focused on rules and making judgments according to rules. Kant come to focus on rules and making judgments according to rules via his interests in the law, natural law, logic, morals, ethics, and aesthetics. Wittgenstein approached the normative via his preoccupation with logic and grammar.

Both Kant and Wittgenstein set out in their mature philosophies to cure people of philosophical quandaries that grow out of misusing a priori concepts outside their proper contexts. In his discussion of the Antinomies in *Critique of Pure Reason* Kant attacked rationalism by showing how the misuse of a priori concepts apart from their proper application to synthesize experience often leads philosophers to irreconcilably opposed metaphysical positions in which there is no way to resolve who is right. For example, on the one hand one might argue, "The world has a beginning in time and is also limited in space," and be opposed by another metaphysician who argues equally persuasively that, "The world has no beginning, and no limits in space; it is infinite as regards both space and time." Such arguments would be unresolvable. Wittgenstein thought that metaphysical quandries involved in statements like "Only my pain is real," or "Nothing in the world is solid," or "The tree in the forest ceases to exist when no one is looking at it," or "Things in the world really have no color but have only the power to stimulate the sensation of color in us, which is an illusion," to be the result of using language outside its usual everyday contexts in ways contrary to the grammar governing its use in these contexts. Those asserting these perplexing propositions do not inform us (because they are often not aware themselves) that they have changed the rules of the game for the use of ordinary terms and are playing a new game in a new context where they declare that we are losing (by their rules) as we try to play by the old rules for these same terms in their original context (Hacker, 1986). The way out of these quandries, Wittgenstein believed, was to get a clear understanding of the rules by which we use our ordinary language and to compel those who wish to play by a different set of rules to make their rules explicit as those of a different language game. Otherwise, by our rules, what they say makes no sense for it is ungrammatical.

Both Kant and Wittgenstein were concerned with neutralizing skepticism. Both also eschewed the idea that there can be essentially private judgments (Kant, *CPR*, A820-821; B848-849; Wittgenstein, 1953).

Where Kant and Wittgenstein differ is in the explicitness with which they focused on language as the vehicle for all thought and communication. Language for Wittgenstein is central to all his mature work. For Kant language lurks in the background implicit in the discursive nature of the contents of the understanding and in the presumption that discourse must proceed according to rules. Kant also engaged in formulating what appear to be psychological theories of the relations between faculties of the mind. But Kant regarded these faculties as having a transcendental ("grammatical") as well as empirical use (Kant, *CPR*, A94). Wittgenstein eschewed psychological theories while concentrating on the abuses of grammar for mental terms in psychology. Aristotle strongly influenced Kant's view of semantics and logic, and Euclid's geometry shaped Kant's view of mathematics. Wittgenstein, on the other hand, had the new non-Aristotelian logics of Frege and Russell to work with as well as against. In the mathematical, Wittgenstein had the benefit of the major developments of non-Euclidean geometries of the 19th century to consider. And perhaps the major difference between them lies in Wittgenstein's abandonment of classical semantics in his formulation of the idea of criteria.

While there are these differences, I think it is important not to exaggerate them nor to emphasize differences based on distorted understandings of these philosophers' works. P. M. S. Hacker (1986), who is one of the few to note previously the similarities between Wittgenstein and Kant, still notes sharp fundamental differences between them, but does so with what I think is a distorted understanding of Kant.

Hacker begins his discussion of differences between Kant and Wittgenstein in the following way:

First there is the deep and ramifying disagreement between Kant and Kantians on the one hand and Wittgenstein on the other over the intelligibility of the notion of synthetic a priori propositions. . . . A synthetic a priori proposition for Kant was a proposition that was *true* of the empirical world, but could be known in advance of experience. It was conceived of as a *necessary* truth about the phenomenal world, and Kant's object was to show that we could have knowledge of such truths insofar as they are conditions of any possible (conceptualized) experience. What Kant thought of as synthetic a priori truths about the world, Wittgenstein held to be norms of representation. (Hacker, 1986, p. 207)

In a later place, Hacker states,

Kant's transcendental arguments constitute attempts to derive synthetic a priori propositions which are true descriptions of the phenomenal world (hence synthetic), but which hold necessarily of it and can be known in advance of experience. (Hacker, 1986, p. 211)

According to Hacker, because Wittgenstein focused explicitly on language, he was able to develop the concept of grammar as the language for the discussion of the rule-following aspects of language use. He was thus able to distinguish between language for expressing experiences of things in the physical world and language (i.e., grammar), about the correct use of such physical-world language. It was Wittgenstein's major insight, Hacker contends, that grammatical propositions do not state truths or knowledge about things as do empirical propositions. Grammatical propositions are not "true to the facts" of the world. Grammatical propositions are neither true nor false as empirical propositions for they are not empirical propositions at all. They are simply the rules and criteria by which we apply language about things to experience and, among other things, provide the rules by which we determine whether any empirical proposition is true or false in experience. For example, if we say objects continue to exist when they pass from view behind other objects on one side and reappear later on the other side, that is not a truth that "accords with" the facts of our experiences but is simply a grammatical norm for speaking about the existence of objects of experience (cf. Rosenberg, 1988). So, Hacker faults Kant for claiming his transcendental method provides a priori truths and knowledge about objects as if this is comparable to truths and knowledge about objects obtained empirically. Kant's transcendental "knowledge" is at best grammatical propositions about how to talk about things in experience.

Hacker's criticisms of Kant would have force if it were indeed the case that Kant made no distinction between empirical knowledge and a priori knowledge about things, if he regarded "transcendental truths" as the same as "empirical truths." But Kant insists that there is a distinction between the two and that it is bad to confound them (Kant *CPR* B ix–x; B 2–3). Hacker, I think, believes Kant confuses the two because Hacker echoes the typical post-Humean empiricist misinterpretation of Kant that conflates "synthetic" with "empirical," and "analytic" with "nonempirical." But this totally distorts the meaning of analysis and synthesis in the rationalist tradition, which Kant shared, going back to Descartes' resurrection and popularization of these concepts from the ancient Greek geometer, Pappas, initially as methods for breaking down, dissolving, or resolving problems into elements (analysis) and composing them together (synthesis) (Schouls, 1980). Kant makes it quite clear that knowledge independent of experience "is entitled *a priori*, and distinguished from the *empirical*, which has its sources *a posteriori*, that is, in experience" (*CPR*, B2). What makes the "synthetic *a priori*" synthetic is that something is joined together, not that it has something to do with phenomena (Kant, *CPR*, B130–131); being a priori, what.is joined together is joined independently of experience. Thus Kant treats synthetic a priori "knowledge" of the a priori forms, for example, *inherence* (synthesis of object and attribute), *causality* (synthesis of an attribute of an object with another attribute of an object by making the second attribute a condition for the first attribute), and *community* (the reciprocal conditioning of the attributes of coexisting objects in a community of objects), by which we think and talk about objects of phenomenal experience as distinct from synthetic a posteriori knowledge. The latter is the joining together of concepts as a result of experience, say, through association, in talking about our concepts of the world as derived *in part* from experience. As long as Kant treated these two so-called forms of knowledge differently, and the a priori or transcendental as rules for thinking about objects in connection with experience, he was not guilty of anything other than using an idiosyncratic vocabulary.

Hacker also glosses over the fact that there is a sense in which one can say that grammatical propositions are "true." Grammatically constrained propositions about things in the world are "true" in a nonempirical sense, that is, they are "correct" ways of speaking about things that may even be used in making empirical inferences with other, empirical propositions according to that grammar. Grammatically "false" propositions about things, on the other hand, are ways of talking that are not in our language about things (i.e., nonsense), at least relative to that language. For example, "When objects pass from view by going behind other objects, they cease to exist," is nonsense in ordinary thing language. I will concede to Hacker that Wittgenstein's insight, that we can call grammatically "false" propositions "nonsense," was an advance over Kant, who failed to see that the appropriate synonym for "transcendentally false" was "nonsense." Thus he missed "Nonsense!" as a marvelous tool for neutralizing the skeptic who takes nonsensical metaphysical propositions seriously but has incurable doubts about them. As for calling "transcendental knowledge," "knowledge," while opposing it to "empirical knowledge," Kant, I believe, was simply using the term in a manner analogous to "mathematical knowledge," as a systematized body of correct propositions.

Finally, Hacker contends that Kant's transcendental arguments (deductions?) were attempts to derive synthetic a priori propositions from premises about knowledge we have directly and incorrigibly about our own inner states, a notion Wittgenstein firmly rejected. But this objection is widely off its mark in two ways: (1) Kant argued we have no direct, immediate, incorrigible knowledge of any *thing*, whether of so-called things in themselves or sense impressions (whether inner or outer) (Kant, *CPR* B 59–62; Schwyzer 1990). (2) Hacker's characterization of Kant's transcendental arguments (deductions?) as syllogistic arguments from premises about knowledge of inner states and inferences about first-person propositions reflects the failure of almost 200 years of Kantian scholarship to understand Kant's special use of the term *deduction*, which he borrowed from the legal language of his time. It also may reflect Kant's inappropriately mixing a partially psychological (quasi-empirical) argument Kant himself recognized as not appropriate to a deduction (Kant, *CPR*, A86–87, B118–119) with his transcendental (grammatical) argument in the Transcendental Deduction in his first edition of *Critique of Pure Reason*. In the second edition this partially psychological argument is stripped out of the Transcendental Deduction in favor of a more explicitly transcendental (grammatical) argument. Both of these points I will seek to amplify upon below.

In any case, my position is that while there are differences between Kant and Wittgenstein, the differences between them insofar as Kant's notion of the transcendental and Wittgenstein's of the grammatical are concerned are not as great or fundamental as Hacker suggests. What I will have to say will also apply in large measure to M. Williams' (1990) more recent attempt to sharpen the differences between Kant and Wittgenstein. My primary aim is to assimilate Kant's "transcendental" to Wittgenstein's "grammatical" rather than Wittgenstein's "grammatical" to Kant's "transcendental" (as traditionally interpreted). In other ways, the differences between them are indeed considerable.

Nevertheless, while it may seem at first that Kant was oblivious to the central role of language in our dealing with experience, there are those like Williams (1987) who argue that Kant was already on the verge of seeing the central importance of language, with one of his students, J. G. Herder (1967), making such a concept explicit in a book on the origin of language published just weeks before Kant finally saw how he could write the *Critique of Pure Reason* (Kant, 1965/1787) after many years of pondering how to begin.

Insofar as Kant was aware of the social and the normative, it is important to recognize that he was an ardent admirer of Jean-Jacques Rousseau who wrote *The Social Contract* (Rousseau, 1762/1913) to articulate the idea that men have no rights except those that arise out of the *social contract* by which they, with mutual consent, form themselves into communities for the common good (Friedrich, 1949). The idea of the social contract can be seen as a metaphor for one idea of the normative basis for language as the common medium of communication in such communities (Rousseau 1781/1967). Inspired by Rousseau but not bound by his concept of the social contract, Kant went on to develop his own theories of natural rights, natural law, and the moral theory underlying the formation of civic communities and states governed by law (Mulholland, 1990). The *Critique of Pure Reason* is but the first book in a series of *Critiques* that arose out of an investigative program that Kant pursued in his mature years into the role of the a priori in forming judgments, not only of objects, but of ethical, moral, legal and aesthetic matters. Kant was deeply interested in understanding the meaning of normativity (Friedrich, 1949). Having implicitly the idea that concepts are used as rules by those within a rational community, that judgments based on rules must be communicable (Kant, *CPR*, A820, B848), Kant would not have been under the pressure to make language salient, although ultimately it needs to be to provide the medium for communication by which the community arises and its activities are regulated by verbally articulated norms. That language is not salient in Kant's work may be seen as a shortcoming (Schwyzer, 1990), but considering that Kant grasps the idea of natural law and has a synthetic a priori concept of the "general will" that constitutes the basis for the concept of a rule-governed rational community (Mulholland, 1990), it is not such a major shortcoming as it may seem. In fact, Kant seemed to recognize what many contemporary advocates of Rousseauan social-based views of language seem to overlook: mutual consent is not by itself the basis for a language community. Those creating a norm-based verbal community by their mutual consent must have a prior concept of community and what it means to have and follow a rule in order for mutual consent to certain rules to give rise to such a norm-based community. It is not that a rule comes into being by a certain community's agreement in certain practices, but rather it is mutual consent to follow a certain predefined but teachable rule that gives rise to the norm-based community.

Kant as professor was not only a teacher of metaphysics and logic but also of natural law. Legal terms occur frequently in his writings. In his *Critique of Pure Reason* Kant sought to justify the use of a priori concepts, not by setting forth an empirical theory of psychology that would locate them in the physiology of the mind as Locke and Hume had done with the associative processes, but by using a legal form of argument, common in the courts of the Holy Roman Empire of his time, known as a *deduction* (Kant, *CPR*, A84, B117). Henrich (1989) has made a major contribution to Kantian scholarship in exposing the obscure legal meaning behind Kant's use of the term *deduction* and what I have to say here benefits from his insight. Although the legal meaning of the term *deduction* was common knowledge in Kant's time, his decision to use it as the vehicle for his own argument was ill-fated, for in less than a generation afterward, its use passed into obscurity when the Holy Roman Empire was ordered abolished by Napoleon (Henrich, 1989). Countless commentators since have puzzled over these deductions because it was assumed that they were tightly argued syllogistic arguments derived from self-evident premises, like those found in Spinoza's writings. They did not have this form at all, however.

According to Henrich (1989), the purpose of a juridical deduction in a legal dispute in the Holy Roman Empire was to trace, with a minimum of philosophical and theoretical digressions, the legal origins for an acquired right, usage, title, or privilege. This aspect of the claim involving the juridical deduction traces origins for a right within a legal or normative framework to that which *originally* sanctions the right. This was quite distinct from setting forth *facts* to substantiate one's claim, such as presenting a birth certificate, a will, or affidavits from witnesses, which would be presented in another aspect of the case.

In choosing a deduction as the form for presenting his case for the use of a priori concepts, Kant, I believe, presumed that the issues he was concerned with were normative, involving rights to a practice. The right to a priori concepts was in dispute, having been challenged in the court of reason by skeptical empiricists like Hume. On the other hand, Kant thought the rationalists abused their right to a priori concepts by using them in metaphysical speculations in ways that were quite beyond the originally sanctioned purpose for a priori concepts in experience. Although Kant provided a psychological hypothesis about the source of a priori concepts in the faculties of the understanding, he had doubts as to its adequacy to persuade the skeptic to drop his case, regarding the psychological hypothesis as but the subjective aspect of his argument. In the end he regarded the psychological argument to be ultimately irrelevant and resorted to simply justifying our right to the use of a priori concepts by describing how they originate not in the material presented by the senses (and so could not be a posteriori) but as the forms by which we self-consciously and/or reflectively synthesize or combine the material from the senses in the making of objective judgments according to concepts. According to Henrich (1989, p. 36), Kant sought to justify the use of his a priori categories by tracing the legitimacy for their use to an original use for which we have a Natural Right analogous to the right to an *original acquisition;* that is, the natural right granted by the collective will of the original civic community to the original physical possessors of land to which all claims to land would have to be traced to establish their legitimacy (Mulholland, 1990). But apart from stating that the purpose of the deduction was "to determine, with regard to origin, the domain and the limits of the [a priori] categories' legitimate usage," Henrich (1989, p. 39) did not spell out in detail what the *original* use was that Kant appealed to, to establish their legitimacy.

But Kant says at the end of the Transcendental Deduction in his first edition (A) of *Critique of Pure Reason,* "Pure understanding is thus in the [a priori] categories the law of the synthetic unity of all appearances, and thereby *first* and *originally* [emphasis added] makes experience, as regards its form possible" (A128). He claims to lay out how all objective judgments are formed in experience using a common set of combining or synthetic a priori concepts, called "categories." Our right to these a priori concepts is the right we would appeal to in any use of them as the fundamental constituent moves in any rational argument seeking an objective determination in experience, such as even the skeptic makes in denying them by appealing to experience, as Hume did. The ultimate legitimacy of a priori concepts is traced to the "*original* synthetic unity of apperception" (B131, 169), that is, the natural right to be able to say self-consciously, "I think . . ." as a synthetic a priori grammatical form ("transcendental unity of apperception") that joins thoughts to a subject in connection with any acts of synthesis in thought concerning experience, granted by the collective will of the rational community, for these concepts are forms of thinking about experience. By implication, their use apart from experience is illegitimate, which undermines the rationalist metaphysicians' claim to use them speculatively.

In Wittgensteinian terms we might describe Kant's transcendental deductions as grammatical expositions or investigations (as Hacker [1986] asserts). They seek to expose the complex web of a priori relationships of usage among a number of interrelated concepts that underlie our concepts of objects and of self-consciousness. The deductions are not designed to prove absolutely that you must use these concepts. Rather, Kant attempts to show how a set of common a priori concepts by which we synthesize the particulars of sensory intuition in discursive thought underlie all forms of what we call "objective judgment." These concepts represent the fundamental logical forms by which we act to form objective judgments. And so he presumes you understand and accept objective judgment as a public form for representing experience just as the syllogism was a public form for stating arguments, regardless of their content.

The key to understanding Kant is to understand the implications of objective judgment. Unfortunately Kant presumes his reader already understands what judgment is generally and does not give an explicit meaning for this term. Those trained in empiricism are easily misled, because they tend to regard judging as a subjective activity of stating how things appear, and so they regard Kant's categories of judgment as something like the associative processes that are driven by the order and arrangement in which impressions appear to consciousness to form the way things appear to be related in experience. But Kant intended something quite different.

The term *judgment* comes from what judges in a legal system do. This is the implicit underlying metaphor of *Critique of Pure Reason*. A judge cannot simply form opinions or make decisions on his own terms, but is constrained by precedent and the law. The law must be taken as the basis for the judge's reasoning and by combining elements of the law the judge reproduces what is legally permitted in the particular case at hand and then determines whether the actual situation is in conformity with this conception of what is legally permitted. But it is not enough that the judge *do* this properly in arriving at a decision. The judge must justify the decision by laying out for others the reasoning used to arrive at the decision. The judge must also be aware of personal biases, personal philosophy, and personal interests, and how any of these might tend to distort judgment of the law's application, and be able to factor these influences out of decisions or even to disqualify him- or herself. This implies that the judge be self-conscious and able to articulate to him- or herself and others not only how a decision is arrived at in terms of the law, but the biases and prejudices that must be avoided and guarded against. Judging is a very self-conscious activity.

Judging is thus the metaphor Kant uses for reasoning about experience. According to Kant objective judgments are distinguished in language from subjective judgments by the copula *is;* for example, "The ball *is* red" makes an objective assertion, whereas "The red ball . . ." does not inform us whether the combining of the predicate "red" with the subject "ball" has been evaluated for its objective validity and thus may be only a subjective assertion (Kant, *CPR*, B142). What Kant wished to demonstrate was that if you analyze the purely logical aspects of judging wherein you ignore the issue of content, you will find 12 synthetic a priori functions by which all logical judgments are formulated. These are the common factors, so to speak, the logical functions of judgment. We display these in Table 1. The meaning of the functions in this table is more

TABLE 1. Kant's Table of Logical Judgments

Quantity	Quality	Relation	Modality
Universal	Affirmative	Categorical	Problematic
Particular	Negative	Hypothetical	Assertory
Singular	Infinite	Disjunctive	Apodictic

fully described in Kant's *Logic* and are like traditional logical forms. But if we consider the application of the logical functions to the formulation of concepts about objects, Kant called the result the categories of judgment, given here in Table 2:

TABLE 2. Kant's Categories of Judgment

Quantity	Quality	Relation	Modality
Unity	Reality	Inherence	Possibility
Plurality	Negation	Causality	Existence
Totality	Limitation	Community	Necessity

Now I do not have the space here to develop a detailed interpretation of these tables; in fact, books have tried to make sense of Kant's tables and to explain how he arrived at them. There are just three conclusions I want to draw from these tables, and they concern Table 2.

The first is that Kant believed this table was exhaustive in setting forth the *logical forms* of synthetic judgments about objects in general. In other words, in considering the *logical forms* of what we mean by judgments about objects in general, Kant says, these are they, and there are no more. This is, in Wittgenstein's terms, an assertion about the grammar of the concept of an object (i.e., norms of a community), and not a psychological or neurological assertion. These are not discovered by a direct and immediate intuition of one's thought processes, as Locke and Hume sought to discover the associative processes, but by an analysis of our discourse about objective matters, performed as logicians discovered the principles of logic or as a grammarian might analyze spoken language to arrive at the grammar of its use.

The second thing I wish to note is the third group of categories, of *Relation*. That is where causality is placed. So, causality is an aspect of making judgments about what we call objective states of affairs. It is a category concerning a relation involving objects.

The third thing I wish to do is briefly note, using the third group of categories, *Relation*, the principle underlying how within each group there are three categories. Kant wrote in a footnote at the end of the "Introduction" to his *Critique of Judgment* (1790/1987):

> That my divisions in pure philosophy almost always turn out tripartite has aroused suspicion. Yet this is in the nature of the case. If a division is to be made a priori, then it will be either *analytic* or *synthetic*. If it is analytic, then it is governed by the principle of contradiction and hence is always bipartite (*quodlibet ens est aut A aut non A* [any entity is either A or not A]). If it is synthetic, but is to

be made on the basis of a priori *concepts* (rather than, as in mathematics, on the basis of *intuition* corresponding a priori to the concept), then we must have what is required for a synthetic unity in general, namely, (1) a condition, (2) something conditioned, (3) the concept that arises from the union of the conditioned with its condition; hence the division must of necessity be a trichotomy (Kant, 1790/1987, p. 38).

To illustrate, we begin in Table 3, therefore, with the relation of inherence in which an attribute is determined to be inherent or essential to an object's existence, which involves joining the attribute to the object in an objective judgment. Next, we may consider how objectively this relationship of attribute to object is conditioned on something else, another attribute of an object, which is what causality is about. Finally, we may consider these previous two relations united as a whole, in the manner by which attributes are mutually or reciprocally determined among mutually coexisting objects.

We are most familiar with the first two cases. The third, reciprocal causation, is a distinct kind of relationship built on the first two. Bandura (1986), for example, would find the relationship of reciprocity of influence what interests him most in discussing the causal relations between per-

TABLE 3. Kant's Categories of Relation in His Table
of Categorical Judgments

	Relation
Condition	**Inherence** Joint attribute to object
A Conditioned	**Causality** How properties of one object are conditioned on those of another
Synthesis of the Condition and the Conditioned	**Community** How the properties of a community of coexistent objects are reciprocally conditioned

son and environment and vice versa. I suggest that Skinner's (1953, 1974) major failing, despite claiming to study the reciprocal relationship of organism and environment, was to force our understanding of this relationship into the procrustean bed of the simpler relationship of causality between environment and organism. Actually Skinner did not ultimately focus on behavior but on stable relationships between different well-defined events in the environment as mediated by an organism's behavior, such that one well-defined event in the environment (e.g., a light turning on) under certain conditions would produce another well-defined event in the environment (e.g., a bar is depressed) through actions of an organism (the actions not being well defined or described in any detail).

It is important to realize that Kant does not claim these categories constitute the meaning of judgment as a self-conscious activity in which one seeks to distinguish what is due to the object from what is due to the subject by means of rules. Nor do the categories by themselves show how one applies them to objects of experience, for that requires a discussion of the schemata (Schwyzer, 1990, p. 17). Nor do they concern how one establishes objective validity in experience because that is an empirical, a posteriori matter. Nor do the categories exhaust all that is a priori in thought. Identifying the categories with prespecified acts of combination applied to the contents provided by the senses, Kant regards the categories as *a priori* because they are simply essential, normatively sanctioned constituent moves of combination or synthesis in the activity of formulating and stating an objective judgment from experience.

Regardless of the ultimate philosophical status of Kant's second table of categorical judgment, it remains an ingenious example of an attempt to elucidate the internal or grammatical relations implied within the concept of objective judgment regarded as a synthetic or combining act of the intellect operating in terms of the schema of an object as the bearer of attributes.

Kant rejected the empiricist and Cartesian assumption that we are immediately conscious of objects presented to us via the senses. For example, the sense impressions of empiricism are supposedly intentional objects of consciousness. But one may argue that they are a metaphor, likely borrowed from Renaissance artists who analyzed paintings into blobs of color superimposed on the spatial framework of a canvas. Blobs of color were objects and when placed in the proper spatial orientation could create the illusion of a physical object. British empiricism regarded sense impressions as objects comparable to blobs of color. These were the bedrock of experience and reality, the only real objects set before us. Physical objects were but mere fabrications of the associative processes applied to these sense impressions just as the viewer of the painting sees an object within the painting that "really" isn't there. But sense impressions are private objects. And here the metaphor breaks down, because what the painter calls blobs of this or that color can be verified objectively. There are external standards ("This is crimson," I say, pointing to a splotch of paint used as a standard; and "patches" and "blobs" also have external criteria to evaluate correct usage). But with sense impressions there are no external, independent criteria of correct talk about them, and one is led into the philosophical quandaries of solipsism: I have no way to determine objectively whether I am using my color language consistently to describe sense impressions, or whether what I call "red" is what others have when they say "red." Nor can I be sure others have sense impressions like I do. All of this is nonsense for Wittgenstein. It was Wittgenstein who by his private language argument demonstrated the incoherence in the empiricist assumption that the knower can act in a rule governed way with essentially private objects (Suter, 1989; Wittgenstein 1953).

In contrast to the empiricist position, Kant argued that being sensibly affected does not in itself constitute consciousness nor does it provide objects (Schwyzer, 1990). Kant's view of how we gain conscious awareness of objects is, I believe, something like the following, which is illustrated in Figure 1:

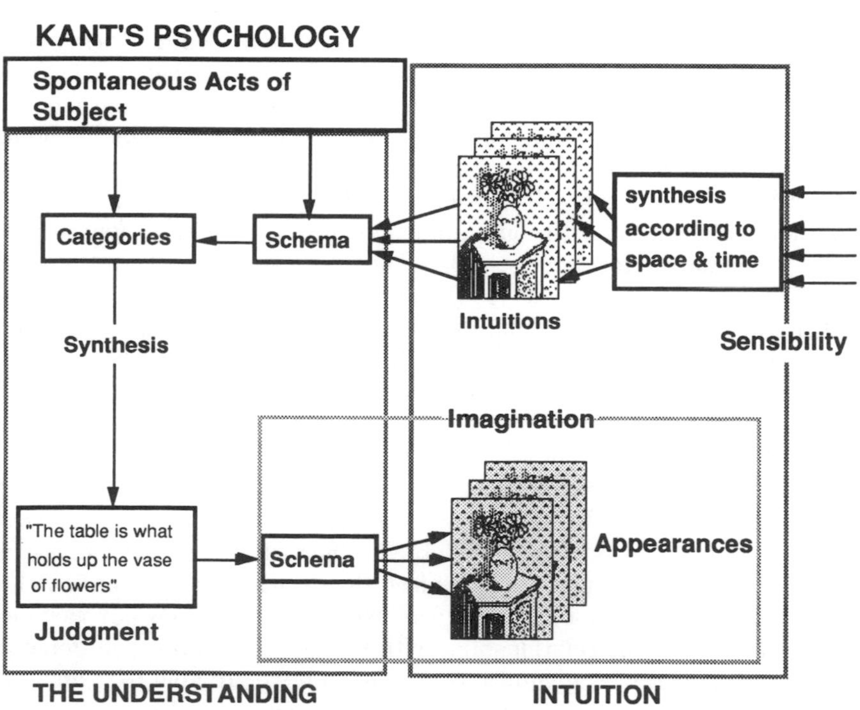

FIGURE 1. Kant's psychology.

We first begin to perform synthetic acts to combine the sensory manifold in the sensibility which organizes or synthesizes the sensory manifold according to space and time in the form of intuitions (which are like instantaneous but uninterpreted snapshots). But we are not immediately conscious of intuitions as objects of consciousness. The intuitions in Kant's analysis are arrived at indirectly by taking away from appearances "everything which the understanding thinks through its concepts, so that nothing shall be left save empirical intuition" (Kant, *CPR*, A22, B36). But intuitions without concepts are blind (Kant, *CPR*, A51, B75; B136–137). The intuitions are next taken up by the understanding by a process that spontaneously combines them via provisionally applied a priori schema into discursive (verbal) thought. These in turn are synthesized by the categories into judgments in discursive thought. The understanding next takes the resulting discursive concepts and guided by them uses schema to transform these again in imagination back into images in pure intuition, which are known as *appearances*. Now, whether this psychological account is empirically valid or not does not matter (Kant drops it from his transcendental deduction in the second edition of *Critique of Pure Reason*, perhaps because, as an empirical argument, it is irrelevant to the legal deduction of the right to a priori concepts). Kant argues that only insofar as there are transcendental (grammatical) forms wherein I can say I am able to recognize and to represent to myself abstractly acts of combination and synthesis in general, and to identify them as *my* acts in my particular acts of forming a concept of an object or reproducing appearances of them in imagination, can I say *I* am conscious of them. And only as I am aware that *I* perform all these acts of synthesis in general can I say I am self-conscious in the process. But this is made possible and legitimate (in our language) by the "original" synthetic a priori grammatical form of "I think" which joins all "my" acts of thinking in general to a single subject "I" (Kant, *CPR*, B137–139). But this "I" is but a transcendental (grammatical) subject empty of any ontological or empirical content or implications, as Kant makes abundantly clear in his discussion of the Paralogisms of Pure Reason (Kant, *CPR*, A341–405; B399–B432; cf. Rosenburg, 1986).

But appearance is not yet our final verdict of the object which we regard now as provisionally imminent in the appearance. As we act and move about we come to have diverse appearances which we may now provisionally regard as of the same object. The task now is to formulate in imagination a conception of the object that synthesizes or unifies the diverse appearances in a coherent way using schema of how our varying acts and concomitant relationships with respect to an object in general varies the appearances given to us. But even if we are able to formulate such a concept of the object unifying those appearances already given to us, that is still not sufficient to establish its objective validity. We must first regard the concept of the object as having provisional universal validity as a rule. This means that by the concept of the object and a general scheme of our possible varying relationships to an object, we are able to anticipate in imagination how the object will appear from additional, novel perspectives. And if we then make the moves to these new perspectives and appearance conforms to what is anticipated, then we can regard our concept of the object as "objectively valid." This by no means implies that at some later time using this concept of an object we will never come across an appearance that disconfirms its anticipated form. When that happens we then say the objective concept is no longer valid. So, we must rethink our concept of the object, or our relationship to it, to account for all the relevant appearances up to that point and test this concept against additional experiences as before. Science adds an additional element. As in the making of legal judgments based on law, in science we make empirical judgments in terms of prior concepts and articulate our reasoning in a public fashion. This makes justification in science a self-conscious activity.

Another way to put this is that

> [A]n object is a concept regarded as universally valid that unites diverse appearances according to a rule that resolves their disparity in the concept while indicating how, on the other hand, the subject may distort, alter, or vary what appears by its movements, actions, perspective, or conceptual schemas or use of observational instruments relative to the object. Once we grasp this dual relationship of appearances (presentations) to object and subject and the role their mutual relationship plays in determining these presentations, we grasp how object and subject may be distinguished while recognizing the internal relation between them that makes them inseparable. (Mulaik, in press, see also Mulaik 1991)

Appearances are to be explained as complex functions of the varying properties of objects, the subject, and their mutual interrelationship. This is illustrated in Figure 2, which has a certain superficial similarity to Brunswik's Lens Model, but is not to be confused with it. The diagram is drawn from the point of view of an external observer rather than from the point of view of the original observer, which makes it somewhat misleading, since the subject, from the point of view of the original observer is not an object.

Another metaphor I have used (Mulaik, in press) of the relationship of Kant's subject, object, and appearance is taken from computer graphics used in computer aided design. Given two-dimensional views of an object taken from different points of view, one first seeks to synthesize them in a conception of a three-dimensional object according to rules of projection. For example, the three-dimensional conception may be repre-

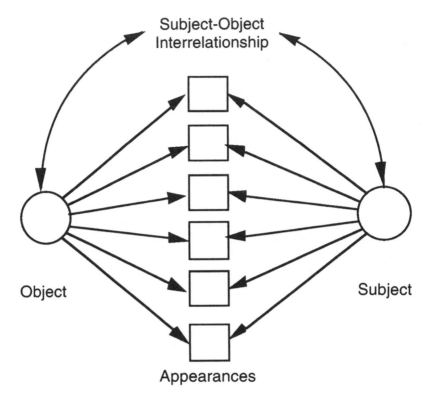

FIGURE 2. The interrelationship of subject, object, and appearances.

sented by three-dimensional coordinates of points in the surface of the object, and these coordinates stored in computer memory. To fill in the gaps between the points on the surface of the object you may use certain interpolating functions to generate the additional points. Then you turn around and determine how the object would appear in two-dimensions from new points of view. As the observer varies his or her position with respect to the position of the object, the two-dimensional view (appearance) varies. And if you alter the representation of the three-dimensional object, this alters in turn the two-dimensional views also. On the other hand, if the observer uses distortive lenses, this also alters the appearance of the two-dimensional views. This metaphor of the subject–object relationship has the advantage of not treating the concept of the subject as an object, for it is not represented as an object in the metaphor. But this metaphor also misleads in giving the impression that the concept of the object is itself an object that causes what appears. But the concept of an object, as concept, is only a rule by which I synthesize the sensory manifold. It is only as I synthesize my sensory manifold that I relate to an object of experience. And I validate a provisional concept of the object by comparing an image of the object reconstructed from my concept (say in a sketch or a description I give) with the actual object seen from a new and independent point of view.

So, what does this all mean for structural equation modeling? Both Kant and Wittgenstein sought to expose the a priori or "grammatical" rules that govern our use of concepts about objects (in the case of Kant) or language generally (in the case of Wittgenstein) so that we would know the limits of their legitimate use. If we look at structural equation modeling in the way Kant and Wittgenstein look at concepts and language use, we will recognize the a priori or grammatical aspects of it, particularly those concerned with its objective application.

Let us begin by observing that a structural equation model involves representing relations between variables. In pure mathematics a variable is a symbol to which may be assigned any one of a number of values from a set of values, which may be quantitative or qualitative. Note too that the act of assignment of a value to the symbol implicitly rules out at the same time the assignment of other values from the same set. The act of assigning a value to a variable would be, for Kant, a synthetic (combining) act, for the act of assignment joins a value to a symbol in thought. He would identify this synthetic act with the judgment of his general logic that joins a predicate to its subject. On the other hand, in using a variable in mathematics to represent the variable properties of physical objects, we are focusing on a variant of this synthetic act that concerns its special application to objects. Kant identifies this synthetic act with the category of inherence, which is the joining of an attribute to an object in thought. Going further, we note that functional relations between latent variables in our models represent causal relations between the attributes of objects. Recall that causal relations represent the second relational categorical judgment in Kant's table of categorical (objective) judgments, that in which the attributes of an object are conditional on other attributes; for example, of another object. Finally, a path diagram representing reciprocal causation allows us to see simultaneously how the attributes, say, of two coexisting objects mutually influence each other. For Kant this is the case of community or reciprocity, which involves "stepping back," so to speak, to see the system of objects and attributes and their mutual causal effects on one another as a whole, which for Kant involves a synthesis of the other two relational categories of inherence and causality into the category of community or reciprocity.

What Kant struggled to convey in often obscure language is really a fairly trivial point by our standards today, once you grasp it: when in science we say, as we frequently do, that our aim is to study the relations between variables we implicitly specify a priori a general framework for the representation of objects and their relations in experience. This is not an empirically determined issue but a "grammatical" or "transcendental" issue. Where empirical considerations enter in is in formulating specific kinds of relation between specifically chosen variables, or in determining the specific magnitudes of values (where magnitude is another a priori concept) in representing the attributes of specific kinds of objects.

The a priori enters in other ways in structural equations modeling. Consider that we have the whole range of mathematics from which to choose our schema for representing relations between attributes of objects. In choosing to confine our study to models involving linear relations, we exclude a priori a whole range of representational schema from further consideration. Whether this is a good prior choice, however, will ultimately be an empirical question.

Consider further that a linear structural equations model in its barest form comes first without any values specified for its parameters, which initially are free variables. We must relate these parameters to observed quantities in formulating a model to reproduce those quantities. A structural equation model seeks to reproduce the variances and covariances of a covariance matrix among observed variables by modeling these variables as linear functions of latent and observed variables. If we are prescient, we will know precisely the values of each of the model parameters that allow us to reproduce the covariance matrix. But normally we start out with little or no knowledge about the model parameters and first seek to estimate their values in some context to be used later for testing purposes in other contexts. We discover right away that because the model equation contains more parameters than the number of observed parameters, we have an underdetermined system of equations, which is inadequate for the purposes of solving for unknown parameters as functions of known parameters. We must prespecify a priori the values of certain parameters of the model equation to reduce the number of unknown parameters to the number of known parameters, just to identify the model, that is, to make it possible to solve for unknown parameters from the known parameters. This involves an a priori choice, because there are many different, equally good ways to do this, all of which will allow us to solve for values of the remaining unknown parameters that will reproduce the observed parameters perfectly. The choice is typically constrained by seeking to embed the phenomena studied in some larger, more general framework, such as a physical conception of the world or our general understanding of the behavior of human beings.

Our model at this point is only just-identified. It is still useless as a scientific model because we cannot test the model against these same covariances. We have estimated the unknown parameters by adjusting their values until they necessarily reproduce the known variance and covariance parameters perfectly. So, where there can be no lack of fit, there can be no test of a model either. What we need to do is prespecify additional parameter values, or place further constraints on the model's free parameters beyond those we use to just-identify the model. When we do this we overidentify the model. When the overidentifying constraints on model equation parameters are not correctly specified, they will constrain the estimates of the free parameters in ways that prevent our being able to reproduce the observed covariance matrix with estimated and prespecified parameter values. Lack of fit, when it occurs, is then due to the overidentifying constraints imposed within the context of the constraints we initially imposed just to obtain identification. Thus overidentification is essential to being able to test a hypothesis against data. What is tested are the prespecified overidentifying constraints in the context of the just-identifying constraints.

What we can learn from this is that a priori schemas, such as are provided by the concept of objectivity and the "grammar" of a language for objects, provide general schemas that serve to reduce but not totally eliminate the indeterminacy in the way we represent experience. Such general schemas in turn govern the choice of mathematical systems and provide a basis for the general semantic rules for the systems' application when we use them to develop mathematical models to represent experience. In mathematical models, identifying conditions, which are imposed somewhat arbitrarily, serve further to eliminate indeterminacy in making it possible to estimate unknown parameters from data. Overidentifying conditions apply even further constraints, making it possible for us to test certain formulations of a model to determine when these conditions are improperly specified because they make the model fail to fit the data. But because along the way at various points we impose arbitrary constraints to reduce indeterminacy, it is always possible for us to model the same data in other ways. Whether that will be interesting will depend on whether some alternative set of constraints will be meaningful in the context of some more general set of constraints that we already accept.

The last issue involving objectivity and structural equation modeling I wish to discuss concerns the concept of latent variables. Kant argued that we seek to analyze our concepts into those common or general concepts by which we reproduce all appearances. Some of these common concepts would concern physical objects and others our own physical and mental operations, as well as general concepts of their interrelation. The set of all common concepts by which we formulate our conception of an objective world and our relationship to it from the diversity of our appearances, Kant called the "analytic unity of consciousness" (Kant, *CPR*, B134f). Common factor analysis is but a mathematical implementation of this idea applied to the realm of variables. For example, Thurstone (1947) wrote:

> It is the faith of all science that an unlimited number of phenomena can be comprehended in terms of a limited number of concepts or

ideal constructs. . . . To discover a scientific law is merely to discover
that a man-made scheme serves to unify, and thereby to simplify,
comprehension of a certain class of natural phenomena. (p. 51)

Nothing could be more Kantian than that. Kant's "synthetic unity of
consciousness," on the other hand, referred to the objective conceptions
formulated from these common concepts as well as their use in the reproduction of appearances in imagination. Its analogues in common factor
analysis are the fundamental equation of factor analysis $X = \Lambda\xi + \Psi\delta$,
which states how what appears is a function of what is objectively and
subjectively the case, and the reproduced correlation matrix $\Sigma = \Lambda\Phi\Lambda' + \Psi^2$, which is a reproduction of appearances.

Common concepts have an objective quality in that they may be
regarded as the invariant universal components of diverse appearances.
But we must beware of stumbling into Platonism wherein we regard
these common concepts as existing independently of experience as things
in themselves. They derive their reason for being only in their role in
formulating concepts of objects in experience. And their status is only
provisional, being accepted as valid only as long as they allow us to
successfully anticipate and reproduce appearances. Latent variables in
common factor analysis and its generalization, structural equations modeling, correspond to general, common concepts in Kant's sense.

There are those in multivariate statistics who abhor the latent variable concept. What I think they react against is the Platonic abuse of the
concept of a latent variable that regards the latent variable as a thing in
itself. It is interesting that one can trace much of this abhorrence of latent
variables to logical positivism's abhorrence of the unobservable, and this
in turn to Ernst Mach's proscriptions against these in physics that
stemmed from his own misreading of Kant's *Prolegomena* as a young man
(Magill and McGreal, 1961, pp. 692–693). Mach believed Kant advocated
the idea of the thing in itself as some kind of metaphysical entity. In a
certain sense he did, but Kant's concept of metaphysics as a science, the
theme of the *Prolegomena*, was an attempt to implement his novel idea of
metaphysics as the systematic analysis of a priori concepts used to structure experience—which we might recognize, after Wittgenstein, as philosophical grammatical investigations. For Kant the idea of the thing in
itself was just the "pure idea" of an object in general, abstracted from all
experiences of objects, and had no status independent of its application to
experience. The thing in itself was but the bare bones, "man-made" schema by which diverse sensible intuitions were synthesized into objects in
experience.

We may similarly regard a latent variable in this way as a schema for
synthesizing diverse variables, not as a function of them as in principal
components or Partial Least Squares (which follow Pearson's and Mach's

maxim that scientific concepts must be summary descriptions, functions of the data) but as diverse functions of a common latent variable that accounts for their observed interrelations and possibly that of other variables not yet studied.

The criticism of latent variables that they are indeterminate and must be avoided in favor of determinate variables rests on a correct major premise and a false minor premise. The correct major premise is that latent variables are mathematically indeterminate; they cannot be uniquely derived from their observed indicators. More than one variable might be found to stand in the same relationship to the observed variables as given by the correlations of these variables with their common factor as yielded by a factor analysis of the variables. But the false premise is that scientific concepts are not and must not be indeterminate with respect to the evidence on which they rest. For one thing it is now recognized by most philosophers of science (Garrison, 1986) that scientific concepts are underdetermined with respect to experience. Nevertheless, even if the common factor of a given set of variables is indeterminate so that there is no unique interpretation we can give to it, we can nevertheless create a use for it by choosing some interpretation consistent with the factor analytic results that allows us to generalize further to other variables. We can then declare the indicators of the factor in the initial factor analysis to be *criteria* for our interpreted factor. I am influenced here by Wittgenstein's (1953) concept of *criteria* (cf. Suter, 1989). Then we can test the hypothesis that not only is this factor common to our criterion indicators but to additional variables we believe have that factor in common as well. We do this by joining the original indicators with these additional variables in a new confirmatory factor analysis wherein we fix the loadings of the common factor on the original variables to the values they had in the initial analysis, leaving free the loadings on the additional variables. If the resulting model fits acceptably, that supports our hypothesis about the connection between the original variables and the additional variables (Mulaik 1990; Mulaik & McDonald, 1978).

Having introduced Wittgenstein's idea of *criteria*, I think I should say more about it. That a proposition p is a criterion for another proposition q is a matter of convention, a norm of grammar that *partially* fixes the meaning of q in specifying grounds for verifying q (Hacker, 1986). For example, "John is doubled over holding his belly and grimacing" is a criterion that John has a stomach ache. But "John has a stomach ache" does not mean "John is doubled over holding his belly and grimacing." We cannot substitute a criterion proposition p for the proposition q it is a criterion for. The propositions p and q do not have the same meaning for they have different verifying criteria. For example, "John is doubled over holding his belly and grimacing" is verified by applying what it means to be doubled over and holding one's belly and grimacing to the situation to which this proposition is applied. One will have been shown in the past what it means to doubled over, to hold one's belly, to grimace, and these are the criteria for this proposition. The criteria for stomach ache are behavioral, but the behaviors themselves are not the stomach ache.

Wittgenstein contrasted *criteria* with *symptoms*, which are states of affairs that have been inductively correlated in experience with those states of affairs that have been already designated by defining criteria. In the 19th century, Davaine and Rayer discovered a certain bacillus in the blood of sheep dying from anthrax. The bacillus in the blood was a symptom then of anthrax, for anthrax in animals was defined in those days by criteria such as bloody discharges from the nose and anus, sudden, greatly enlarged spleen, acute and often rapidly fatal onset of the disease, and in those animals that resisted the disease, the formation of carbuncles or pustules (Birkeland, 1949). But Wittgenstein recognized that often in science what were at first symptoms often later became new defining criteria, which in effect changed the meaning of the phenomenon. Once Koch in 1877 had isolated the anthrax bacillus and demonstrated he could cause the disease by inoculating it into animals, the meaning of anthrax changed, and finding the anthrax bacillus in the blood of diseased animals with greatly enlarged spleens became defining criteria for anthrax, while the bloody discharges and enlarged spleens now became symptoms. Today when the veterinarian wishes to diagnose for anthrax, he submits a sample of the diseased animal's blood to a bacteriologist to discover if the anthrax bacillus is present; that is his or her criterion. But before the germ theory of disease existed, the meaning of anthrax was different and had different criteria.

But in many other situations there is no clear distinction between what are criteria and what are symptoms. Having unbearable fatigue might be a symptom of AIDS, especially if the person who has this symptom belongs to a group at high risk for AIDS. But losing immunity to certain common diseases is a criterion for AIDS. Still one might have AIDS and not show the immunity difficulties or exhibit immunity difficulties and not have AIDS but something else that also attacks the immune system. So, what are criteria and what are symptoms sometimes fluctuate. At one time, for example, an acid was something that tasted sour and was able to dissolve metals. After someone discovered that dropping a metal into acid yielded hydrogen, generating hydrogen gas upon reaction with a metal became the defining criterion for a substance called an "acid" (Suter, 1989). And a more recent criterion for an acid might be that it is a "proton-donor" (Bennett, 1986). But such new criteria usually are accompanied by a new framework for understanding or representing the phenomena in question, for with new criteria there are new meanings.

But criteria are neither necessary nor sufficient conditions for something. Criteria do not logically entail anything. I may know that a child knows how to speak, because I have heard him speak spontaneously to report things or ask for things, which are criteria for a person's ability to speak. But when in front of strangers, I ask him to say something, he remains silent. Has he lost the ability for speech? No. We may say he is shy. So speaking is not a necessary condition for knowing how to speak. On the other hand, a parrot may be taught to "speak" in the sense that it makes sounds we recognize as sounds of speech. But this is not a sufficient condition that the parrot is able to talk and use language like a human. An opera singer may be trained to sing in a foreign language, but not understand the words, which we would know if we asked her to order food in that language. Thus singing in the foreign language is not a sufficient condition that the person can speak and understand that language, although singing in that language might in certain contexts be a criterion for that understanding, if we come upon the person by surprise and hear him or her singing a popular song in that language (Suter, 1989).

Often there are several criteria of something, and one may satisfy one of these criteria for a certain state of affairs, but not others, and then even criteria for this state of affairs not being the case. So, criteria are not logically decisive (Suter, 1989) and are even defeasible (Baker, 1974). A person may put on the act of being in pain and fool us, but then tell us he was only fooling, which defeats the act as a criterion for being in pain.

Finally, Wittgenstein argues that if p is a criterion for q, and one knows that p is true, then one is fully justified in saying that q is true. Criteria are conclusive and establish certainty. One is not permitted skeptical doubt that presents doubts without any basis for the doubts. One must provide reasons and evidence for doubting. As Baker puts it, "Wittgenstein identifies what is certain with what is actually beyond doubt, not with what is beyond all possible doubt" (Baker, 1974, p. 163).

Wittgenstein's theory of meaning in connection with his concept of criteria departs radically from previous theories of meaning. According to Baker (1974) traditional theories of meaning allowed one to be able to determine the sense of a proposition independently of the criteria one uses to determine its validity. Furthermore certainty was identified with absolute impossibility of doubt (Descartes). By merely doubting something one rendered it as uncertain and only probable opinion, if not irrelevant. Next, only rational deductions can transmit certainty from one proposition to another. And finally, rational inference is either inductive or deductive. But as we have seen, Wittgenstein differs with each of these views.

Wittgenstein used the concept of criteria to show how we come to understand certain mental terms through behavioral criteria. Some have thought he was then a behaviorist, but this is not so, for he clearly distinguished between criteria for behavioral statements and behavioral statements as criteria for traits and mental states of the individual, show-ing how they have distinct meanings in use. The aim of Wittgenstein was to put psychological constructs on a public basis. But the importance I see for Wittgenstein's notion of criteria relates to the way we use constructs and latent variables in psychological theorizing and structural equation modeling.

First, the meanings we ascribe to latent variables and constructs are not independent of the criteria or indicators we link these latent variables to. Furthermore when our theories satisfy our criteria that they are true or approximately true, this does not allow one to raise all kinds of doubts without good reasons and supporting evidence for those doubts. At the same time we must recognize that the evidence we offer to support our theories can be defeated by other evidence. But before everything we must establish criteria and not confuse these with inductive inference.

Lack of progress in the use of factor analysis in studying the struc-ture of the intellect, for example, has resulted from our failure to see that in their exploratory forms these methods do not provide definitions of the latent variables they point to. We cannot discover the meaning of intel-ligence through empirical research that yields latent variables. Meaning is not discovered but given by establishing conventions of language use, that is, through laying down criteria. We must break the indeterminate impasse of latent variables by assigning a use for these latent variables and proceed to study the consequences and implications of that use in additional studies, using the initial indicators of our factors as criteria for them. How many researchers take the variables from one study and in confirmatory analyses with addition variables believed to be influenced by the same factors, fix the original variables' loadings to the values they had on the presumed factor in a previous factor analytic study to test their hypothesis about the relation of the criteria to the additional vari-ables? But it is only by proceeding in this iterative way that we will make progress (cf. Mulaik, 1987b, 1990).

It is not mathematically impossible that a set of determinate compo-nents of a given finite set of observed variables (e.g., as in partial least squares) can be common factors of a domain of variables. But it is highly improbable that we will ever encounter such a situation, or if we do, that we will regard it as of general interest. For it implies that the observed variables themselves are common components of the domain of variables, representing a different basis for the common factor space of this domain. Such a situation would occur where the domain consists of all the vari-ables measuring "downstream" effects of the specific set of observed variables to which have been added, perhaps, other unique components such as various disturbances. But we are more likely to be interested in causes that are not only causes of the original set of variables but of other variables as well that are not effects of the original set of variables. Such causes will be objective in being not dependent on any specific phenomena from any particular point of view. These common causes cannot be determinate linear combinations of the initial set of observed variables if the original variables each contain a unique disturbance as well. The dimensions of the explanatory space of common causal factors and disturbance variables then exceeds the dimensions of the space of observed variables. And you cannot uniquely determine a common or a unique factor from the observed variables. Our desire for universally general common concepts by which to explain all phenomena, which is the basis for objective explanations, impels us to accept indeterminate concepts. Our concept of a set of general common causes of which all phenomena are (probabilistic) functions is but a regulative schema for achieving objective conceptions. The indeterminacy in the schema's implementation also makes possible for surprises that lead to those recurrent revolutions in science that we regard as progress.

REFERENCES

Baker, G. P. (1974). Criteria. A new foundation for semantics. *Ratio, 16*, 156–189.

Bandura, A. (1986). *Social foundations of thought and action: A social cognitive theory.* Englewood Hills, N.J.: Prentice-Hall.

Bennett, P. W. (1986). Wittgenstein and defining criteria. In J. V. Canfield, (Ed.), *The philosophy of Wittgenstein: Criteria.* (Vol. 7, pp. 373–387). New York: Garland Press.

Birkeland, J. (1949). *Microbiology and man.* Baltimore: Williams & Wilkins.

Canfield, J. V. (1986). The grammar of grammar. In J. V. Canfield, (Ed.), *The philosophy of Wittgenstein: Logical necessity and rules.* (Vol. 10, pp. 138–172). New York: Garland Press, 1986. [Originally published in Canfield, J. V. (1971). *Wittgenstein, language and world* (pp. 172–203, 225–226)].

Ellington, J. The unity of Kant's thought in his philosophy of nature. In I. Kant, *Metaphysical foundations of natural science.* Indianapolis: Bobbs-Merrill, 1970.

Friedrich, C. J. (1949). Introduction. *The philosophy of Kant: Immanuel Kant's moral and political writings.* New York: The Modern Library/Random House.

Garrison, J. W. (1986). Some principles of postpositivistic philosophy of science. *Educational Researcher, 15*, 12–18.

Hacker, P. M. S. (1986). *Insight and illusion: Themes in the philosophy of Wittgenstein.* Oxford: Clarendon Press.

Henrich, D. (1989). Kant's notion of a deduction and the methodological background of the first critique. In E. Förester, (Ed.), *Kant's transcendental deductions.* Stanford, CA: Stanford University Press.

Herder, J. G. (1967). Essay on *The Origin of Language.* In *On the origin of language,* A. Gode, trans. New York: F. Ungar.

Kant, I. (1965). [The critique of pure reason]. Tra. N. K. Smith. New York: St. Martin's Press, [Originally published 1781 as *Critik der reinen Vernunft.* Riga: Friedrich Hartknoch. Revised in 1787].

Kant, I. (1911). [Critique of judgment]. Werner S. Pluhar, trans. Indianapolis: Hacket Publishing Co. (Originally published in Prussia in 1790).

Kant, I. (1970). [Metaphysical foundations of natural science]. J. Ellington trans. Indianapolis: Bobbs-Merrill. [Original published 1786 as *Die metaphysichen Anfangs-gründe der Naturwissenschaft*].

Kant, I. (1977). [Prolegomena to any future metaphysics]. P. Carus, trans. 1902; revised by J. Ellington. Indianapolis: Hackett Publishing Co. [Originally published 1783]

Kant, I. (1988). [Logic]. R. S. Hartman & W. Schwarz, trans. New York: Dover Publications, 1988. [Originally published 1800 as *Immanuel Kants Logik: Ein Handbuch zu Vorlesungen*. Königsberg: Friedrich Nicolovius.]

Magill, F. N., & McGreal, I. P. (Eds.) (1961). The analysis of the sensations—Ernst Mach. In *Masterpieces of World Philosophy in Summary Form*. New York: Harper & Row.

Mulaik, S. A. (1985). Exploratory statistics and empiricism. *Philosophy of Science, 52*, 410–430.

Mulaik, S. A. (1986). Toward a synthesis of deterministic and probabilistic formulations of causal relations by the functional relation concept. *Philosophy of Science, 53*, 313–332.

Mulaik, S. A. (1987a). Toward a conception of causality applicable to experimentation and causal modeling. *Child Development, 58*, 18–32.

Mulaik, S. A. (1987b). A brief history of the philosophical foundations of exploratory factor analysis. *Multivariate Behavioral Research, 22*, 267–305.

Mulaik, S. A. (1988). Confirmatory factor analysis. In R. B. Cattell, & J. R. Nesselroade, (Eds.), *Handbook of Multivariate Experimental Psychology*. New York: Plenum.

Mulaik, S. A. (1990). Blurring the distinctions between component analysis and common factor analysis. *Multivariate Behavioral Research, 25*, 53–59.

Mulaik, S. A. (1991). Factor analysis, information-transforming instruments, and objectivity: A reply and discussion. *British Journal for the Philosophy of Science, 42*, 87–100.

Mulaik, S. A. (in press). The critique of pure statistics. In B. Thompson (Ed.), *Advances in social science methodology, Volume 3*, Greenwich, CT: JAI Press.

Mulaik, S. A., James, L. R., Van Alstine, J., Bennett, N., Lind, S. & Stilwell, C. D. (1989). Evaluation of goodness-of-fit indices for structural equation models. *Psychological Bulletin, 105*, 430–445.

Mulaik, S. A. & McDonald, R. P. (1978). The effect of additional variables on factor indeterminacy in models with a single common factor. *Psychometrika, 43*, 177–192.

Mulholland, L. A. (1990). *Kant's system of rights*. New York: Columbia University Press.

Pearson, K. (1911). *The grammar of science. Part I: Physical*. London: Adam & Charles Black. [Originally published 1892]

Rosenberg, J. F. (1986). *The thinking self*. Philadelphia: Temple University Press.

Rousseau, J. J. (1967). Essay on the origin of language. In J. Moran, Trans., *On the origin of language*. (First published posthumously in 1781).

Rousseau, J. J. (1762/1913). *The Social Contract*. G. D. H. Cole (translator). London: J. M. Dent. (Originally published 1762.)

Schouls, P. A. (1980). *The imposition of method: A study of Descartes and Locke*. Oxford: Clarendon Press.

Schwyzer, H. (1990). *The unity of understanding*. Oxford: Clarendon Press.

Skinner, B. F. (1953). *Science and Human Behavior*. New York: Macmillan.

Skinner, B. F. (1974). *About behaviorism*. New York: Knopf.

Suter, R. (1989). *Interpreting Wittgenstein*. Philadelphia: Temple University Press.

Thurstone, L. L. (1947). *Multiple factor analysis*. Chicago: University of Chicago Press.

Williams, M. (1990). Wittgenstein, Kant, and the "Metaphysics of Experience." *Kant-Studien, 81*, 69–88.

Williams, T. C. (1987). *The unity of Kant's critique of pure reason*. Lewiston/Queenston: The Edwin Mellen Press.

Wittgenstein, L. (1953). *Philosophical investigations*. New York: Macmillan.

CHAPTER ELEVEN

On the Quality of Test Statistics in Covariance Structure Analysis: Caveat Emptor

Peter M. Bentler

Structural equation modeling, and its important special cases of covariance structure analysis and confirmatory factor analysis, has become an important tool for testing theories with nonexperimental data (see Bentler, 1986; Bollen, 1989a; Loehlin, 1987). Some of the useful properties of structural modeling methods in theory testing are: the requirement for explicitness of a theory, so that it can be represented in path diagram form; the emphasis on a distinction between the variables of true interest, typically constructs or latent variables, and particular operationalizations of these; the capability to distinguish between direct, indirect, and total effects of certain variables on others; the ability to provide a statistical evaluation of the adequacy of the theory as a whole; the availability of tests to compare competing, nested models for their relative adequacy; the possibility of isolating potential problems with a theory via tests on missing parameters; and so on. Clearly, structural modeling has provided a useful methodology for theory testing in situations where more traditional or alternative methods may not work.

The availability of statistical goodness of fit tests to help evaluate the adequacy of models seems to have been an indispensable ingredient to the growth of structural modeling. This may be due to the implied objectivity

Peter M. Bentler • Department of Psychology, University of California, Los Angeles, Los Angeles, California, 90024-1563.

Cognitive Assessment: A Multidisciplinary Perspective, edited by Cecil R. Reynolds. Plenum Press, New York, 1994.

in model evaluation that such tests help to promote. An illustration of the importance of such tests, and the important role that computerized methods have for being able to calculate the tests, can be seen in the context of factor analysis. Methods of exploratory factor analysis, and a statistical test for evaluating the number of factors based on the assumption of multivariate normality of the measured variables (Lawley, 1940), had been around for decades. The test could not effectively be computed, however, until Jöreskog (1967) showed how the maximum likelihood (ML) estimator required for this test could be practically computed based on recently developed methods of nonlinear programming. As a result, the normal theory ML method for factor analysis became popular (Lawley & Maxwell, 1971). Yet, questions about the empirical quality of the statistical test in exploratory factor analysis were raised as soon as it became practically available (Linn, 1968), and alternative methods for evaluating ML results in exploratory factor analysis were proposed (Tucker & Lewis, 1973). Somewhat more generally, methods of oblique transformation help evaluate factor analytic models with correlated factors (Mosier, 1939) and concepts of restricted factor models (Anderson & Rubin, 1956) had been around for some time prior to the introduction of a practical computerized method for confirmatory factor analysis that yielded a goodness of fit χ^2 test statistic (Jöreskog, 1969). The test statistic and the associated statistical machinery, as well as the availability of computer programs to implement the estimation and testing, seem to have helped settle on confirmatory factor analysis as the preferred way to evaluate hypotheses about measurement models. Yet, empirical problems with the statistics (Boomsma, 1983; Harlow, 1985; Muthén & Kaplan, 1985) were noted and continue to be studied (Muthén & Kaplan, 1992). Similarly, alternatives to statistical tests due to potential problems with such tests (Bentler & Bonett, 1980) were noted quite early, and also continue to be developed (Bentler, 1990; Bollen, 1989b, Tanaka & Huba, 1985).

The past decade has seen the development of more general mathematical models, statistical methods, and computer programs in structural equation modeling. It may be of interest to see whether these recent developments, especially in statistical theory, have improved the quality of model tests in structural modeling beyond that noted in earlier work on factor analysis. It is possible that recent theories on the robustness of normal theory statistics, on elliptical and heterogeneous kurtosis statistics, on asymptotically distribution-free tests, and on tests based on models for categorical variables are a substantial improvement over prior work that provide more accurate evaluations of theories of psychological process. I shall concentrate my discussion on the studies of Hu, Bentler, and Kano (1992) and Lee, Poon, and Bentler (1991). While these studies do not cover all tests and modeling situations that are likely to be encountered in practice, they cover several of the popular ones. These studies show that some of the problems first noted in the context of factor analysis have not been mitigated by recent developments. In fact, the results show serious limitations in many modern test statistics, and verify that reviews made only a few years ago (Cuttance, 1987; Tanaka, 1987) cannot be considered as a guide to action today.

METHODS FOR CONTINUOUS VARIABLES[1]

Estimation methods in covariance structure analysis are traditionally developed under an assumption of multivariate normality (Bollen, 1989a; Browne, 1974; Jöreskog, 1969). This assumption is usually violated in practice. For example, Micceri (1989) reported that, among 440 large-sample achievement and psychometric measures taken from journal articles, research projects, and tests, all were significantly nonnormally distributed. Yet, normal theory methods such as maximum likelihood (ML) and generalized least squares (GLS) are frequently applied even when normality assumptions are not tenable. It has been found that a violation of the multivariate normality assumption can seriously invalidate statistical hypothesis testing (Browne, 1982, 1984; Harlow, 1985). As a result, a normal theory test statistic may not adequately reflect the quality of a covariance structure model under such a violation. Asymptotic (large sample) distribution-free methods, for which normality assumptions need not be made, therefore have been developed (Bentler & Dijkstra, 1985; Bentler, Lee, & Weng, 1987; Browne, 1982; 1984; Chamberlain, 1982) and made routinely available (Bentler, 1989; Jöreskog & Sörbom, 1988). Despite the preferable theoretical properties of these asymptotically distribution-free (ADF) methods, their wide application has been hampered due to the need for computing the fourth-order moments of the measured variables, which are both computationally expensive to obtain and unstable as estimators. In fact, empirical studies using Monte Carlo procedures have raised some questions about the relevance of the elegant theory for practical data analysis. In particular, the basic goodness of fit test for model adequacy under arbitrary distributions may behave quite poorly (i.e., not close to a theoretical χ^2 variate, as expected) when sample size is relatively small or model degrees of freedom are large (Chou, Bentler, & Satorra, 1991; Muthén & Kaplan, 1985, 1992; Tanaka, 1984). The limits of adequate performance are hardly known, but enough questions have been raised to again peak interest in simpler estimators.

A recently developed theory offers hope for the appropriate use of normal theory methods even under violation of the normality assumption. Based on initial work by Amemiya (1985) and Browne (1985), the asymp-

[1]This material is substantially taken from Hu, Bentler, and Kano (1992).

totic robustness of normal theory methods has been extensively studied (Amemiya & Anderson, 1990; Anderson & Amemiya, 1988; Browne, 1987; Browne & Shapiro, 1988; Mooijaart & Bentler, 1991; Satorra & Bentler, 1990, 1991; Shapiro, 1987). This literature has appeared only in statistical journals, so that it is hardly known to psychological researchers. The main point of this technical literature is to determine conditions under which models with nonnormally distributed variables can still be correctly described and evaluated by use of normal theory based methods such as ML or GLS. It is difficult to summarize this technical literature succinctly, but it has been shown that asymptotic optimality and correct standard errors of factor loadings can be obtained under normal theory methods when the common factors are not normally distributed and the unique factors have a multivariate normal distribution, and hence the observed variables are also nonnormal. For example, Anderson and Amemiya (1988) and Amemiya and Anderson (1990) have found that the asymptotic χ^2 goodness of fit test in factor analysis can be insensitive to violations of the assumption of multivariate normality of both common and unique factors, if all factors are mutually independently distributed and the elements of the covariance matrices of common factors are all free parameters. With an additional condition of the existence of the fourth-order moments of both unique and common factors, Browne and Shapiro (1988) and Mooijaart and Bentler (1991) also demonstrated the robustness of normal theory methods in the analysis of a general class of linear latent variate models. Satorra and Bentler (1990, 1991) obtained similar results for a wider range of discrepancy functions, estimators, and test statistics. In these results, the standard errors based on normal theory of some parameters, usually the variances of nonnormal variables, need correction, but the relevant computation is minor compared to that required by the distribution-free methods. Thus, asymptotic robustness theory promises to extend the range of applicability of the computationally simpler ML and GLS estimators to situations where the more difficult distribution-free methods might seem to be needed.

In practice, the applied researcher may be tempted to use a normal theory method in data analysis with nonnormal variables, justifying such a choice on the basis of asymptotic robustness theory. It is not at all certain that this theory can be invoked in practice, however, since nothing is known about the robustness of the asymptotic robustness theory; that is, whether asymptotic robustness theory can be applied when its assumptions such as large sample size and independence of latent variates may not hold. Adequate procedures to evaluate whether latent factors or errors are not only uncorrelated, but furthermore are mutually independent, do not exist. It will be remembered that independence is a much stronger condition than uncorrelatedness, and that these concepts are equivalent only when variables are normally distributed.

Estimation methods based on distributional assumptions more general than normal, but more restricted than arbitrary, also have been developed. Browne (1982, 1984) introduced multivariate elliptical theory to covariance structure analysis. Elliptical distributions are, like the normal, symmetric, but they have tails that can be identical to those of a normal distribution as well as heavier or lighter. Browne's work was followed up by Bentler (1983; Bentler & Berkane, 1986) and Shapiro and Browne (1987), and computer implementations (e.g., ERLS) have been available for some years (Bentler, 1989). In these distributions, only one additional parameter beyond the usual normal theory parameters is needed to yield asymptotically optimal estimators and simple χ^2 goodness of fit tests. This extra parameter is a kurtosis parameter reflecting the assumed common kurtosis of the variables; that is, the extent to which the distribution of variables is heavier-tailed or lighter-tailed as compared to the normal. Normal distributions are a special case that has no excess kurtosis. Computations are particularly simple when the model meets a scale invariance condition (Shapiro & Browne, 1987). Although elliptical theory is by now quite old, little is known about the robustness of elliptical theory statistics to violation of assumptions. One might expect that, since normal theory is a special case of elliptical theory, and elliptical methods reduce to normal theory methods, elliptical methods should perform at least as well as or substantially better than normal theory methods. However, this does not appear to be the case. Harlow (1985) found that elliptical χ^2 tests could be more misleading than normal theory statistics, but this work has not been followed up.

A recent extension of elliptical distribution theory by Kano, Berkane and Bentler (1990); Bentler, Berkane, and Kano (1991) has revealed that a simple adjustment of the weight matrix of normal theory, using marginal kurtosis estimates, results in an asymptotically efficient estimator of structural parameters within the class of estimators that minimize a general discrepancy function. This method, called here heterogeneous kurtosis (HK) theory, is hardly more difficult computationally than elliptical theory, but applies to a wider class of multivariate distributions that is allowed to have heterogeneous kurtosis parameters. That is, while these distributions are assumed to be symmetric, they need not be equally heavy- (or light-) tailed for all variables. Elliptical and normal theory statistics are special cases that occur when the variables have homogeneous kurtoses, or no excess kurtosis, respectively. Thus, one might expect that HK theory should perform at least as well as normal or elliptical methods.

An attractive feature of HK theory is that fourth-order moments of the measured variables do not need to be computed as they do in ADF theory, since these moments are just a function of the variance and covariances and the marginal kurtoses. As a result, the HK method can be used on models based on a substantially larger number of measured variables. For example, while ADF methods cannot be implemented in practice with 30, 40, or more variables due to the large size of a matrix that is required, this is not a limitation of the HK method. Except for an illustration given in the initial report, nothing is known, about the performance of HK theory under violation of its assumptions, or even when its assumptions are met as when the data are normal or elliptical.

When normal, elliptical, or heterogeneous kurtosis theory distributional assumptions are false, statistics based on these assumptions can be corrected using a method developed by Satorra and Bentler (1988a,b) and further studied by Kano (1990). In their approach, a scaling correction is computed based on the model, estimation method, and sample fourth-order moments, and the given test statistic is divided by this correction factor. The correction factor has no impact when the distributional assumption is correct. This approach, which is a type of Bartlett correction to the χ^2 statistic, has not been evaluated widely even though it has been available in the EQS program (Bentler, 1989) for some years. Preliminary indications are that this corrected test statistic, here called the SCALED statistics, can perform as well as, or perhaps better than, the ADF method under violation of distributional assumptions (Chou, Bentler, & Satorra, 1991). However, nothing definitive is known.

Hu, Bentler, and Kano (1992) evaluated the performance of six goodness of fit test statistics obtained from a variety of estimators under violation of assumptions, that is, the empirical robustness of these statistics. In all cases, under an assumed distribution and a hypothesized model $\Sigma(\theta)$ for the population covariance matrix Σ, these statistics have an asymptotic χ^2 distribution that describes the mean, variance, and tail performance of the statistics. Three ways of violating theoretical conditions, chosen for their relevance to the data analysis practice and recent theoretical results, were investigated. First, distributional assumptions were violated. Second, assumed independence conditions were violated. Third, asymptotic sample size requirements were violated. The effects of these conditions on normal theory maximum likelihood (ML) and generalized least squares (GLS), elliptical theory (ERLS), heterogeneous kurtosis (HK), asymptotic distribution-free (ADF), and scaling-corrected (SCALED) test statistics (T_{ML}, T_{GLS}, T_{ERLS}, T_{HK}, T_{ADF}, T_{SCALED}) were studied in an extensive Monte Carlo sampling experiment. Technical definitions for these statistics are given in the Appendix of the Hu et al. paper.

HU, BENTLER, AND KANO'S METHOD

The confirmatory factor model $\underset{\sim}{x} = \Lambda\xi + \epsilon$ was used to generate measured variables $\underset{\sim}{x}$ under various conditions on the common factors ξ and unique variates ("errors") ϵ. In the usual approach, factors and errors are assumed to be normally distributed, factors are allowed to correlate with covariance matrix ($\mathscr{E}(\xi\xi') = \Phi$, errors are mutually uncorrelated with factors, i.e., $\mathscr{E}(\xi\epsilon') = 0$, and various error variates are mutually uncorrelated and have a diagonal covariance matrix $\mathscr{E}(\epsilon\epsilon') = \Psi$. As a result, $\Sigma = \Sigma(\theta) = \Lambda\Phi\Lambda' + \Psi$, and the elements of θ are the unknown parameters in Λ, Φ, and Ψ. In one condition, factors and errors were created to be multivariate normally distributed, so that the latent variates that are uncorrelated in the factor model are also independent of each other. Additional conditions were created in which the factors and/or errors are not normally distributed; in some of these conditions, factor–error variates that are uncorrelated under the model also are independent, but in other conditions variables that are uncorrelated as assumed by the factor model are not also independent. After generation of the population covariance matrix Σ under the assumed conditions, random samples of a given size from the population were taken. In each sample, the parameters of the factor model were estimated using the methods ML, GLS, ERLS, HK, ADF, SCALED, and the associated test statistics T_{ML}, T_{GLS}, T_{ERLS}, T_{HK}, T_{ADF}, and T_{SCALED} were computed. Results for each sample were saved. The performance of the test statistics across the sampling replications at a given sample size represents the main data of the study.

In particular, the confirmatory factor analytic model studied by Hu, Bentler, and Kano was based on 15 observed variables with three common factors. The factor loading pattern is Λ (15 $\times$ 3) was a simple one in which a variable is influenced by one, and only one, common factor, and the three common factors were allowed to correlate. The factor loading matrix (transposed) Λ' had the following structure:

$$
\begin{bmatrix}
.70 & .70 & .75 & .80 & .80 & .00 & .00 & .00 & .00 & .00 & .00 & .00 & .00 & .00 & .00 \\
.00 & .00 & .00 & .00 & .00 & .70 & .70 & .75 & .80 & .80 & .00 & .00 & .00 & .00 & .00 \\
.00 & .00 & .00 & .00 & .00 & .00 & .00 & .00 & .00 & .00 & .70 & .70 & .75 & .80 & .80
\end{bmatrix}.
$$

Variance of the factors were 1.0, and the covariance among the three factors were taken to be 0.30, 0.40, and 0.50. The unique variances were taken as values that would yield unit-variance measured variables under normality. In estimation, the factor loading of the last indicator of each factor was fixed for identification at 0.80, and the remaining nonzero parameters were free to be estimated. The behavior of the various test statistics $T = (n - 1)\hat{F}$ (for variously defined functions F) was observed at sample sizes of 150, 250, 500, 1000, 2500, and 5000. In each condition at each sample size, 200 replications (samples) were drawn from the population. The various estimators and goodness of fit tests were computed in each sample using a modification of the simulation feature of EQS (Bentler, 1989). A statistical summary of the mean value and standard deviation of T across the 200 replications, and the empirical rejection rate

TABLE 1. Asymptotic Expected Goodness-of-Fit Statistics under 7 Conditions

Distribution[a]		Method of Estimation[b]			
Factor	Unique Factor	ML and GLS	ERLS	HK	ADF and SCALED
1. NORMAL	NORMAL	87	87	87	87
2. NON[c]	NON	—	—	—	93
3. NON	NON	87	$87/\kappa_3$	—	87
4. NORMAL	NON	87	$87/\kappa_4$	—	87
5.[d] NORMAL/Z	NORMAL/Z	87*3	87	87	87
6.[d] NORMAL/Z	NON/Z	87*3	$87*3/\kappa_6$	—	87
7.[d] NON/Z	NON/Z	87*3	$87*3/\kappa_7$	—	87

[a]NON denotes a nonnormal distribution.
[b]See text for explanation.
[c]Factor covariance matrix ϕ is taken as known and fixed.
[d]Common and unique factors are divided by the same variate $Z = \chi_{(5)}^{2}{}^{1/2}/\sqrt{3}$.

at the $\alpha = .05$ level based on the assumed χ^2 distribution, was used to compare the various methods.

Table 1 presents the experimental design and the expectations (or the first-order moments) of the asymptotic distributions of the goodness of fit test statistics T in each condition. Under the modeling conditions, the expectations in Table 1 would be very close to the corresponding empirical mean value of the test statistics, one of the statistical summaries in the Hu et al. experiment, if the sample size and number of replications are large enough. In some conditions, these are the expected values of a central χ^2 variate, that is, the degrees of freedom, but in other cases these are other values as based on predictions from the current literature and the rationale given below. Seven conditions are examined as shown in the rows of the table. These conditions correspond to various distributional specifications on the common and unique (error) factors. In condition 1, all factors were normally distributed, with no excess kurtosis. In conditions 2 and 3, all factors were nonnormally distributed. In these conditions, the true kurtoses, using the formula $\sigma_{iiii}/\sigma_{ii}^2 - 3$, for the non-normal factors in the various conditions were -1.0, 2.0, and 5.0, while the true kurtoses of the unique variates for conditions 2 through 4 with nonnormal errors were -1.0, 0.5, 2.5, 4.5, 6.5, -1.0, 1.0, 3.0, 5.0, 7.0, -0.5, 1.5, 3.5, 5.5, and 7.5. In conditions 1 through 4, all the factors and unique variates were mutually independently distributed regardless of whether or not they were normally distributed. Additionally, in condition 2, all elements in the factor covariance matrix Φ were fixed at their true value. Thus, while conditions 3 and 4 were designed to be consistent with asymptotic robustness theory, the fixed covariance matrix invalidates this theory, and asymptotic robustness of normal theory test statistics would not be expected in condition 2. In conditions 5 through 7, the factors and error variates were divided by a random variable $Z = (\chi^2_{(5)})^{1/2} / \sqrt{3}$ that is distributed independently of the original common and unique factors. The division by $\sqrt{3}$ was made so that $E(Z^{-2}) = 1$, that is, the variance and covariances of the factors remain unchanged by the division (Kano, 1990), but the kurtoses of the factors and errors became modified. A consequence of the division by a random variable is that the factors and errors were mutually dependent, even though they remain uncorrelated. Because of the mutual dependency, asymptotic robustness of normal theory statistics was not to be expected under conditions 5 through 7.

Under the model $\Sigma(\theta)$, as can be seen in the table, in many conditions the predicted values of the asymptotic goodness of fit statistics are the degrees of freedom. The degrees of freedom for the model in all conditions but the second is 87, whereas the degrees of freedom for the model in condition 2 is 93. Under other conditions, the predicted values of the test statistics depend upon the kurtosis of the variables as well. These predicted values were computed using the known relation of normal to elliptical theory as well as the results of Kano (1990). In all cases, the expectations of Table 1 are based on the assumption of the correctness of the model $\Sigma = \Sigma(\theta)$ and the assumption of infinite sample size. As noted above, in the simulation, the correctness of the model was maintained in all sampling situations and conditions, but sample size was varied in a standard range.

The simplest predictions were made for condition 1 (row 1) and the ADF and SCALED statistics (last column) of Table 1. In row 1, all variables are normally distributed and hence $E(T) = 87$ for all testing conditions. The predicted value of T_{ADF} and T_{SCALED} is the degrees of freedom, regardless of the seven types of distributions and conditions that are considered. The results of T_{ML} and T_{GLS} (in the column marked ML & GLS) depend upon the independence of factors from errors as noted above. When they are mutually independent, as in conditions 1 and 3 through 4, asymptotic robustness conditions apply and $E(T_{ML}) = E(T_{GLS}) = 87$, but the fixed factor covariance matrix in condition 2 invalidates robustness theory, and no prediction was made there. Lack of robustness for normal theory methods in conditions 5 through 7 leads to expectations of $261 = 87 \times 3$ as the mean value of the normal theory test statistics, which is obtained from a chi-squared variable multiplied by $E(Z^{-4})/E(Z^{-2})^2 = 3$ (Kano, 1990). The predicted value of the statistic T_{ERLS} of elliptical theory is given by the predicted value under the ML method divided by $(\kappa + 1) = E((\chi - \mu)\Sigma^{-1}(\chi - \mu))^2/p(p + 2)$, which is the rescaled Mardia kurtosis parameter for multivariate distributions. Note that κ_3, κ_4, κ_6, and κ_7 in Table 1 are the specific values of the Mardia kurtosis defined for different distributions. They have the following relationships: $3 \times \kappa_3 = \kappa_7$ and $3 \times \kappa_4 = \kappa_6$. Predictions were made for the HK theory only under normality (condition 1) and elliptical (condition 5) distributions. Of course, HK should yield the same result as the normal theory statistic in condition 1, and, since the distribution in condition 5 is elliptical, and ERLS and HK methods were expected to work correctly.

SUMMARY OF HU, BENTLER, AND KANO'S RESULTS

Only the results of Conditions 1, 3, and 7 will be summarized here since they demonstrate the major effects found in the study. The original report, of course, provides information on all conditions studied.

Tables 2 through 4 present summaries of the results of the simulation, one table per condition. These tables are organized the same way. The columns of each table give the sample size used for a particular set of 200 replications from the population. At each sample size, a sample was drawn, and each of the six methods shown in the rows of the table (ML, GLS, ERLS, HK, ADF, SCALED) was applied to estimate the parameters of the model and compute the resulting test statistic T; this process

TABLE 2. Summary of Simulation Results for Condition 1

Method	Sample Size					
	150	250	500	1000	2500	5000
ML	92.674[a]	90.540	87.771	86.166	87.136	86.583
	(13.175)[b]	(14.622)	(12.617)	(12.450)	(12.232)	(11.728)
	20[c]	21	9	5	4	8
GLS	85.491	86.546	85.355	85.214	86.779	86.328
	(12.440)	(13.667)	(12.212)	(12.490)	(12.154)	(11.578)
	5	12	5	5	3	7
ERLS	89.887	88.905	87.250	85.812	86.986	86.573
	(12.363)	(14.496)	(12.558)	(12.241)	(12.205)	(11.794)
	11	18	7	5	5	9
HK	87.747	88.031	86.180	85.579	86.882	86.373
	(13.441)	(14.103)	(12.634)	(12.575)	(12.084)	(11.531)
	8	15	5	7	2	7
ADF	229.118[d]	144.930	109.333	96.077	91.096	88.447
	(48.426)[d]	(27.487)	(17.613)	(15.017)	(13.222)	(12.057)
	191/191[d]	184	100	32	12	9
SCALED	94.469	91.540	88.251	86.398	87.251	86.654
	(13.485)	(14.732)	(12.644)	(12.426)	(12.246)	(11.750)
	23	22	8	5	6	9

[a] Mean goodness of fit test statistic across 200 replications.
[b] Standard deviation of test statistics across 200 replications.
[c] Frequency of rejection of the null hypothesis (critical value from $\chi^2_{(p^*-q)}$ at $\alpha = .05$).
[d] Statistic based on number (<200) of converged replications.

TABLE 3. Summary of Simulation Results for Condition 3

Method	Sample Size					
	150	250	500	1000	2500	5000
ML	91.752[a]	90.800	87.571	88.531	88.766	87.517
	(14.481)[b]	(13.401)	(14.227)	(14.620)	(14.056)	(13.559)
	20[c]	20	14	16	10	10
GLS	85.072	86.138	85.450	87.366	88.320	87.228
	(12.342)	(12.274)	(13.353)	(14.239)	(14.043)	(13.441)
	8	5	8	14	12	9
ERLS	82.491	81.682	78.242	78.582	78.549	76.547
	(13.255)	(12.487)	(13.197)	(13.408)	(12.486)	(11.763)
	8	4	3	5	4	2
HK	73.854	71.818	69.112	69.216	68.499	67.493
	(12.733)	(12.242)	(12.757)	(12.978)	(11.899)	(11.077)
	3	0	0	1	0	0
ADF	216.807[d]	143.761	108.541	97.816	91.983	88.899
	(39.495)[d]	(25.163)	(18.668)	(16.441)	(14.311)	(13.476)
	188/188[d]	185	89	44	18	11
SCALED	93.777	92.066	88.160	88.914	88.896	87.568
	(14.403)	(13.427)	(14.372)	(14.786)	(14.083)	(13.551)
	25	25	16	18	12	10

[a]Mean goodness of fit test statistic across 200 replications.
[b]Standard deviation of test statistics across 200 replications.
[c]Frequency of rejection of the null hypothesis (critical value from $\chi^2_{(p*-q)}$ at $\alpha = .05$).
[d]Statistic based on number (<200) of converged replications.

was repeated 200 times. For each estimation method, the resulting T statistics were used to compute (1) the mean of the 200 T statistics; (2) the standard deviation of the 200 T statistics; and (3) the frequency of rejecting the null hypothesis at the .05 level. These are the three entries in each cell of each table. As noted in the columns of each table, these procedures were repeated at sample sizes of 150, 250, 500, 1000, 2500, and 5000. When converged solutions were not obtained in each of the 200 replications of a given cell of the table, the statistics reported in the table are based on the results for those replications that did converge. If a cell had convergence problems, these are noted in footnote d. The ADF method at the smallest sample size provided the only consistent lack of convergence.

The results of condition 1 are easiest to understand, since it is the baseline condition in which the factors and errors, and hence measured variables, are multivariate normally distributed. The results are tabulated in Table 2. Asymptotically, each estimation method should yield a mean test statistic T of about 87, a standard deviation of $13.19 = \sqrt{174}$

TABLE 4. Summary of Simulation Results for Condition 7

	Sample Size					
Method	150	250	500	1000	2500	5000
ML	166.485[a]	175.366	191.309	199.481	215.325	225.643
	(45.844)[b]	(47.955)	(70.507)	(65.989)	(70.836)	(81.001)
	194[c]	195	200	199	200	200
GLS	128.266	144.718	165.662	181.992	204.578	217.556
	(20.923)	(25.089)	(33.047)	(40.587)	(53.465)	(60.689)
	162	185	199	198	200	200
ERLS	106.482	100.633	95.455	88.795	84.535	81.369
	(30.482)	(25.031)	(25.156)	(20.558)	(17.377)	(15.355)
	64	50	31	14	11	7
HK	67.711	70.218	70.166	70.130	71.966	70.487
	(13.147)	(14.124)	(14.022)	(13.864)	(14.983)	(14.731)
	0	1	3	1	3	1
ADF	206.609[d]	137.762[d]	108.634	96.721	91.343	89.150
	(37.517)[d]	(20.131)[d]	(15.645)	(12.365)	(13.433)	(13.360)
	177/177[d]	183/199[d]	93	27	11	10
SCALED	92.032	89.154	87.539	86.359	86.114	85.625
	(12.474)	(12.653)	(11.628)	(12.681)	(12.859)	(12.805)
	14	11	4	7	6	5

[a]Mean goodness of fit test statistic across 200 replications.
[b]Standard deviation of test statistics across 200 replications.
[c]Frequency of rejection of the null hypothesis (critical value from $\chi^2_{(p^*-q)}$ at $\alpha = .05$).
[d]Statistic based on number (<200) of converged replications.

$(174 = 2 \times 87)$, and $10 = .05 \times 200$ rejections. The last column of the table gives the results for n = 5000, which is as close to asymptotic sample size as was considered in this study. It will be seen that for all 6 estimation methods, the mean goodness of fit statistic T was quite close to 87; the standard deviations were a bit smaller than 13.19, and the rejections were just slightly below 10. Clearly, however, these results are very close to the theoretical values, indicating that the Monte Carlo procedure as implemented in the computer program was working correctly. In addition, one can note the following features. As can be seen in the first row, the ML method worked well when sample sizes were equal or greater than 500, but the rejection frequency was higher than nominal at smaller sample sizes. Similar results have been reported by Boomsma (1983). The GLS method performed better than ML at the smaller sample sizes, though at the smallest sample size models were rejected too infrequently. The ERLS and HK methods seemed to perform equally well, and a bit better than ML at the two smallest sample sizes. The ADF method yielded unacceptably high rejection rates and test statistics at all sample sizes up to 1000, with performance being completely unacceptable at $n = 250$ or below, where almost all true models were rejected. At $n = 150$, only 191 replications yielded converged solutions, all of which rejected the null hypothesis. In contrast, the SCALED statistic, based on the ML statistic, performed about the same as the ML statistic itself.

For condition 3, where asymptotic robustness for normal theory statistics had been predicted, ML and GLS indeed performed well as is shown in Table 3. That is, at sample sizes of 2500 and 5000, the statistics yielded their expected behavior. As with the results under normality, GLS performed somewhat better than ML at the smaller sample sizes, with ML tending to reject models somewhat too frequently. ERLS and HK tended to overcorrect, that is, to accept models too readily. While ADF performed well at $n = 5000$, at smaller sample sizes it rejected models far too frequently. At $n = 150$, about 5% of the replications did not yield converged solutions. In all the converged solutions, the true model was rejected. Condition 3 thus represents a situation where ML and GLS methods indeed perform better than ADF methods at all but the largest sample size. The SCALED test statistic performed better than ADF at all but the largest sample size, where it performed equally well. It performed about the same as the ML statistic, though with marginally greater rejection of true models at the smaller sample sizes.

When the factors and errors were mutually dependent on each other; that is, in condition 7 as summarized in Table 4, asymptotic robustness theory was not relevant, and the results indicate that empirical robustness completely broke down. Specifically, the normal theory methods (ML, GLS) essentially always rejected the true model even at the largest sample sizes. The ERLS method performed substantially better than the normal theory methods. The HK method performed considerably better than all but the SCALED statistic across the different sample sizes, though it retained its tendency to accept models too frequently. As under independence of factors and errors, when the sample sizes were smaller than 2500, ADF consistently yielded test statistics that were too large and rejection rates that were too high. The SCALED statistic performed better than the ADF method at all sample sizes below 2500, though it tended to overreject models at the largest sample size.

IMPLICATIONS OF HU ET AL. RESULTS

Regarding the ADF method, the Hu et al. results provide support for, and extend, the cautions raised, for example, by Chou, Bentler, and Satorra (1991), Harlow, Chou, and Bentler (1986), and Muthén and Kaplan (1992). ADF theory originally was introduced as a general purpose solution to the problem of nonnormal distributions of variables in structural modeling (Browne, 1982; Chamberlain, 1982); that is, it was expected that the ADF method would work well for any arbitrary distribution. The results of the present study indicate that this expectation is correct asymptotically; T_{ADF} does perform as a χ^2 variate when the sample size is about 5000 cases under the modeling conditions studied. However, applications in practice typically have substantially smaller sample sizes. In more than half of the Hu et al. conditions, a sample size of 2500 was not large enough to yield the number of model rejections expected on the basis of the assumed χ^2 distribution, and in none of the conditions was a sample size of 1000 large enough to yield a nominal rejection rate. At sample sizes of 250 or less, the ADF statistic, when it could be computed, yielded model rejections from 93 to 99.9% of the time; that is, it almost never correctly diagnosed that a true model was being evaluated. This spectacularly poor performance occurred even with multivariate normal data that would be expected to show the best behavior of the statistic. Thus, clearly ADF is not a general panacea to the problem of nonnormal variables in structural modeling. In fact, like the normal theory methods ML and GLS, under some conditions it will yield completely misleading results. Typically, models that are true would be rejected far too frequently when using the ADF method. Hu, Bentler, and Kano provide an explanation of the poor performance of the ADF method in terms of the variability of the weight matrix used in estimation.

Under conditions where latent common factors and unique factors were distributed independently of each other (conditions 1–4), which is a basic requirement of asymptotic robustness theory, normal theory methods (ML, GLS) outperformed ADF at all but the very largest sample sizes. This occurred even when the data were quite nonnormally distributed, and even under a condition where asymptotic robustness theory has not been shown to hold (condition 2). Thus conditions certainly exist in which nonnormal data are better analyzed for model adequacy using normal theory methods than those specifically developed for nonnormal data. Hu et al. emphasized, however, that the word *asymptotic* in asymptotic robustness theory requires careful attention. At the smaller sample sizes, this theory also had some limitations. For maximum likelihood, sample sizes of 2500 were needed before the rejection rate approached nominal levels. Generalized least squares performed much better, performing near nominal levels at even the smallest sample sizes, with only a few exceptions. As yet, there is no theory to explain the differential behaviors of ML and GLS, nor to explain the robustness observed in condition 2 where the common factor covariance matrix was fixed rather than free to be estimated.

On the other hand, the practitioner certainly cannot blindly trust normal theory test statistics to yield correct results with nonnormal data. The Hu et al. results show that normal theory methods performed extremely poorly when there is a dependency among latent variates. In fact, under those conditions even the poorly performing ADF method always outperformed the normal theory methods, which for all practical purposes were completely useless at evaluating model adequacy at all sample sizes, since they almost always rejected the true model. These results must give serious pause to the covariance structure analysis practitioner. It would be inappropriate for a practitioner to use normal theory methods in their analysis on the hope that "asymptotic robustness theory verifies that nonnormal data can be appropriately analyzed using ML or GLS." Without some diagnostic about the relevance of this theory to the particular model and data analysis situation, it is entirely possible that the data being analyzed comes from a data generation mechanism that does not yield asymptotic robustness for ML or GLS test statistics.

Elliptical and heterogeneous kurtosis theory promise a methodology to correct for normality that requires only trivially heavier computations than normal theory methods. These methods performed variably. When the latent common and error variates were independently distributed, both methods tended to accept models more frequently than expected. When these variates were dependent, ERLS tended to reject models more frequently than expected, while the HK method accepted models too often, though both performances were certainly substantially better than those obtained by the normal theory methods which essentially always rejected true models. The performance of the new HK method was remarkably consistent across all conditions, yielding mean test statistics T_{HK} and associated standard deviations that were reasonably close to the theoretically expected values under a χ^2 distribution, though the number of rejections were consistently smaller than nominal levels. Except at the largest sample sizes, HK theory performed better than ADF theory, though improvements in HK theory are clearly still needed. It is possible that a new implementation of this theory (Bentler, Berkane, & Kano, 1991) would yield better performance. In any case, the HK method seems to be the most promising of all methods when considering extremely large models, in which normal theory methods can be misleading (under dependence of factors and errors) and in which alternative methods like ADF and SCALED basically cannot be implemented at all due to the size of the matrices involved.

The best performance across all conditions was shown by Satorra and Bentler's (1988a,b) SCALED test statistic, which has been documented and available in EQS since 1989. Although preliminary positive research on its performance has previously been obtained (Chou, Bentler, & Satorra, 1991), the Hu et al. study is the first comprehensive study of its behavior. It performed better than ADF at all but the largest sample sizes. When considering the closeness of the empirical mean of the statistic to the expected value (87, or 93 in condition 2), the SCALED statistic was closer than the ADF statistic 42 times out of 42 comparisons. In terms of closeness to the expected 10 rejections at $\alpha = .05$, at sample sizes up to and including 1000, the SCALED statistic performed better than the ADF statistic in 28 out of 28 comparisons. At $n = 2500$ or $n = 5000$, the SCALED and ADF statistics were closer to nominal levels an equivalent number of times.

While the SCALED statistic performed extremely well overall, it had a tendency to overreject models at smaller sample sizes. The same tendency was observed for ML as compared to GLS when these statistics performed adequately (conditions 1–4). Since the SCALED statistic as implemented was based on the T_{ML} statistic (using METHOD = ML, ROBUST in EQS), it is likely that closer to nominal rejection rates would be observed if the GLS statistic had been scaled instead (using METHOD = GLS, ROBUST). Of course, the scaling correction can work with many other estimators as well. It is interesting to speculate whether the tendency of the HK method to overaccept models would be eliminated if the scaling correction were used on the T_{HK} statistic. Clearly more work is needed in this area.

The reason for the superior performance of the SCALED over the ADF statistic is not known. Hu et al. suggested that, while both statistics rely on the sample fourth order moments of the variable as part of their estimation, the SCALED statistic uses a matrix computed from these moments directly while ADF requires the relevant matrix to be inverted. This inverse may not even exist in sufficiently small samples, and there may be accuracy problem in intermediate-size samples.

Although the Hu et al. study evaluated the empirical behavior of a larger variety of test statistics under a more varied set of conditions than has previously been attempted, clearly any simulation has its limitations. Some of these are noted in their report, and suggestions for further research; for example, in better corrections for small sample behavior, are made in the technical report. It should also be noted that the Hu et al. study concentrated on the overall goodness of fit χ^2 test. On the basis of the general relations among various test statistics used in structural modeling (e.g., Bentler & Dijkstra, 1985; Satorra, 1989), one can expect that related statistics such as the Lagrange Multiplier test (Lee & Bentler, 1980; Bentler, 1989, chapter 10) should be subject to the same difficulties noted in the Hu, Bentler, and Kano (1992) simulation. This suggestion awaits further research.

METHODS FOR CATEGORICAL VARIABLES[2]

Since many variables in social science research are not continuous, a separate methodology has been developed for structural equation models

---

[2]This material is based on the results of Lee, Poon, and Bentler (1991).

with categorical variables. In general, this methodology assumes that continuous underlying multivariate normal variables have been categorized, that linear structural relations describe the interrelations among the continuous underlying variables, and that a probit-type relation holds between the categorical indicators and the underlying continuous variables. Estimation and testing in these models is somewhat more complicated than for continuous variables, since product moments (means and covariances) are not the usual summary statistics to be analyzed.

There are a variety of estimators and tests based on categorical variable methodology, but the best known are those of Jöreskog and Sörbom, and Muthén. In their LISREL computer program, Jöreskog and Sörbom (1988) provide procedures for categorical variable models. Unfortunately, nothing has been published on the mathematical and statistical basis of their approach so it has not been studied further. Muthén (1984) developed the most general structural model available today in computerized implementation that allows both continuous and ordered categorical variables (although more general approaches are being developed: Arminger & Küsters, 1989). A three-stage estimation method based on limited information conditional maximum likelihood and generalized least squares approaches was proposed and integrated into the LISCOMP program (Muthén, 1987). Moreover, an approach analogous to Muthén (1984) was applied to factor analysis with censored variables and made available in LISCOMP, the premier program for modeling categorical variables available today. Lee, Poon, and Bentler (1991) studied the behavior of the goodness-of-fit χ^2 test statistics and standard error estimates of Muthén's categorical variable methodology, using LISCOMP. Unlike the Hu et al. study, the distribution of the underlying continuous variables was taken as assumed under the methodology, i.e., multivariate normal. Thus robustness and distributional misspecification were not at issue. The simpler question of performance under nominal conditions was addressed.

LEE, POON, AND BENTLER'S METHODS AND RESULTS

A variety of models and statistics were studied, but only a subset of these will be summarized here. One of the models studied was a 15-variable two-factor confirmatory factor analysis model. In one condition, 12 of the 15 variables were taken to be continuous, and 3 polytomous. In another condition, 8 were taken as continuous, and 7 as polytomous. Thresholds for the categorical variables were based on symmetric and asymmetric polytomous distributions, with two sets of values for each. The performance of the statistics at two sample sizes of 1500 and 2500 observations were tabulated, based on 100 replications of each condition. The results on the χ^2 test are reproduced in Table 5.

The left part of the table shows the experimental conditions, namely,

TABLE 5. Empirical Cumulative Frequency of the Goodness of Fit Statistics, and p-Values of K-S test. Model with 15 Variables

N	Threshold Type	Theoretical Percentage of χ^2_{89}							K-S test's P-value
		80	70	50	30	20	10	5	
Combination	C_1^*								
1500	S1	94*	87*	67*	44*	33*	17	11	0.005
	S2	91*	84*	70+	47*	39*	17	12	0.000
	AS1	87	80	53	39	31*	20*	16*	0.160
	AS2	83	79	60*	45*	41+	18	11	0.000
2500	S1	87	81*	69*	47*	38*	27*	12	0.001
	S2	85	77	63	42*	35*	23*	8	0.020
	AS1	88	80	61*	39	25	12	8	0.160
	AS2	85	81*	66*	46*	36*	19	11	0.010
Combination	C_2^*								
1500	S1	88	77	64*	47*	32*	18	9	0.005
	S2	91*	83*	69*	53+	44+	26*	16*	0.000
	AS1	89	81*	71+	51+	42+	23*	15*	0.000
	AS2	91*	82*	65*	45*	33*	22*	14	0.020
2500	S1	89	78	62*	44*	33*	20*	12	0.035
	S2	92*	84*	67*	46*	30*	17	9	0.005
	AS1	85	73	53	38	31*	19	12	0.160
	AS2	88	79	71+	53+	40+	22*	10	0.000

the two sample sizes and the four types of thresholds under two sets of combinations. The middle of the table shows, for each condition, the theoretical percentage of the χ^2 distribution with 89 degrees of freedom, and the empirical rejection rate observed at the value that corresponds to the theoretical percentage. For example, in Combination C_1 with threshold type S1, 11% of the replications rejected the true model as an $\alpha = .05$ level. The right-hand side gives the Kolmogorov-Smirnov test statistic evaluating whether the observed distribution can be considered χ^2. It will be seen that 13 out of 16 conditions yielded p-values less than .05, that is, rejection of the hypothesis that the LISCOMP test statistic was χ^2-distributed, even at these larger sample sizes. The typical tendency, at $\alpha = .05$, was for models to be rejected perhaps twice as frequently as they ought to have been based on chance alone. Lee et al. also found that the standard error estimates were typically biased by a factor of 2 when compared to the empirical variability of the estimates. These and other results are not shown in the table.

A similar simulation study was undertaken for censored variables based on Muthén's (1989) theory as implemented in the LISCOMP program. A confirmatory factor analysis model was used with a smaller model based on 8 variables and a larger model with 15 variables. In each case all, or only some, of the variables were censored. Sample sizes ranging from 100 to 2500 were studied with 100 replications using the LISCOMP program. Results on the χ^2 test statistics are reproduced from Lee et al. in Table 6. It will be seen that 16 of the 20 conditions yielded K-S statistics with p-values less than .05, i.e., the χ^2 distribution was systematically rejected as the appropriate reference distribution to describe the empirical distribution of the LISCOMP test statistic. At the $\alpha = .05$ level, models were rejected about 2 to 3 times as often as expected. Not shown in the table are the standard error results, which demonstrated that the theoretical formula used by LISCOMP typically was off by a factor of two, when compared to the empirical variability of the estimates.

IMPLICATION OF LEE ET AL. RESULTS

Ad hoc procedures, whose statistical foundation is uncertain, have long been used in the analysis of categorical variables. An example of an ad hoc procedure might be to ignore the categorical nature of the variables and apply a method developed for continuous variables. Actually, this approach can work quite well, in fact, there are instances in which such procedures have worked better than presumably more correct methods. For example, Collins, Cliff, McCormick, and Zatkin (1986) found that the "wrong" correlations (phi coefficients) generally performed better than the theoretically correct correlations (tetrachorics) in a simula-

TABLE 6. Empirical Cumulative Frequencies of the Goodness of Fit Statistics, and p-Values of K-S Test from Analysis of Censored Variables

N	Censoring Point	Theoretical Percentage of χ^2 Dist.							K-S test's P-value
		80	70	50	30	20	10	5	
All variables are censored:									
				Analysis with the smaller model					
100	0.25	88	76	62*	47*	42+	25*	16*	0.000
	0.85	92*	87*	79*	59+	45+	32+	22*	0.000
200	0.25	83	73	54	38	30*	21*	15*	0.104
	0.85	84	78	64*	41*	33*	14	10	0.005
500	0.25	85	78	59	38	25	17	14	0.165
	0.85	86	79	62*	34	29	15	10	0.062
Four variables are censored:									
100	0.25	90*	87*	72+	46*	37*	27*	18*	0.000
	0.85	88	82*	69*	54+	46+	34+	22*	0.000
200	0.25	86	73	57	46*	37*	21*	14	0.001
	0.85	81	78	61*	41*	28	21*	13	0.036
500	0.25	86	78	55	41*	31*	16	9	0.036
	0.85	82	70	53	40*	30*	21*	14	0.165
				Analysis with the larger model					
All variables are censored:									
1500	0.25	85	78	66*	47*	29	15	8	0.005
	0.85	81	78	63*	45*	32*	17	7	0.019
2500	0.25	89	85	66*	43*	29	18	14	0.010
	0.85	88	77	64*	39	25	17	11	0.035
Eight variables are censored:									
1500	0.25	87	79	65*	49*	33*	18	13	0.001
	0.85	91*	84*	62*	45*	31*	17	13	0.019
2500	0.25	89	79	62*	49*	33*	21*	12	0.001
	0.85	90*	84*	66*	46*	29	16	5	0.011

tion dealing with recovery of factors in binary data. Nonetheless, it would be desirable to have a coherent categorical variable methodology that has a well-developed theoretical rationale and also performs better than its less rationalized competitors. The main advantage of a theory such as Muthén's (1984), and the theoretically driven program LISCOMP, is that it is supposed to provide accurate statistical measures of goodness of fit, and sampling variability of the estimators. However, the Lee et al. study shows that under some conditions that meet the assumptions of the method, the goodness of fit test provided by Muthén (1984, 1987, 1989) for his methodology cannot be trusted to yield statistically correct decisions about model acceptance or rejection, even with samples as large as 2500 cases. One might suspect that the test would perform even more poorly when assumptions of the methodology, such as multivariate normality of latent variables, are also violated. Further research will need to establish whether the conjecture is correct. Of course, it might be possible to modify Muthén's statistic to yield improved behavior. In the meantime, it is hard to know under what conditions the LISCOMP test statistic can be relied upon to yield appropriate decisions about models studied in the real world; for example, models that are designed to evaluate important psychological processes.

CONCLUSIONS

Although structural modeling is by now quite a mature field of study, it is surprising that one of the basic elements of the modeling process, and one of its major "selling points"—the ability to evaluate hypothesized process models by statistical means—remains an immature art form rather than a science. Of course, under classical conditions, those in which the observed variables of a model are continuous and multivariate normally distributed, and the sample size is relatively large, the ML and GLS test statistics do perform about as expected, as was shown in Table 2. In fact the GLS statistic did quite well at even the smallest sample sizes in this particular study. Of course, most of the other test statistics also do well under these same conditions. But when data are nonnormal, it seems that all bets are off. Normal theory methods may do well or badly, depending upon unknown model conditions, such as independence or dependence of factors and errors, that are not yet routinely able to be diagnosed. Certainly the widely touted general solution to nonnormal data, the ADF method, cannot be relied upon except at sample sizes that are so large to be unlikely to be generally available. The SCALED statistic, a correction to the ML statistic in this study, does seem to perform quite well over the entire range of conditions of continuous variables studied. Nonetheless, further theoretical work is required to yield adjustments that would provide more accurate behavior at the smaller sample sizes.

Only a small start was made in the Lee, Poon, and Bentler (1991) study regarding the behavior of tests on structural models with categorical variables. Clearly, a lot of further work is needed, including evaluations by others of newer approaches such as those espoused by Lee, Poon, and Bentler (1990, 1992).

REFERENCES

Amemiya, Y. (1985). On the goodness-of-fit tests for linear structural relationships. *Technical Report No. 10*. Stanford University.

Amemiya, Y. & Anderson, T. W. (1990). Asymptotic chi-square tests for a large class of factor analysis models. *The Annals of Statistics, 18*, 1453–1463.

Anderson, T. W. & Amemiya, Y. (1988). The asymptotic normal distribution of estimators in factor analysis under general conditions. *The Annals of Statistics, 16*, 759–771.

Anderson, T. W., & Rubin, H. (1956). Statistical inference in factor analysis. *Proceedings of the Third Berkeley Symposium on Mathematical Statistics and Probability, 5*, 111–150.

Arminger, G., & Küsters, U. (1989). Construction principles for latent trait models. In C. C. Clogg (Ed.), *Sociological methodology 1989* (pp. 369–393). Oxford: Basil Blackwell.

Bentler, P. M. (1983). Some contributions to efficient statistics for structural models: Specification and estimation of moment structures. *Psychometrika, 48*, 493–517.

Bentler, P. M. (1986). Structural modeling and Psychometrika: An historical perspective on growth and achievements. *Psychometrika, 51*, 35–51.

Bentler, P. M. (1989). *EQS structural equations program manual*. Los Angeles: BMDP Statistical Software.

Bentler, P. M. (1990). Comparative fit indexes in structural models. *Psychological Bulletin, 107*, 283–246.

Bentler, P. M., & Berkane, M. (1986). The greatest lower bound to the elliptical theory kurtosis parameter. *Biometrika, 73*, 240–241.

Bentler, P. M., Berkane, M., & Kano, Y. (1991). Covariance structure analysis under a simple kurtosis model. In E. M. Keramidas (Ed.), *Computing science and statistics* (pp. 463–465). Fairfax Station, VA: Interface Foundation of North America.

Bentler, P. M., & Bonett, D. G. (1980). Significance tests and goodness of fit in the analysis of covariance structures. *Psychological Bulletin, 88*, 588–606.

Bentler, P. M., & Dijkstra, T. (1985). Efficient estimation via linearization in structural models. In P. R. Krishnaiah (Ed.), *Multivariate analysis VI* (pp. 9–42). Amsterdam: North-Holland.

Bentler, P. M., Lee, S.-Y., & Weng, J. (1987). Multiple population covariance structure analysis under arbitrary distribution theory. *Communications in Statistics-Theory, 16*, 1951–1964.

Bollen, K. A. (1989a). *Structural equations with latent variables*. New York: Wiley.

Bollen, K. A. (1989b). A new incremental fit index for general structural equation models. *Sociological Methods & Research, 17*, 303–316.

Boomsma, A. (1983). *On the robustness of LISREL (maximum likelihood estimation) against small sample size and nonnormality*. Ph.D. Thesis, University of Groningen.

Browne, M. W. (1974). Generalized least squares estimators in the analysis of covariance structures. *South African Statistical Journal, 8*, 1–24.

Browne, M. W. (1982). Covariance structures. In D. M. Hawkins (Ed.), *Topic in Applied Multivariate Analysis* (pp. 72–141). Cambridge: Cambridge University Press.

Browne, M. W. (1984). Asymptotically distribution-free methods for the analysis of covariance structures. *British Journal of Mathematical and Statistical Psychology, 37*, 62–83.

Browne, M. W. (1985). Robustness of normal theory tests of fit of factor analysis and related models against nonnormally distributed common factors. Paper presented at the Fourth European Meeting of the Psychometric Society and the Classification Societies, Cambridge.

Browne, M. W. (1987). Robustness of statistical inference in factor analysis and related models. *Biometrika, 74*, 375–384.

Browne, M. W. & Shapiro, A. (1988). Robustness of normal theory methods in the analysis of linear latent variate models. *British Journal of Mathematical and Statistical Psychology, 41*, 193–208.

Chamberlain, G. (1982). Multivariate regression models for panel data. *Journal of Econometrics, 18*, 5–46.

Chou, C.-P., Bentler, P. M., & Satorra, A. (1991). Scaled test statistics and robust standard errors for non-normal data in covariance structure analysis: A Monte Carlo study. *British Journal of Mathematical and Statistical Psychology, 44*, 347–357.

Collins, L. M., Cliff, N., McCormick, D. J., & Zatkin, J. L. (1986). Factor recovery in binary data sets: A simulation. *Multivariate Behavioral Research, 21*, 377–391.

Cuttance, P. (1987). Issues and problems in the application of structural equation models. In P. Cuttance & R. Ecob (Eds.), *Structural modeling by example* (pp. 241–279). Cambridge: Cambridge University Press, 1987.

Harlow, L. L. (1985). *Behavior of some elliptical theory estimators with non-normal data in a covariance structure framework: A Monte Carlo Study*. Unpublished Ph.D. dissertation, University of California, Los Angeles.

Harlow, L. L., Chou, C. P., & Bentler, P. M. (1986). *Performance of chi-square statistic with ML, ADF, and elliptical estimators for covariance structures*. Paper presented at the Annual Meeting, Psychometric Society, Toronto, Canada.

Hu, L., Bentler, P. M., & Kano, Y. (1992). Can test statistics in covariance structure analysis be trusted? *Psychological Bulletin, 112*, 351–362.

Jöreskog, K.G. (1967). Some contributions to maximum likelihood factor analysis. *Psychometrika, 32*, 443–482.

Jöreskog, K. G. (1969). A general approach to confirmatory maximum likelihood factor analysis. *Psychometrika, 34*, 183–202.

Jöreskog, K. G., & Sörbom, D. (1988). *LISREL 7, A guide to the program and applications*. Chicago: SPSS.

Kano, Y. (1990). *A simple adjustment of the normal theory inference for a wide class of distribution in linear latent variate models*. Technical Report, University of Osaka Prefecture.

Kano, Y., Berkane, M., & Bentler, P. M. (1990). Covariance structure analysis with heterogeneous kurtosis parameters. *Biometrika, 77*, 575–585.

Lawley, D. N. (1940). The estimation of factor loadings by the method of maximum likelihood. *Proceedings of the Royal Society of Edinburgh, 60*, 64–82.

Lawley, D. N., & Maxwell, A. E. (1971). *Factor analysis as a statistical method*. London: Butterworths

Lee, S.-Y., & Bentler, P. M. (1980). Some asymptotic properties of constrained generalized least squares estimation in covariance structure models. *South African Statistical Journal, 14*, 121–136.

Lee, S.-Y., Poon, W.-Y., & Bentler, P. M. (1990). A three-stage estimation procedure for structural equation models with polytomous variables. *Psychometrika, 55*, 45–51.

Lee, S.-Y., Poon, W.-Y., & Bentler, P. M. (1991). *Some theoretical and empirical problems with LISCOMP*. Technical Report, The Chinese University of Hong Kong.

Lee, S.-Y., Poon, W.-Y., & Bentler, P. M. (1992). Structural equation models with continuous and polytomous variables. *Psychometrika, 57*, 89–105.

Linn, R. L. (1968). A Monte Carlo approach to the number of factors problem. *Psychometrika, 33*, 37–72.

Loehlin, J. C. (1987). *Latent variable models: An introduction to factor, path, and structural analysis*. Hillsdale, NJ: Erlbaum.

Micceri, T. (1989). The unicorn, the normal curve, and other improbable creatures. *Psychological Bulletin, 105*, 156–166.

Mooijaart, A., & Bentler, P. M. (1991). Robustness of normal theory statistics in structural equation models. *Statistica Neerlandica, 45*, 159–171.

Mosier, C. I. (1939). Determining a simple structure when loadings for certain tests are known. *Psychometrika, 4*, 149–162.

Muthén, B. (1984). A general structural equation model with dichotomous, ordered categorical, and continuous latent variable indicators. *Psychometrika, 49*, 115–132.

Muthén, B. (1987). *LISCOMP: Analysis of linear statistical equations using a comprehensive measurement model*. Mooresville, IN: Scientific Software.

Muthén, B. (1989). Tobit factor analysis. *British Journal of Mathematical and Statistical Psychology, 42*, 241–250.

Muthén, B. & Kaplan, D. (1985). A comparison of some methodologies for the factor analysis of non-normal Likert variables. *British Journal of Mathematical and Statistical Psychology, 38*, 171–189.

Muthén, B. & Kaplan, D. (1992). A comparison of some methodologies for the factor analysis of nonnormal Likert variables: A note on the size of the model. *British Journal of Mathematical and Statistical Psychology, 45*, 19–30.

Satorra, A. (1989). Alternative test criteria in covariance structure analysis: A unified approach. *Psychometrika, 54*, 131–151.

Satorra, A., & Bentler, P. M. (1988a). Scaling corrections for chi-square statistics in covariance structure analysis. *Proceedings of the American Statistical Association*, 308–313.

Satorra, A., & Bentler, P. M. (1988b). *Scaling corrections for statistics in covariance structure analysis*. Los Angeles: UCLA Statistics Series #2.

Satorra, A., & Bentler, P. M. (1990). Model conditions for asymptotic robustness in the analysis of linear relations. *Computational Statistics & Data Analysis, 10*, 235–249.

Satorra, A., & Bentler, P. M. (1991). Goodness-of-fit test under IV estimation: Asymptotic robustness of a NT test statistic. In R. Gutiérrez & M. J. Valderrama (Eds.), *Applied Stochastic Models and Data Analysis* (pp. 555–567). Singapore: World Scientific Publishing Co.

Shapiro, A. (1987). Robustness properties of the MDF analysis of moment structures. *South African Statistical Journal, 21*, 39–62.

Shapiro, A. & Browne, M. (1987). Analysis of covariance structures under elliptical distributions. *Journal of the American Statistical Association, 82*, 1092–1097.

Tanaka, J. S. (1984). *Some results on the estimation of covariance structure models*. Ph.D. Thesis, University of California, Los Angeles.

Tanaka, J. S. (1987). "How big is big enough?": Sample size and goodness of fit in structural equation models with latent variables. *Child Development, 58*, 134–146.

Tanaka, J. S., & Huba, G. J. (1985). A fit index for covariance structure models under arbitrary GLS estimation. *British Journal of Mathematical and Statistical Psychology, 38*, 197–201.

Tucker, L. R., & Lewis, C. (1973). A reliability coefficient for maximum likelihood factor analysis. *Psychometrika, 38*, 1–10.

Author Index

Subject Index